ALSO BY DAVID D. HALL

WAYS OF WRITING
The Practice and Politics of Text-Making
in Seventeenth-Century New England

CULTURES OF PRINT
Essays in the History of the Book

WITCH-HUNTING IN SEVENTEENTH-CENTURY NEW ENGLAND
A Documentary History, 1638–1693

WORLDS OF WONDER, DAYS OF JUDGMENT
Popular Religious Belief in Early New England

THE FAITHFUL SHEPHERD
A History of the New England Ministry in the Seventeenth Century

THE ANTINOMIAN CONTROVERSY, 1636–1638
A Documentary History

A Reforming People

A Reforming People

PURITANISM AND THE TRANSFORMATION
OF PUBLIC LIFE IN NEW ENGLAND

DAVID D. HALL

Alfred A. Knopf · New York · 2011

THIS IS A BORZOI BOOK
PUBLISHED BY ALFRED A. KNOPF

Copyright © 2011 by David D. Hall
All rights reserved. Published in the United States by Alfred A. Knopf,
a division of Random House, Inc., New York, and in Canada
by Random House of Canada Limited, Toronto.
www.aaknopf.com

Library of Congress Cataloging-in-Publication Data
Hall, David D.
A reforming people : Puritanism and the transformation of public
life in New England / David D. Hall.—1st ed.
p. cm.
Includes bibliographical references and index.
ISBN 978-0-679-44117-5
1. New England—History—Colonial period, ca. 1600–1775.   2. New England—
Politics and government—To 1775.   3. New England—Church history—17th century.
4. Puritans—New England—History—17th century.   5. Local government—New
England—History—17th century.   6. Religion and politics—New England—
History—17th century.   I. Title.
F7.H227 2011
974'.02—dc22   2010051851

Jacket design by Mary Jane Callister

Manufactured in the United States of America
First Edition

For Hannah

When we first set up Reformation in our Church way, did not this expose us to as greate an hazard as we could run both from abroad and at home? Did not our frends in England many of them forewarne us of it ere we came away? Did not others send letters after us, to deterre us from it? Did not some among our selvs (and those no meane ones) inculcate our inevitable dangers at home from no smale Company left out of Church fellowship, and Civill Offices, and freedome hitherto? Yet we trusted in God (though there appeared no meanes of safety) and went on our way. . . .

—John Winthrop (1643)

Contents

Preface

Good titles are like eels, slipping away just as you reach out to catch hold of one. As this book was beginning to form in my mind, an eel-like title appeared and, almost as suddenly, disappeared: "Why They Mattered." Remembering that moment, I realize that it grew out of my aspiration to change how we think about the English people—the "Puritans"—who created the institutions and social practices I describe in these pages. Should I do so by characterizing these people as forerunners of the American Revolution and the democratic nationalism of the nineteenth century? A project of this kind would have the sanction of John Adams, who did something like it in *A Dissertation on the Canon and Feudal Law* (1765), and of orators in the nineteenth century, one of them Henry David Thoreau, whose way of eulogizing the anti-slavery fanatic John Brown in 1859 was to link him with Oliver Cromwell and the Puritans. Intrigued though I am by this connection-making, in the end I wanted to write about the seventeenth century on its own terms. This is what I have attempted, in particular by emphasizing the pre-liberal aspects of the colonists' thinking and practice. But I have allowed myself a brief look forward in the Conclusion.

The argument that runs through this book is plain enough: the people who founded the New England colonies in the early seventeenth century brought into being churches, civil governments, and a code of laws that collectively marked them as the most advanced reformers of the Anglo-colonial world. Not in England itself but in New England did the possibilities for change opened up by the

English Revolution, as the period of English history between 1640 and 1660 is commonly named, have such consequences. Most of us have been reluctant to recognize a transformation of public life well under way in the 1630s, several years before anything like it was attempted in England. I hope I have made the colonists' accomplishments more visible and compelling.

In counterpoint to this argument, I resist the temptation to turn the colonists into nineteenth-century liberals or twentieth-century social gospelers and democrats. Nowhere in their own thinking did they endorse the premises of liberalism or democratic theory, although some aspects of both can be found in what they did and said. To mention in advance one critical point of difference, the colonists assumed that there was a right way of doing things. Any modern reader who lingers on the passage I quote in the Introduction in which John Cotton evokes the colonists' determination to establish "purity" is abruptly confronted with this assumption. Purity is purity, and purity is God's law, a premise Cotton translated into the argument that Scripture mandated how the true church should be organized and religion practiced. No one of this mindset expects a referendum to decide whether God got it right; no one anticipates being in a voting booth and hesitating between alternatives. There are none, save for the wholly perverse extremes of idolatry and the Antichrist.

Nor would anyone of Cotton's milieu have made room for personal autonomy or "self-interest rightly understood" of the kind Adam Smith and Alexis de Tocqueville introduced as the ground of liberal politics. Instead, the moral and social imperative was to enact the reign of Christ. Liberty there was, and plenty of it, a liberty reserved for the saints who had cast off the Antichrist and submitted to Christ as king. The many allusions to liberty in the chapters that follow should not be understood, therefore, as denoting an autonomy that releases each of us as individuals from the enclosing webs of custom, obligation, and circumstance. Similarly, the "liberties" enumerated in the Massachusetts "Body of Liberties" (1641) were, for the most part, protections against unauthorized and unjust actions of the civil state, not doorways to personal freedom.

A second thread of argument concerns the workings of everyday politics. I owe the shape of this argument to the historians, most of them British, who study the Tudor-Stuart period in English history, and to elements of that history itself, especially the many attempts to curtail the royal prerogative. Again, there is nothing new about finding in English history some of the keys to understanding the colonists. What makes my doing so a little unusual is that I rely on the revisionists who, in recent decades, fashioned an alternative to the "Whig" interpretation of seventeenth-century English history, the key premise in dispute being the Whig argument that the civil war that broke out in 1642 was the outcome of a long-developing constitutional crisis. Did English politics before 1642 revolve around clear-cut ideological divisions or a strong hostility to royal governance? To both these questions the revisionist answer is no.

The perspective I employ is spelled out in more detail in the Introduction, but two aspects of it are worth mentioning here. The first is a tempered understanding of political and social authority—tempered because the exercise of power by kings, bishops, sheriffs, and others depended on the cooperation of local agents and agencies. The second is a more robust understanding of the possibilities for participation in affairs of church and state. Officially, England was a top-down society. Unofficially, it was this and also something quite different. For some readers, the section of Chapter Two on the possibilities for participation in early New England may be unexpected, although to most historians of early-seventeenth-century England they will have a familiar ring.

My reading of Stuart society and culture also incorporates a reluctance bordering on active resistance to making serious changes in political and religious institutions. This conservatism had several sources, among them a near-instinctive preference for local interests, the entitlements of the more socially privileged, and, as the politics of the Long Parliament would amply demonstrate, a traditional respect for monarchy and a comprehensive (including everyone), centralized Church of England. Hence the singularity of the colonists in attempting far-reaching reform. The churches, the civil institutions, and the system of justice they brought into being curtailed the prerogatives and privileges of the few, and aligned political and social life with an ethics of equity and justice.

Inevitably, this book is also about the religious and social movement known as Puritanism—always capitalized in "American Puritan Studies," but not in English scholarship, in order to sidestep the implication that the term denotes a coherent and consistent program. The roll of the dice that brought some people and not others to New England makes it easier to capitalize the word, for colonization served to shorten a highly diverse and internally contentious movement that, at one end, encompassed reform-minded bishops of the church and, at the other, Separatists who renounced those very bishops and withdrew into congregations of their own. As I have learned from trying out some of this book on other historians, the Puritanism in these pages does not coincide with the entrenched opinion that the movement was authoritarian or "theocratic." For persons of this mind-set, the most "Puritan" aspect of my story may be the migrants' confidence in the "saints" and the attempts to establish "godly rule" (Chapter Three). But in contrast to interpretations that focus on social discipline or the suppressing of dissent, I bring other aspects of Puritanism as we now understand it into the story, including the currents of popular or insurgent religion that can be discerned in fears of "arbitrary" rule and ecclesiastical "tyranny," the emphasis on participation, and the importance given to consent. Nowhere do I presume that Puritanism embodied a particular political ideology, and nowhere is it translated into social control or top-down authoritarianism, for reasons I spell out in the Introduction and in more detail in succeeding chapters.

In keeping with recent scholarship, moreover, I take for granted that argument, compromise, experiment, failure, and complaint were persistent features of the movement—and, for that matter, of all social, religious, and political programs attempted during this period. Religious movements often have their moments when expectations for reform accelerate and when what seemed impossible to undertake is suddenly within reach; at other moments, hopes become tempered and compromises emerge. This perspective on Puritanism has the warrant of such excellent scholarship as Stephen

Foster's *The Long Argument: English Puritanism and the Shaping of New England Culture, 1570–1700* (1991), Patrick Collinson's *The Elizabethan Puritan Movement* (1967), and Mark A. Peterson's *The Price of Redemption: The Spiritual Economy of Puritan New England* (1997). My interest in the contradictions or ambiguities that inhere in social practice has been shaped by other studies, among which I would single out Alexandra Walsham's *Charitable Hatred: Tolerance and Intolerance in England, 1500–1700* (2006).

This is a book about social practice and the workings of politics during a relatively brief period of time, the twenty-year period between 1630 and 1650, though I venture outside this period in order to set the stage and, at the other end, to document more fully the parallels with English history or provide a telling bit of evidence. Some of the innovations of the 1630s and early 1640s came under pressure during the 1650s and 1660s; the percentage of men who voted in colony-wide elections declined, economic inequality widened, and apocalyptic evocations of liberty gave way to complaints about "declension." Touching on these aspects of change in the Conclusion, I also call attention to certain continuities. Writing about hopes for reform in the early seventeenth century at a moment in contemporary American history when any serious, emphatic reform of out-of-control capitalism seems impossible, and when a president so attuned to an ethics of accountability, responsibility, and equity is reviled by some of his fellow citizens, has made me appreciate the aspirations of the colonists. As I point out from time to time, however, it was not the case that everyone who arrived in New England in the 1630s and 1640s agreed with or fully shared in the transformation of public life. Even so, I have chosen to focus on the institutions and practices favored by a majority of the colonists, institutions that proved remarkably persistent.

The past is rich in the unexpected, and my sense of surprise, even a feeling of enchantment, colors many of the pages that follow—the appeal of words such as "equity" to the colonists, the role of petitions in their political lives, and especially the complex parallels and differences between 1630s New England and England during the period of the English Revolution. Perhaps the greatest surprise I felt was when I realized how close the colonists came to fulfilling the program of the Levellers, the most substantial and democratic of the groups that wanted to transform English politics and society. Most readers of this book will not be accustomed to seeing the Levellers take second place to the colonists, but perhaps the description of legal reform in Chapter Four and the summary that concludes Chapter One will persuade them that the comparison is worth attempting for the light it throws on the "further reformation" the colonists were undertaking. So, too, the case study of Cambridge, Massachusetts (Chapter Five), begins with a surprise that I try to exploit within the limits of the evidence.

IT IS a pleasure to acknowledge the people and institutions that have abetted the making of this book. Much of the research for the book was accomplished during the academic year 2004–5, when I was Mellon Senior Fellow at the American Antiquarian Society. I am deeply grateful to John Hench and the senior staff of the Society for appointing me to this fellowship, and to the staff of Readers' Services for the skillful assistance they offer everyone who uses the Society's collections. No other library where I have worked makes so much available on such generous terms of access.

I am grateful as well to those who have enabled me to try out versions of the argument on informed audiences. The initial version of Chapter Five was presented to an Omohundro Institute conference on "micro-history" at the University of Connecticut in November 1999. Aspects of the general argument were shared with members of the Columbia University Seminar in Early American History and Culture in 2005, and with Japanese scholars of American culture in January 2006. I have benefited from informal exchanges with several members of this group, especially Naoki Onishi, Shitsuyo Masui, Izumi Ogura, and Hiromichi Sasaki. More recently, other aspects of my argument were critically appraised by participants in the Center for British Studies at the University of California, Berkeley, and the University of Southern California/Huntington Library Early Modern Studies Institute. On home ground, the members of the North

American Religions Colloquium (Harvard Divinity School) were, as is their custom, vigorously suggestive in responding to a near-final version of Chapter Four.

My debts to the several persons with whom I have shared chapters and ideas are substantial. In particular, I am grateful to Daniel W. Howe, Alan Taylor, David Hempton, and Roger Thompson. Richard W. Fox will recognize the impress of his response to the Introduction on the pages that follow. So will James Simpson. Bill Stott's skillful pen improved the prose of a chapter, and David Little has been the best of partners in debating the nature of Puritanism. No one could be better served than I have been by these friends and fellow historians. As research assistants, Emma Anderson and Jenny Wiley Legath provided some of the research that underlies Chapter Five, and I gladly acknowledge Gloria Korsman's remarkable skills as a reference librarian both for this project and for others that preceded it. The endnotes indicate a great many others whose work has made this book possible. Jane Garrett's unwavering support has been indispensable. Any errors of fact or interpretation are my own responsibility.

In reproducing quotations, I have expanded ampersands, eliminated italics, and made other modest changes in spelling, though for the most part I have adhered to the sources as closely as possible. Quotations from Scripture conform to the King James Bible.

A REFORMING PEOPLE

INTRODUCTION

S HORTLY AFTER Charles I received the Petition of Right in 1628
and agreed to its provisions, he changed his mind and inserted a
speech justifying the royal prerogative in the journal of the House of
Commons. In a Boston where muddy tracks and half-built houses
were visible signs of a newly founded town, a magistrate in the
Massachusetts government, angered by reports that "the people"
wanted to clamp down on the authority of officers like himself,
raged in 1632, "Then we should have no government, but . . . everye
man might doe what he pleased." Five years later, as "freemen" gathered on the Cambridge common to vote, a minister got up into a
tree and harangued the crowd about the dangers of "antinomianism." When Thomas Wentworth, Earl of Strafford, the chief adviser
of Charles, had been sentenced to death for treason, thousands of
people thronged the streets around Parliament in May 1641, shouting out, "Justice and Execution."[1]

At moments such as these, people of high rank and low, in both
metropolitan London and colonial New England, weighed in on the
two great issues of their day. These were the dual challenge of incorporating the "liberties" of the people into the workings of a politics
premised on the preservation of authority and of deciding which
version of Protestantism would prevail in England, the one preferred by the people stigmatized as "Puritans," the more "catholic"
version preferred by the king and most of his bishops, or the compromise (in effect, the status quo, with its many loopholes) accepted
by the large numbers of people indifferent to reform of any kind. In
their introduction to a treatise on church government published in

the mid-1640s, two ministers gave succinct expression to the first of these challenges, citing the great "commotions" that "have . . . been raised and maintained for and about power, and liberties of the rulers and the ruled, together with the due bounds and limits of either." At about the same moment, a minister in New England was phrasing the problem as "balancing . . . the liberties or privileges of the people . . . and the authority of the magistrate." In sermons that the same minister had preached a few years earlier, he contrasted two forms of religion, the one embodied in the "tyranny" of Roman Catholicism, the other in a form of church government grounded on "liberty."[2] No wonder so much seemed at stake in the early decades of the seventeenth century, or that a sense of crisis would prompt thousands of people to immigrate to New England in the 1630s. Many more who disliked the regime of Charles I stayed at home, only to find themselves engaged in civil war in the 1640s.

This book is about a multi-sided process of reform that unfolded in New England between 1630 and 1650, a process driven by the colonists' unhappiness with the Church of England, the monarchy, and certain features of English society. Reform was also driven by a particular interpretation of the Bible and the history of the Christian church. To grasp the significance of this process, we must look across the Atlantic and compare the colonists' accomplishments with what was happening during the period of English history known as the "English Revolution" (1640–60). These included a daring revision of church government that eliminated any centralized authority, a thorough revamping of law and judicial practices that jettisoned most of the cruelty and abuses rampant in the English system, and a remaking of civil government that limited central state power in ways that a few colonists described as "democratical." Less original in the substance of their social ethics, the colonists were unusual in taking seriously the concept of equity and in attempting to implement a special kind of fellowship.

So much happened in New England, so little in old. The English Revolution was fragmented and inconclusive, thwarted by the drag of local interests, the fractures that emerged within the groups most in favor of significant reform, and the conservatism of a coalition temporarily held together in 1640–41 by fears of "popery" but collapsing into disarray when bolder steps were proposed or enacted.[3] The Long Parliament did curb the king's authority and revamp the Church of England, but hesitantly and without lasting consequences. Religious unity gave way to confusion, with different branches of the Puritan movement at odds, and groups such as the Baptists and, eventually, the Quakers heightening the fray. In political affairs, a faction of the army sanctioned the execution of Charles I in January 1649, a turn of events that led to Oliver Cromwell's becoming Lord Protector in what was formally a republic. In the aftermath of a series of failed or ineffective Parliaments during the Interregnum of the 1650s, few of them commanding much popular support, the monarchy was restored in 1660, when Charles II ascended the throne from which his father had been removed. Again, New England was unusual. The institutions and social practices created during the 1630s and early 1640s remained in place, though touched by change in certain respects.

The chapters that follow lay out the program of the colonists and follow them as they put it into practice. To say that they succeeded is quite different from saying that reform happened easily, or that the principal actors in the story were satisfied with the outcome. It takes only a grain of common sense and a glance back at the past to make us realize that reform is always and everywhere a complicated process—consider, for instance, the history of anti-slavery before the American Civil War. Reformers have to wrestle with the irony that their projects may (and almost certainly will) have unexpected consequences. They must contend with differences in their own ranks, some hesitating, others calling for a thorough transformation. So it was within the Puritan movement as it arose in sixteenth-century England, for Puritanism was never a monolith. Nor did the Puritans who questioned the policies of Charles I and his bishops adopt a consistent program, much less one committing them to overthrowing either monarchy or state church. Before 1640, anyone who dared imagine dismantling the Church of England and replacing it with some version of voluntary religion risked his life for doing so.

These realities make it all the more important to follow the decision-making of the colonists as closely as the records allow. Who should have the vote, and what kind of rulers did they want? How should the inheritance of property be arranged, and what ways of voicing dissent or criticism were acceptable? What role should the civil state play in matters of religion, and vice versa? And how should land be distributed, the task that animated every town meeting? Dry though they seem at first glance, town, church, and colony records provide fascinating evidence of the colonists' attempts to answer these questions. And thanks to an unusually articulate minister, Thomas Shepard of Cambridge, Massachusetts, we can look over someone's shoulder as reform unfolded in a single community.

This, then, is a book about politics in the broadest sense of that term, a politics animated by strong feelings about what was good and right or, as I emphasize in Chapter Four, what was equitable. This was also a politics driven by the English contexts that I will describe more fully in a moment and, in the colonists' New World communities, by elements of self-interest, localism, and participation. It is a little unusual to emphasize the ethical context and the possibilities for participation, but I do so in part because the excellent scholarship on which I build has not adequately acknowledged the role of petitioning or principles such as equity. The story begins in Chapter One, with the making of colony governments, followed by a chapter on towns. Then comes a chapter on churches and church and state, another on the social ethics of the colonists and the law, and, finally, a close study of Shepard's church and town.

The point of departure for these chapters is the political culture of Stuart England in the 1620s and 1630s. Shedding some features of this culture, the colonists retained others. From it they took a language in which references to Old Testament kings and the moral law mingled with evocations of the common law and Magna Carta. From it they absorbed a discomfort with Charles I and his policies so charged that it moved a young minister in Massachusetts to describe the king as an agent of the Antichrist.[4] Always shaped by the experience of authority the colonists had known in England, the making of civil and religious society in the New World was also affected by particular circumstances and contingencies. Any hopes of being faithful to the colonists' decision-making about church, state, and society depend on holding together the continuities of culture with contingency and circumstance, and on recognizing the interplay of civil and religious ways of thinking. If only in this respect, the political culture of the colonists was significantly different from ours.

I

NONE OF us is innocent when we look back at the past, for what we see or choose to emphasize is shaped by long-enduring stories of heroes and villains, reformers and their enemies, battles won and battles lost. So it is with early New England and the people who came there in the seventeenth century, a people who bear the very complicated name of "Puritan." My version of their history is, like all others, affected by the stories I inherit—in essence, two powerful stories that collide in these pages. Both date from the seventeenth century, though they owe their currency to what was said about the Puritans in the nineteenth and twentieth.

According to one of these stories, the colonists and especially their clerical and civil leaders set up a tightly run, authoritarian regime that repressed (or attempted to repress) any expression of dissent. Supposedly this regime entrusted political power to the relatively few men who were church members and withheld it from a much larger number who never joined. As an occasional critic complained at the time, the men who ran civil governments exercised their power in an "arbitrary" manner not in keeping with traditional English "liberties."[5]

A second version turns this story upside down, or nearly so. The first two Stuart kings regarded all Puritans as anti-authoritarian malcontents given to "seditious" behavior because of their refusal to abide by the rules of the Church of England, their complaints of "popery" (a code word for arbitrary governance), and their emphasis on the moral law as more binding than the king's commands.[6] Once New England came into being, the anti-authoritarianism of the

7

colonists dismayed moderate Puritans in England, who accused the immigrants of going too far. In New England itself, a local minister echoed this complaint, telling John Winthrop in 1639 that "the spirits of people runne high" and opining that "both Common-wealth and Churches have disended to[o] lowe already." A year later, after deciding not to immigrate to New England, Lord Saye and Sele warned Winthrop that the people in New England were exaggerating the importance of "liberty." What "wise man" would want to "live whear every man is a master" or "wise men propounde and fooles determine," he asked rhetorically.[7]

Stigmatized on the one hand as arbitrary and authoritarian, stigmatized on the other as overly democratic or undermining of authority—thus were formed two interpretations that have persisted to the present day. Each version has its proponents, each its critics. In the middle of the nineteenth century, some historian-antiquarians insisted that the New England town and, more generally, the stubborn anti-authoritarianism of the Puritans were sources of democratic practice and ideology in the nineteenth century, an argument accepted by Alexis de Tocqueville, who wove it into the fabric of *Democracy in America* (1835–40), his prescient study of social, political, and cultural life in the new nation.[8] Simultaneously, others pointed to events like the Salem witch-hunt of 1692 and the suppression of insurgent groups such as Baptists and Quakers as demonstrating the abuses of power in a "theocracy" sanctioned by the authoritarianism of Calvinist theology.[9] Following out this line of argument, critics argued that a politics centered on rights and liberties emerged only after prolonged struggle *against* a monolithic Puritan regime.[10] Of the many who have reiterated these themes in the twentieth century, I single out the literary historian Vernon L. Parrington, who delighted in quoting John Winthrop and John Cotton whenever they distanced themselves from "democracy."[11] Although astoundingly original in many respects, the mid-twentieth-century scholar Perry Miller echoed Parrington's assertions, describing the leaders of Massachusetts (and all Puritans) as bent on "uniformity" and the ecclesio-political structure they created as an "oligarchy."[12] In recent years, the "orthodoxy" of the colonists has come under fire for being patriarchal and imperialistic. One way or another, the image and idea of Puritans as excessively authoritarian remains alive and well, sustained by present-day expectations about diversity and, for interpreters who descend from Parrington, a secular or theological liberalism that emphasizes the rights of each individual.

Of course it is not so simple. Never for a moment did the colonists assume that they were practicing democratic politics of the kind Americans would attempt in the nineteenth century. No colonist—and, for that matter, no one in early-modern Europe— would have agreed with George Bancroft's assertion in 1836 that the voice of the people is the voice of God. No one would have resonated to (much less understood) the Emersonian ethics of "self-reliance" or a theory of natural rights that overrode differences of social rank, race, and gender.[13] Forward-looking in certain respects, in others the colonists were very much of their age. Context is crucial. We must remember that the drift of political thought and practice in seventeenth-century Europe was toward oligarchy and absolutism, and that, in the political and religious history of England, the severest repression of religious dissent happened during the Restoration of Charles II, in the 1660s and early 1670s.[14]

Better to change the question, then, and open up the range of possibilities for understanding the politics of the colonists. At once, four dimensions of political culture and practice in early-seventeenth-century England come into view, four dimensions that, partially recast, were replicated on the other side of the Atlantic.

1. The first of these was the everyday experience of accepting the authority of those above you. No one was spared this experience, not even the Stuart kings, who repeatedly were told (and sometimes said themselves) that they were God's servants. Treatises on household governance, sermon series on the imperative of subordination, and catechisms all counseled the willing acceptance of authority and the benefits that flowed from being dependent, chief among them the uniting of divergent social groups or interests into a peaceful whole, a true commonwealth or kingdom. Likening the state to a

ship at sea, commentators noted the crucial role of the person who served as pilot; quoting Matthew 12:25, they warned that a "house divided against itself shall not stand." Without a center, without obedience to a higher authority, without "Sovereraignty," no society could sustain an ethics of the common good. So an English minister pointed out, evoking the "adulteries, incests . . . robberies . . . and savage cruelty" that "would overflow" the earth in its absence. So John Winthrop insisted in his "little speech on liberty" of 1645, when he contrasted the "natural liberty" of people trapped like animals in the anarchy of self-interest with the "civil liberty" made possible by subordination and obedience.[15]

Everywhere, the practical workings of civil society and social life turned on this principle. Parliaments acknowledged the higher authority of the king, ministers in the Church of England the superiority of bishops. The men who had aristocratic rank and the many more who were of the gentry took for granted that important offices in county and royal government were theirs.[16] Husbands presumed to rule in households, children were taught to obey, and the "little commonwealth" of a well-ordered family was universally regarded as the foundation of order, peace, and obedience in society as a whole. As for cultural practices, only a handful of writers commanded the stylistics and genres of Renaissance humanism, and many remained illiterate in the triple sense of knowing neither Latin nor how to read and write their own language. Near the close of the century, a young New England minister invoked these hierarchies in characterizing a prose narrative written by a mason as "in his own Style . . . by an Hand used only to the Trowel." Hierarchy was inscribed in culture, politics, religion, and society; obedience or submission was normative.[17]

2. Yet, always and everywhere in seventeenth-century England, authority was mediated, its capacity to influence or control what people thought and did compromised by structures, practices, and assumptions. A historian pondering how to define totalitarian fascism in twentieth-century Italy and Germany has shown that, in Mussolini's Italy, significant elements of traditional political society persisted alongside the revolutionary structures of the dictator's regime, with the result that fascist power was significantly curtailed.[18] So it was in Stuart England, only more so. James I and Charles I huffed and puffed about their powers of governance, but they had to depend on intermediaries (or, as one historian has termed them, "brokers") to carry out royal policy. Great families, county magnates and sheriffs, guilds and chartered corporations, city governments such as London's, courtiers and favorites of the king, bishops of the church—all inserted their own preferences into the practice of governance. The geography of governance also mattered. As a historian of administration in Stuart England has emphasized, the "Stuart magistracies were poised between the regimes which appointed them and the people of the English villages and market towns," a situation that made for "numerous disincentives" to adhere to law or social policy prescribed from far away. Referring to the Book of Orders published by the government of Charles I in 1631, the same historian describes it as a failure "because it was not properly enforced." Inconsistency at the center—spasms of zeal followed by periods of indifference or distraction—made it easier or more likely that local enforcement would waver. To many in Parliaments of the 1620s, a particular version of laxness was the intermittent curtailing of English Catholics, who by law were to be fined, and their priests arrested. Cumulatively, these aspects of governance limited the effectiveness of royal and parliamentary rule. So did the alliances that emerged among disaffected members of the elite.[19]

A contradiction in English society accounted for much of this confusion, the difference between loyalty or subordination and the acute fractures—religious, social, cultural, regional, economic—that divided the English people. Of these fractures, the most apparent to contemporaries concerned religion. Catholicism remained the religion of choice for certain groups or regions, even as many others were attempting a stricter, more explicitly "Reformed" version of Protestantism than what was authorized by the Church of England. From one diocese to the next in the church, bishops, priests, and church wardens behaved in different ways, so much so that some of the ministers who came to New England in the 1630s had never conformed to the Canons of 1604 or the rules William Laud as archbishop of Canterbury was attempting to impose in the 1630s. A few congregations broke with the church altogether, and in the 1620s and 1630s a handful of ministers tested the boundaries of orthodoxy by preaching a theology known as "Antinomianism."[20] In the kingdoms of Ireland and Scotland, moreover, the Church of England was secondary to Catholic and Presbyterian preferences. Alongside these differences lay fractures arising out of economic life. Port towns wanted one kind of taxes and foreign policy, agricultural counties another, and in some counties a proto-industrial sector was at odds with landed interests.[21] The financial needs of the Crown were a wild card in this deck, for the revenues of the government failed to match its expenses, a gap that expanded whenever soldiers were sent overseas or the navy reinforced. Granting a monopoly on some product or service was one means of raising extra funds, but in doing so the Stuarts provoked an outcry against "oppression." Rival groups competed for economic advantage in the great metropolis of London, and courtiers who gathered around the king and staffed his administration were also rivals in the quest for economic gain.[22]

To make matters worse, the signs and sounds of conflict were amplified in printed books and pamphlets and handwritten texts. In principle, the government regulated the making of books through a machinery of licenses, supplementing their control with severe measures against printers and writers who criticized the regime. None of these measures, and especially not the system of licensing, kept the press in hand. As many as a third of all the books published in London in the early seventeenth century were never registered or received a license, and licensing itself was a process full of loopholes.[23] Books printed elsewhere in defiance of all regulation—in Leiden, at the press owned by the future "pilgrim" William Brewster, for example—were another means of circumventing the state. Speech was also subject to regulation, but rumor and gossip outran all methods of control.[24]

3. Authority mediated through local agencies, interest groups, a fractured Church of England, and a discordant media was also an

authority constrained by certain principles. The Stuart kings willingly acknowledged one of these, that God was *their* sovereign, and frequently acknowledged two others, the presence of "ancient liberties" and the necessity of having Parliament "consent" to grants of money. For many English people, the most deeply felt political principle may have been the rule of law, an aspect of the "ancient liberties" much extolled by Edward Coke, the great jurist of the day and member of Parliament during these early decades. Coke became famous for insisting that a timeless common law guarded the English against the possibility of royal absolutism.[25] Most of his contemporaries understood the law as protecting their bodies and their property unless the state had the warrant of law and the consent of Parliament to tax or imprison them. So both houses of Parliament asserted in the Petition of Right, directed at Charles I, and in "The Form of an Apology and Satisfaction" (1604), directed at his father, James. The message to James was that Parliament regarded its privileges as "immemorable" and of a piece with "the rights and liberties of the whole commons of your realm of England." The message to Charles was more pointed, that no one could "be compelled to make or yield any gift, loan, benevolence, tax or such like charge without common consent by act of parliament."[26] Although neither king followed these principles to the letter, both acknowledged them on some occasions, and both repeatedly justified their power by making it conditional on their service to the nation—offering protection from its enemies, caring for the poor or those in need, sustaining justice. Local magistrates spoke of themselves in the same way, evoking fairness or "equity" as the principle that guided their administration of the law.[27] Rarely was power described as an end in itself. Instead, it was entrusted to rulers so that, in their role as fathers and in imitation of Old Testament kings like Asa, they could suppress idolatry and do other good things for the people who depended on them.[28]

4. There was little space in this political culture for explicit theorizing about sovereignty and the ideal forms of government. To be sure, there was much to learn from the examples of republican

Venice and conflict-filled Florence as filtered through the reflections of continental humanists on liberty, order, and the prince. One lesson was the value of liberty and how precarious it was; another, the importance of central state authority and therefore the perils of a "republic." The wars of religion in sixteenth-century France held other lessons, as did the history of ancient Greece and Rome and the writings of Aristotle, Polybius, and Cicero. But for any Englishman to argue in favor of a republic or to represent Parliament as in opposition to the king or (as happened in mid-sixteenth-century France) to propose that an immoral king could be deposed or assassinated was out of the question.[29] The alternative, to extol an extreme version of princely rule, as began to happen in England in the 1620s, aroused a storm of criticism. When one faction within the Long Parliament argued for significant changes in the structure of the Church of England and for greater limits on the monarchy, many of the country gentry recoiled. Grand schemes were few and far between; the "free-standing printed political tract" did not become a medium of argument until 1642.[30] Instead, the rhetoric of politics revolved around satire, sarcasm, and stereotypes—the Puritan as rabble-rouser, the Jesuit as relentless plotter, the bishops of the church as greedy parasites.

A significant constraint on explicit theorizing was the flexibility of key words or categories at a moment when "everyone spoke the same language."[31] A maxim like *salus populi suprema lex,* which to a modern ear may sound proto-democratic, was invoked everywhere along the political spectrum, from kings and supporters of the Long Parliament to the more daring group known as the Levellers. So was the image or idea of "mixed" government.[32] The term "democracy" could be narrowly descriptive, a reference to one of three elements in classical theories of mixed government (the others being "aristocracy" and "monarchy"), but could also allude to the premise that sovereignty rested with "the people," empowering them to limit the authority of civil officers. As well, it was a term in popular polemics about a restless "spirit" among the people, or a world "where all are Masters."[33] To some members of Parliament, consent denoted the privilege of participating in decision-making; to others, its meaning was akin to a more passive acceptance.[34] Was a republic necessarily the opposite of monarchy? Not so, in some speculation.[35] Allusions to "liberty" were everywhere, in part because English Protestants appropriated the concept from passages in the New Testament where St. Paul contrasted the obligations of Jewish law with the freedom of Christians "called unto liberty" (Galatians 5:13). Here as elsewhere, the word denoted responsibility or obedience, in contrast to a liberty that was lawless—hence licentious or antinomian, a crude synonym for dispensing with all rules. To a modern sensibility, it may seem that millenarian evocations of the new liberty associated with Christ's coming kingdom implied the overthrowing of civil governments, but a political reading of this theme is partially contradicted by its prevalence in the seventeenth century, and by explicit assertions that it pertained only to the church.[36]

Nonetheless, the agitation that drew on such terms had political consequences, as did the outcry against "popery." Real, imagined, or merely a convenient means of criticizing certain policies of the Crown and church, the rhetoric of anti-popery shared important motifs with the rhetoric of the coming kingdom. Both condemned abusive, unconstrained authority, both extolled Christian liberty, and both implied that church and commonwealth were better off in the hands of the "godly" who adhered to Scripture. Within these frameworks, moreover, sovereignty was usually construed as Christ's, with civil magistrates serving as his stewards. These motifs were not the same as a political program, and certainly not a program pointing toward the abolition of the monarchy or even the overthrow of episcopacy. But they were a bridge to the near-revolutionary themes of the Scottish National Covenant of 1638 and the demands of the "Grand Remonstrance" signed by thousands and presented to Parliament in 1641. Their implications for the colonists will, I trust, become apparent in what follows.[37]

Religion figures in the story in another major respect. Around the Puritan movement swirled the themes of disruption and exclusivity: if church and community were not aligned with the will of God, then they should be confronted, even if the price was conflict; if the mass of the people would not accept the rule of Christ, then the self-proclaimed godly should either withdraw into congregations of their own or impose that rule upon others. These quite different possibilities open the way to exploring "godly rule" and its consequences in a colonial society where, unlike Stuart England, a certain kind of Puritan came into power. The question of whether the godly in New England pursued such an agenda informs this book as well, though addressed most fully in Chapters Two, Three, and Five.[38]

The language of politics in Stuart England—the exaggerations, the pairing of two terms, the one praised, the other condemned, as though all of politics was constructed within fiercely different categories—is another reason for deferring certain interpretive frameworks, including the category of "radical."[39] Otherwise, we run the risk of substituting modern usage for nuances of meaning and practice in the seventeenth century. Those nuances, and, in particular, the difficulty of thinking outside the box of kingship and royal sovereignty, stand in the way of classifying Parliaments in the 1620s and their spokesmen in the early 1640s as proto-liberal or democratic.[40] Re-entering the seventeenth century, we must be prepared for improvisation, uncertainty, and rhetorical excess.

II

THE COLONISTS brought some elements of this political culture with them to New England, but only some. Not only were their aspirations for religion at odds with how the Church of England was organized, they had become wary of the Crown and the policies it was pursuing. Affected, too, by circumstances, the political culture that took shape in the colonies was remarkably daring in certain respects and, in others, marked by elements of continuity.

A central question for this culture was the meaning and practice of authority. Knowing that dissension had brought the English colony in Virginia close to self-destruction, the leaders of Massachusetts reacted swiftly to any signs of disrespect in their midst, imposing in 1634 an oath of loyalty on all "freemen" and, several months later, extending this requirement to every male sixteen and older.[41] Already the importance of putting the good of the whole before individual needs had been emphasized in two publications prompted by the "great migration" of 1630, which brought nearly a thousand persons to Massachusetts, John White's *The Planters Plea* (1630) and Winthrop's sermon "Modell of Christian Charitie," also dating from 1630. The opening sentence of the "Charitie" discourse evoked another aspect of authority, a divinely ordained hierarchy that empowered the few to expect the deference of the many. Aspects of patriarchy passed intact from old to New England, as did the coding of criticism as sedition and liberty as easily giving way to licentiousness. Indeed, John White warned the leaders of the new colony to be on guard against the breakdown of order, reminding Winthrop in 1637 that "as Liberty is sweet soe it is apte (as it is with sweet meats) to allure men to Excess."[42]

White may also have realized that, once under way, a program of reform could get out of hand. A crucial circumstance would abet this process in the 1630s, William Laud's campaign to eradicate Puritan-style nonconformity. In response, outbursts against church and Crown intensified in England, as when, in publications both licit and illicit, William Prynne, Henry Burton, and John Bastwick subjected the bishops of the church to "scandalous" ridicule. Describing to one of the Winthrops the public punishment of these men by branding and other mutilations in 1637, an English correspondent emphasized the "applauding . . . and clapping and shouting for joy to see so great courage and comfort" in the three men by the "many thousands" who witnessed the scene. Here was a portent of things to come in England, Scotland, and the colonies. That very year, as Charles I was attempting to impose the full apparatus of the Church of England on the Scots, a woman hurled a stool at a high-ranking cleric during a church service in Edinburgh. Some months later, a popular uprising swept across the Scottish lowlands, its manifesto, the National Covenant, a "confession" committing those who signed it to defend "the true Christian faith and religion" against the king's attempts to introduce episcopacy.[43]

Lacking the wisdom of his father, who realized that the stability of the English state depended on allowing differences of religious practice as long as dissident groups did not question his legitimacy, Charles and the bishops he favored were determined to impose uniformity. As this campaign unfolded, some disaffected ministers and laypeople survived as best they could in England. Others decided on immigration, a few to the Netherlands, and a great many more to New England. Moved by a heightened animosity against the Church of England and all things associated with Catholicism, the immigrants were agreeing by the mid-1630s that, in the words of John Cotton, the time had come to "enjoy the libertye, not of some ordinances of god, but of all, and all in Puritye." Compromises were a thing of the past. As Puritan clergyman John Davenport explained his own change of mind to an English friend, he could no longer "practice" the liturgy of the church "as formerly I have done," adducing verses in Romans 14 that the Geneva Bible glossed as a warning to "weaklings" not to "blaspheme the Gospel." Cotton, too, had undergone a change of heart about the importance and direction of reform, as had the ministers who, in a letter that reached the English moderate John Ball, spoke of having for the first time "an open door of libertie" to fulfill the Gospel.[44] Thus it happened that, across New England, ministers and laypeople welcomed a thoroughgoing transformation of ministry, church, and political structure. No more "tyrannical" government, no more "popery," no more curtailing of liberty of conscience—with such goals in mind, the colonists took on the task of establishing frameworks of government and an ecclesiastical system.

Accomplishing these tasks would have been impossible had the colonists not gained a remarkable freedom from church and Crown by coming to New England. This freedom was briefly threatened in the mid-1630s, when the English government began to review the Massachusetts charter and talked of sending a governor general to rule the colony. Once these efforts faltered because of the king's political troubles at home, the colonists were on their own, though always in need of English merchants for supplies and of markets in the wider Atlantic world. Meanwhile, they were experiencing another kind of freedom made possible by the differences in social structure between colony and nation. No cohort of county aristocrats made its way to New England, and only a few gentry.[45] Absent these, and without a king who dispensed privilege, wealth, and power, the structure of politics was substantially altered. Other long-entrenched practices and institutions also vanished—the privileged situation of lawyers, the inequalities of power built into the episcopal structure of the Church of England, the economic monopolies that kings used to reward their favorites or raise more money for the government, city governments (as in London) controlled by the few, ecclesiastical courts, and the Court of Chancery. Crucially, the colonists also escaped the attempts of the Long Parliament in mid-1640s England to marginalize any and all religious groups that broke with the traditional synthesis of church and state.

Thanks to these circumstances, the people who colonized New England were virtually unique in establishing a system of church governance that, as their critics angrily complained, shifted authority from the clergy to the laymen of the congregation and made church membership voluntary and selective. They were unique in accomplishing a thorough reform of the legal system that some in England wanted but could never accomplish.[46] They were virtually unique in the care with which they built participation into every level of governance, from town and congregation to colony and confederation. They were singular in distributing land to households in the form of tenure known as freehold—that is, private ownership. Remarkably, a few colonists broke with the norms of English political culture and called their form of government a "democracy."[47] Others broke with those norms by entrusting political power to the "saints" as part of a program of godly rule.[48]

These accomplishments stand in sharp contrast to the pace and nature of reform during the English Revolution.[49] Early in its history, the Long Parliament curtailed the prerogatives of the king and asserted a greater role for itself in governance. In 1643, it abolished the episcopal structure of the Church of England and entrusted the Westminster Assembly with the responsibility for defining a better system. Purged of its more conservative members, or as reorganized under Cromwell, Parliament made a few attempts at moral and social reform. Thanks to Cromwell's sympathies and the severe weakening of central state authority, a de facto toleration of religious difference (but not of Catholics) arose. But the "further reformation" advocated by one wing of the Puritan movement neither became law nor was comprehensively practiced. The Levellers, who emerged in the mid-1640s, advocated an ambitious program of political, legal, and social reform—described more fully in subsequent chapters—none of which passed into law. Nor did Cromwell's government succeed in remaking civil courts, Parliament, and churches. Although Charles I went to the scaffold in January 1649, monarchy, aristocracy, and episcopacy returned in full force in 1660.

Amid the tumult of English popular politics of the 1640s, the colonists were enacting an "English Revolution" of their own.[50] The chapters that follow trace out these accomplishments and transformations, beginning with the organization of colony-wide governments, then of town governments and aspects of participation, followed by the making of the "Congregational Way" and other aspects of godly rule. Chapter Five, a case study of Cambridge, Massachusetts, provides a closer look at a controversial practice, the privileging of church members and its effects on a community in which some remained outside the church. Never was the program of the colonists without complications; never did the most ardent reformers accomplish everything they wanted or was everyone included. The new or innovative aspects of political culture coexisted with others that were thoroughly traditional, like the imperative to sustain authority. More tellingly, reform was compromised by contradictions both old and new. Differences of economic, political, and religious power, as well as those between towns or regions—differences that became more prominent by the 1650s—proved difficult to reconcile with evocations of communal love and unity. Empowering the godly and limiting church membership to the saints were exciting accomplishments, but could the saints always and everywhere be trusted to do the right thing? Claiming to know the truth and enlisting the authority of civil governments to suppress "heresy," magistrates, ministers, and communities had to decide whether the price of doing so was too high. Even in New England, politics was a matter of negotiation and compromise.

Mine is not a story, therefore, of a proto-democratic society in the making, although elements of such a system were certainly present in the transformations described in these pages. Even more emphatically, it is not a story of resurgent authoritarianism as mediated through the narrow lens of Puritanism. The Puritan movement and its aspirations play a key role in the story, but a role, I trust, that is broader, more appealing, and more complex than what is usually understood to be the case.

CHAPTER ONE

"ARBITRARY" OR "DEMOCRATICAL"?
The Making of Colony Governments

Two months after arriving in Massachusetts in June 1630, the officers of the Massachusetts Bay Company held a "court" in their new capacity as administrators of a colony. That day, the business at hand was deciding how to pay the ministers the Company had recruited and what to do about the soaring prices of supplies and servants' labor. By year's end, this little group was enacting rules to ensure the validity of commercial contracts and the distribution of property left by those who died. It was crucial, too, that the group arrange for grants of land so farming could begin, negotiate with the local Indians, and discipline abuses of speech, sex, and alcohol. All these were preliminary acts of statecraft, prelude to decision-making of far greater consequence about the structure and practice of civil government.[1]

One aspect of this process, the implementing of "godly rule," is taken up in Chapter Three. Here the focus is on the creation of five different colony-wide governments; the making of town governments follows in Chapter Two. Telling this story for Massachusetts, where the process is most fully documented, carries us from the early 1630s, when arguments first broke out about civil governance, to the mid-1640s, when these disputes reached something of a climax. Elsewhere, people were deciding much more promptly on what to do—the Plymouth colonists between 1636 and 1639, the founders of Connecticut in 1638 and 1639, the founders of New Haven between 1638 and 1643, and the towns in what became Rhode Island between 1639 and 1647, the year in which these towns came together in a colony-wide federation with a charter from Parliament.

Everywhere, the process turned on how to answer questions about statecraft so difficult to resolve in England that civil war broke out in 1642. For many Englishmen—and certainly for the colonists, had they lingered in their homeland—the great difficulty at the beginning of the 1640s was the insistence of Charles I on his authority as monarch and the corollary he added to this argument, that "Parliaments are altogether in my power" (as he told the Parliament of 1626) "for their calling, sitting and dissolution," an assertion he amplified by likening that body to a "council" and "therefore" limited in what it could undertake. To the dismay of many, Charles was extending his protection to clergymen who defended the divine right of kings to rule and using that argument to validate imposing taxes without the consent of Parliament.[2] No one of Puritan sympathies in late-1620s England had much love for Charles I, and although the people who sailed for Massachusetts in 1630 could not have foreseen that he would reign without the advice of a Parliament for eleven years (1629–40), they sympathized with the provisions of the Petition of Right (1628), one of them the principle, already noted, that "no tax, tallage, aid or other like charge" could be levied by the Crown unless "by common consent in parliament." In his response, the king stigmatized such statements as "innovations" because they broke "through all respects and ligaments of government, and . . . erect[ed] an universal over-swaying power" in Parliament, "which belongs only to us and not to them."[3] Like most members of the Parliament that Charles eventually convened in December 1640, the colonists wanted structures and rules to protect them from a leader who asserted that, in his capacity as king, he had an "absoluta potestas" in matters of justice and was accountable only to God.[4]

Well before the Long Parliament began its quest for constitutional means of curtailing the king's authority, the colonists were devising forms of government that anticipated and, in significant ways, surpassed what their countrymen would accomplish. But, like their counterparts in the Long Parliament, the colonists struggled with a series of questions that successive regimes in revolutionary England could not resolve: Where did sovereignty lie, and what was the proper balance between authority (government) and liberty? The resonance of these questions owed something to debates within continental humanism and the historical examples of republican Venice, princely Florence, and the wars of religion in sixteenth-century France. Yet their more immediate source was the political culture of early-modern England.

I

STATE-MAKING in Massachusetts Bay was repeatedly contentious, for what men such as John Winthrop wanted by way of government displeased many others. Protest erupted in 1632, reached a temporary peak in 1634, when Winthrop was voted out of office as governor, and returned in full force in the late 1630s and early 1640s. Sometimes a specific policy or ruling led people to mobilize for change, as when Winthrop's resistance to judicial constraint provoked a near paranoia about his intentions "to have the government arbitrary," the same anxiety aroused by the policies of Charles I.[5] In continuity with English politics, the underlying issue concerned the structure of government or, more abstractly, the challenge of combining liberty and authority without allowing either to veer off into excess: liberty as anarchy, authority as "arbitrary" or tyrannical. For many of the Massachusetts colonists, the most important business of state-making was to prevent arbitrary rule. For Winthrop and those who shared his thinking, the most important goal was to preserve the authority of the men who held office as governor and magistrates (technically, in Massachusetts, the "Assistants"). Winthrop campaigned persistently for an understanding of "office" that freed it from any direct dependence on consent. Wary of majority rule in a General Court where the deputies outnumbered the magistrates, he insisted on the privilege of a "negative voice" (veto) for the latter. His great bugaboo was "democratie," which he equated with an absence of authority. He would have agreed with his sometime ally John Cotton's remark: "Democracy, I do not conceyve that ever God did ordeyne as a fitt government eyther for church or commonwealth. If the people be governors, who shall be governed?"[6] But for others in New England, this word was much more positive.

The particular questions of statecraft that roiled the colonists emerged in this context. The earliest concerned the levying of taxes, a dispute coinciding with complaints that Winthrop was amassing too much power as the colony's governor. By 1634, the colonists were disputing whether the legislative aspects of governance belonged solely to the governor and magistrates or were shared with the deputies who began to represent each town in the General Court. That year also saw the earliest protest against the negative voice the magistrates were claiming and, simultaneously, a dispute over whether the "freemen" elected all of the colony's officers or only some of them. A few years later, a coalition of deputies and magistrates was challenging Winthrop's insistence on a "Standing Council" empowered to act when the General Court was not in session. Meanwhile, another group that included ministers, magistrates, and laypeople was calling for a written code of laws, a veritable "Magna Carta," as a counterpoint to judicial discretion, which Winthrop favored. For some, the deeper challenge was to articulate the "liberties" shared by everyone in the commonwealth and to code those liberties as "Fundamentall," that is, forever binding on governors and governed. Early and late, some were also insisting on rotation in office.

The starting point for these disputes was the charter of the Massachusetts Bay Company, which laid out a structure of governance based on a "General Court" of freemen (stockholders, who in 1629 numbered about 125), a smaller group of eighteen "Assistants" to be elected out of the freemen, and a governor and deputy governor. As was typical of such charters, it specified four meetings a year of the General Court, one of them for the purpose of electing officers and the others for doing Company business. In between these sessions, a "Council" of assistants and other officers was in charge. Once the decision was made, in late 1629, to transfer the government of the Company to Massachusetts and the great migration of 1630 had taken place, the effective rulers of the new colony were Winthrop, who became governor in October 1629; Thomas Dudley, named deputy governor shortly before the fleet sailed; and the seven stock-holders (now regarded as assistants) who came with them. In October 1630, this small group broke with the charter by admitting 116 men, none of them stockholders, to the status of freemen. No one informed these new freemen of the privileges that were theirs according to the charter, and none of them had access to the actual document.

Some sixteen months later, the "people" of Watertown protested a tax the council had levied on each of the towns. At the heart of their complaint lay the principle of consent on which every Parliament of the 1620s had insisted, and the rhetoric of their protest—"it was not safe to paye monyes after that sorte for feare of bringinge themselves and posteryty into bondage"—echoed what had been said by Parliamentarians protesting the extraordinary levies Charles I was exacting. Winthrop and the magistrates responded forcefully, insisting on an apology from the leaders of the protest and requiring them to read a "retraction and submission" to the townspeople. Winthrop may have specified the contents of that retraction, that he and the council, but not the freemen, had the "power to make lawes or rayse taxation," a point he supported by likening the small group of magistrates and governor to Parliament, an analogy that, from his point of view, supported the practice of confining the role of the freemen (or people) to electing the magistrates. Possibly as a fillip, he added that anyone with a grievance could voice it at any session of the General Court.[7]

Three months later, at the May session of the court, Winthrop had to concede some of the high ground he was claiming. With the power to tax again in dispute, the council agreed that each town could send two men "to be at the nexte Court to advise with the Governor and Assistantes about the raysinge of a public stocke." At this same May meeting of the court, the council also granted the freemen the privilege of electing the governor directly, instead of having him chosen by the magistrates. By August, the uneasiness about the concentration of power in the hands of the few had reached someone as high-placed as Dudley, the deputy governor, who "demanded" that Winthrop specify "the gronde and limittes of his Authoritye whither by the Patent or otherwise." An impassioned back-and-forth between the two men about the scope of the governor's authority—whether the person in that office "had no more Authoritye then everye Assistante (excepte power to call Courtes and precedencye for honor and order)," as Dudley alleged—reached its climax in the accusation that "the Governor intended to make himselfe popular, that he might gaine absolute power, and bring all the Assistantes under his subiection."[8]

This "iealousye" (as Winthrop termed it) extended well beyond the person of Thomas Dudley. In the weeks leading up to the General Court session of May 1634, when a fresh election would determine who held higher office in the colony, the freemen arranged for a grand meeting of delegates from each town to "consider of suche matters as they were to take order in" once the session began. Insisting that Winthrop show them the charter, the group learned from reading the document that the power of making laws belonged to the entire group, freemen as well as magistrates and governor. Winthrop offered to compromise. Alleging it was impractical to call all the freemen together four times a year, he agreed to let delegates from each town "review all Lawes . . . but not to make any newe Lawes" with the exception of taxes, for he accepted the point that "no Assessment should be layd upon the Countrye, without the Consent of suche a Comittee." He acknowledged another constraint on executive authority, that no land be "disposed off" without a similar process of approval.[9] But the freemen wanted more. At the May session, Winthrop was temporarily turned out of the governorship and replaced by Dudley. In a toneless description of what followed, Winthrop noted that the new court immediately empowered the delegates or "deputyes" from each town by allowing them to participate in the "makinge" of "Lawes" and "disposinge" of "landes &c." Overnight, as it were, the General Court became a place where deputies outnumbered magistrates, with both having the same authority to make laws.[10]

Winthrop and the men who agreed with him were quick to insist on other forms of authority. Returning to the charter, they interpreted it as saying that no measure could pass the court unless it gained the approval of the majority of the council. A fresh crisis in the fall of 1634 brought home the possibility of the magistrates being outvoted when, with deputies and magistrates meeting together, the court found itself at odds on whether to approve the request of the people living in Newtown (renamed Cambridge in 1638) to remove to Connecticut. Most of the deputies and a few of the magistrates agreed to let them leave, whereupon the other magistrates demanded the privilege of a negative voice or veto over any such measure.[11] For the moment, conflict was averted when the Newtowners withdrew their request. But the magistrates' insistence on a veto dramatized the difference between two versions of authority and governance. Some, and especially Winthrop, continued to argue that their authority was greater than (or different from) the authority of the deputies and freemen; the deputies could consent, as could the freemen, but only the magistrates could legislate and act as judges or justices of the peace. Most of the deputies countered that everyone in office shared the same authority to legislate.

Winthrop's critics had a further point to make. Late that fall or during the winter, Israel Stoughton of Dorchester disputed any negative voice on the basis of a long-existing distinction—frequently employed in the context of discussing the relationship of the supreme sovereignty of Christ to the powers of the clergy who served him—between "magisterial" and "ministerial" modes of authority. In a paper he may have circulated within the General Court, Stoughton declared that, according to the charter, the governor and assistants had only the weaker of these modes, a "ministerial" authority allowed them by "the greater vote of the general courts, and not Magisterial according to their own discretion." "Denying the magistracy among us" was how Winthrop construed this argument. In one respect he was right, for the insistence on ministerial authority implied that the basis of civil power was located in the people. Stoughton also recommended that the deputies have the same negative voice as the magistrates, though his preference was certainly for majority rule.[12] Had his suggestions been adopted, much of what differentiated the magistrates from the deputies would have vanished.

A year later, and even more emphatically in 1636, most of the magistrates found another way of defending an authority they continued to regard as different in kind. Initially they declared themselves a Standing Council empowered to act when the General Court was not in session, and in 1636 claimed a grander role for three of themselves—Winthrop, Dudley, and the young aristocrat Henry Vane, Jr.—as a "Council for Life." The deputies would have none of this, and the Council for Life died aborning, although not the Standing Council. Meanwhile, the magistrates were facing charges that, in their capacity as judges in civil and criminal cases, their authority to impose penalties for wrongdoing was dangerously broad. Out of these complaints about judicial discretion came a movement to establish a written code of laws, an impulse that resulted in a "Body of Liberties" the General Court adopted in 1641.[13]

Amid these scenes of tension, consensus had been reached on some principles. John Cotton sketched these in a manuscript that, when printed in London in 1641, bore the misleading title *An Abstract of the Lawes of New-England, as They Are Now Established.* In the section on the General Court, he specified that it "call[ed] the Governour . . . into place" and could hold all such officers accountable "for the breach of any laws established." Otherwise, the business of the court was "to make and repeale lawes," "dispose of lands," and levy taxes "for the publique service of the commonwealth." Recommending a Council for Life, Cotton proposed that no law pass unless it was approved by a majority of both magistrates and deputies. Like Stoughton before him, Cotton seemed to suggest in his summary that ultimate authority rested with the people.[14]

Yet any clear-cut, and especially any secular, version of sovereignty was not yet on the table. For the men in Massachusetts as for their contemporaries in 1630s England, the categories of political discourse remained uncertain, ambiguous, and charged with tensions arising out of Stuart rule. That a negative voice was so provocative owed a great deal to the fact that Charles I was claiming the very same privilege. That so many people listened impatiently when Winthrop declared that magistrates were like "gods" (as the Old Testament and Calvinist tradition warranted his saying) had something to do with the fact that James I had used exactly the same language in addressing Parliament in 1610. And when Winthrop extolled consent, the colonists may have remembered that James had done so through an intermediary in 1610 when he acknowledged that "he had no power to make laws of himself . . . without the consent of his three Estates." But was his or Winthrop's the same version of consent that the deputies and freemen were claiming?[15]

The answer was certainly no, for the limited meaning it had for Winthrop did not satisfy the colonists who, like Stoughton, regarded any emphasis on magistracy as veering too close to arbitrary rule. One way of framing their discontents was to describe the "liberties" of the people as "Fundamentall." A second was to reiterate the distinction Stoughton had employed in 1634 to parse the nature of sovereignty. In this regard, Stoughton's successor as a proto-theorist of sovereignty was Henry Vane, Jr. Son of a senior figure in the government of Charles I, and therefore the one person in Massachusetts who indisputably outranked gentry such as Winthrop, Vane was also theocratic in his approach to politics. He squared off with Winthrop in mid-1637 by criticizing a law allowing the magistrates the power to turn away certain immigrants.[16] From Vane's point of view, the statute gave the magistrates far too much discretion. As though he were back in Stuart England, Vane warned that allowing them "unlimitted" power was inherently "unsafe." He warned, too, that such discretion violated the normative politico-theological rule that civil authority in a Christian commonwealth was always and everywhere secondary to the sovereignty of Christ. Given this premise, Vane could easily conclude that the magistrates' authority was properly (and merely) "ministeriall," that is, delegated to them: "Neither hath church nor common wealth *any other than ministeriall* power from Christ, who is the head of the church, and the prince of the kings of the earth." Vane did not spell out the practical workings of this argument or specify, except in very general terms, the "rule for the magistrates to walke by"—others were already attempting this—but the basic point he made was incontestable: rulers and people were alike in being servants of Christ and subordinate to the moral principles he had established.[17]

Apart from playing the card of reason of state (a state is entitled to defend itself), the best Winthrop could say in response was to insist on his own politico-theological version of authority: the oath of office taken by the magistrates, and their devotion to the "wellfare" of the people, were sufficient to keep their powers of office from becoming arbitrary.[18] What Vane was arguing may have had more resonance among the colonists. Like Stoughton before him, he wanted to curtail the claims being made for "magistracy"—hence his attempt to substitute "ministerial" for "magistratical." In doing so, he implied that sovereignty rested elsewhere than with the magistrates—certainly with Christ, possibly with the people or the entire General Court. Magistracy implied something quite different, an authority intrinsic to certain offices or officers.

With regard to "liberties" (always, in the context of these debates, counterpoised to authority, "prerogative," or the necessity of government), a broad coalition of magistrates, deputies, ministers, and people pushed to establish a documentary record of what these were. This record, the Body of Liberties, represented the provisions it embodied as "fundamentall," a term the Massachusetts government had used as early as 1636, when it asked a group of magistrates and ministers to "make a draught" of "the Fundamentals of this Commonwealth," and one that reappeared in the "Fundamental Orders" of Connecticut (1639) and the laws of Plymouth Colony, always signifying foundational rules and principles. Parliamentarians in 1620s England evoked the same foundational character of certain privileges or liberties whenever they referred to the English as having a "birthright in the laws of the kingdom." The opening sentences of the Plymouth law code made this way of thinking explicit: "These foregoing Orders and Constitutions, are so Fundamentally essential to the just Rights, liberties, Common good and special end of this Colony, as that they shall and ought to be inviolably preserved."[19] Permanence was the aura of Magna Carta, and to those who worked to bring the Body of Liberties into being, it had the same status. As did the law codes eventually adopted in the other New England colonies, it opened with a grand assertion: "The free fruition of such liberties, Immunities and priveledges as humanitie, Civilitie, and Christianitie call for as due to every man in his place and proportion without impeachment and Infringement hath ever bene and ever will be the tranquillitie and Stabilitie of Churches and Commonwealths."[20]

This was language informed by the Petition of Right and evocations of consent in English political debate. The importance of consent was underscored in 1635, when the ministers in Massachusetts declared that "in a free State no Magistrate hath power over the bodies, goods, lands, liberties of a free people, but by their free consents." The seventh point in the Body of Liberties brought this point to bear on the Standing Council (the governor and magistrates) by specifying that this body could not act on its own but only with the "consent of a Court generall, or by authority derived from the same." Putting things this way was utterly opposite to Winthrop's position that the charter—or, if not the charter, something other than the people—was the source of political authority. In two ways, therefore, the Body of Liberties drew on widely felt anxieties about arbitrary power: first, in how its provisions were represented as fundamental, and, second, in how it tied the workings of magistracy to the consent of a broader group.[21]

Yet there was still no consensus on the practical workings of magisterial office. General Court sessions in the early 1640s became increasingly contentious, sometimes in response to circumstances, sometimes because of persistent anxieties about arbitrary power. One such circumstance was an effort by the magistrates to reduce the number of deputies each town elected; another, the factionalism that emerged among the magistrates as some became critical of Winthrop. At a General Court session in May 1642, Richard Saltonstall, a magistrate from Ipswich, shared a critique he had written of the Standing Council. It does not survive, but Winthrop characterized some of its "passages" as "very unsound, reproachful and dangerous," and persuaded the court to seek the advice of the ministers.[22] At the same session, "there fell out a great business upon a very small occasion," a dispute about the ownership of a stray sow that grew into a "great business" (in Winthrop's apt phrase) because of another circumstance, popular dismay with the deflation that struck the Massachusetts economy after 1640. Politically, the case found the magistrates and deputies divided on whether justice had been done. In the context of fresh complaints about arbitrary government, the negative voice resurfaced as an issue. A year later, in the fall of 1643, Winthrop was struggling to uphold this privilege for the magistrates.[23]

The back-and-forth of 1642, 1643, and 1644—statements by Winthrop; one (no longer surviving) by Richard Bellingham, a defector among the magistrates; another by one of the ministers; and a treatise collectively written by the clergy—revolved around a familiar array of terms and the deputies' persistence in declaring that "the govenour and assistants had no power out of court but what was given them by the general court." This assertion drew from Winthrop a clear retort to notions of popular sovereignty or, as he put it, assertions that "the Cheif Ordinary Power and administration thereof is in the people." Condemning such a thesis as pointing toward "Democracie," he argued in response that the deputies "were but Counsellors" and, for the first time, employed the language of "mixed" government that Charles I was using at almost the same moment in his response to a parliamentary document aimed at limiting his prerogative, the "Nineteen Propositions" (June 1642). In his answer, Charles described himself as participating in a government composed of three units—"monarchy," "aristocracy," and "democracy."[24]

Different though their politics were in every other respect, Winthrop and Charles turned to this model for the same reason: it warranted a leading role for the few while assuring the people (or, for Charles, the people as represented in Parliament) that the powers assigned to monarchy and aristocracy would not mutate into "tyranny." The model was especially appealing because it curtailed the meaning of democracy, eliminating any possible connotations of popular sovereignty by making it synonymous with one of the tiers—effectively, the least important tier—of mixed government. Solicited by Winthrop to support his position, one of the ministers, probably John Norton of Ipswich, struggled with this terminology in a brief essay defending the negative voice. In his few pages Norton attempted to align the structural and social meanings of "aristocracy" and "democracy." He was clearer about the democratic aspects than about the aristocratic, describing the first as a civil state in which "the supreme civil power is by the people committed or betrusted for the execution thereof" to others, and the second as a civil state in which "the supreame civill power" is in the hands of "the cheifer sort," a category he associated with the aristocracy and the gentry, though parenthetically he recognized that few persons of such rank were actually present in Massachusetts. In keeping with Winthrop's anxieties about respect for social hierarchy, Norton warned that "no popular State" had survived and urged the critics of the negative voice to respect the "eyes" of the commonwealth, or the best men among them; almost in passing, he suggested that "annual elections" and a body of law were adequate safeguards against any undue concentration of power. In the long run, he may have been right, but no one paid him much attention in 1643.[25]

This give-and-take gave way in 1644 to attempts at reconciliation, and a practical reshaping of the General Court. Responding to questions referred to them by the General Court, the ministers sketched a series of propositions that gave each side some of what it wanted. Warranting the Standing Council against critiques such as Saltonstall's, the ministers limited its discretionary powers to "express" rules or, if these did not exist, to the guidance of "the word of God." Splitting the difference on another critical matter, whether the deputies and freemen could establish the scope and authority of any office, the ministers acknowledged that this was one of their privileges but only for "particular matters," leaving the "constant" work of the magistrates to their own discretion. Other distinctions figured in the ministers' analysis of authority. Asked by the deputies if the entire General Court had both judicial and "magistraticall authority," a question aimed at eliminating office of the kind so important to Winthrop, the ministers made matters more compli-

cated by subdividing "magistraticall" into three versions of authority. "Legislative," the first of these, clearly belonged to the freemen,
deputies, and officers. So did "consultative" power. On the other
hand, "judicial" authority was sometimes singular to the magistrates
and sometimes shared. Near the end of their deliberations, the ministers arrived at the heart of the matter. Agreeing with the deputies
that any differentiating of "power of authority" from "liberty of
counsell in the people" was inconsistent with other rulings, they
offered yet another compromise that tilted in Winthrop's direction.
Yes, the General Court was "the chiefe civill power of the common
wealth" and therefore could "describe the power of the magistracy,"
but the patent gave "magistraticall power . . . to the Governor &c."
Effectively, the Massachusetts government was "mixt," with judicial
authority resting mainly with the magistrates, to be "aristocratically
dispensed."26

One more spasm of conflict lay ahead, the attempt of some of the
deputies to have Winthrop censured for intervening in a militia
company's election in Hingham. But a compromise calmed these
troubled waters, the decision to end the practice of having deputies
and magistrates meet together and, with them separated, allowing
each the privilege of rejecting what the other proposed. Adopting
this practice, along with a "libertie" (clarified in the mid-1640s) that
at any Court of Election the freemen could "discharge" someone
from office "without shewing cause," and a ruling in 1641 that no
court could be "dissolved or adjourned without the consent of the
major part thereof" (an echo of agitation in the Long Parliament),
helped to lower the pitch of debate.27 Winthrop gave up warning
against democracy, and the magistrates and deputies who had taken
sides against him their cry of arbitrary rule. In 1646, both groups
agreed to reject a petition asking that many more men be allowed
the privilege of voting in colony elections.

What motivated the colonists who wanted to expand the role of
the freemen and deputies in the General Court and curtail the
authority of the magistrates? No single answer will suffice, if only
because the reasons why deputies, freemen, and (sometimes) people
became so anxious about power changed from time to time. In 1632,

it was taxes; in 1634, a General Court order about stray pigs; in 1642, a lawsuit that seemed to favor an unpopular merchant—to name a few immediate complaints. It is doubtful that the high-status men—Stoughton, Vane, Saltonstall, William Hathorne, Bellingham—who challenged Winthrop wanted to dispense with hierarchy altogether. "Arbitrary," the master word in their rhetoric, was almost boundless in its overtones. In its strongest sense, it referred to officers named without consent and whose authority was unchecked by "a Rule";[28] in a weaker one, any practices or principles that enlarged the power of governor and magistrates at the expense of deputies and freemen. Whether of ordinary or elite status, the "people" who campaigned against the negative voice, the Standing Council, and judicial discretion wanted clear safeguards against the abuse of power. The example of Stuart rule and the Long Parliament's attempts at curtailing the king's prerogative surely weighed on them, as did the "tyranny" of the Church of England, which the ministers were denouncing as they put together the people-centered structure of the "Congregational Way." Out of these disparate sources emerged a version of popular sovereignty, an insistence on a "ministerial" interpretation of the magistrates' office, and, correspondingly, an assertion that "all Authoritye bothe Legislative, consultative and Iuditiall, must be exercised by the people in their bodye representative." Hence the agitation around the negative voice, which contradicted both of these principles.

Massachusetts politics in these years also reflected a tug of war between towns or counties and the central state.[29] As in English politics, where the same tug of war existed, regional interests were involved. Saltonstall and Hathorne lived in Essex County, to the north of Boston, and their dismay at Winthrop's intervention in French colonial politics—another of the circumstances that aggravated many in the General Court—stemmed from local anxieties about being exposed to French attacks. Other local circumstances—Dorchester's in the early 1630s, Newtown's in 1634–35, Hingham's in the 1640s—were also in play.[30]

For Winthrop and those allied with him, the key challenge was to create and sustain government itself. Not, of course, a government that was arbitrary, for Winthrop agreed with his critics that authority was legitimate only if it was constrained by certain rules. In his thinking, three rules sufficed: the structures spelled out in the Massachusetts charter, certain "fundamentals" (of which consent was one), and the will of God.[31] Where he differed from his critics was in wanting to separate the office of magistracy from any version of popular sovereignty. Hence the distinction he drew in 1644 between the "Libertye" of "the people" and the "power of Authoritye" belonging to the governor and magistrates—coincidentally, the same categories John Cotton used in the mid-1640s to preserve the independence of clerical "office" from the "liberty" of church members. Winthrop reinforced this point by glancing sideways at the wrong way of doing things, a situation in which "all were Gouernors, or magistrates, and none lefte, to be an objecte of Gouernment."[32]

Another aspect of Winthrop's thinking was loosely sociological, his low opinion of "the people." As he was reasoning his way in 1629 to taking part in the colonization of Massachusetts, he or someone else pointed out that other attempts at founding colonies had failed because "they used unfitt instruments viz. a multitude of rude and misgoverned persons the very scumme of the land." Once he reached Massachusetts, he insisted that people of the "common ranke" should never "beare equall weight" with "the wisest and cheifest magistrates." In the privacy of his journal, he repeatedly voiced his resentment that some of his opponents tried to mobilize "the people" against his policies. As the Body of Liberties was taking shape in 1639, he may have shared a worried Nathaniel Ward's perception that things were getting out of hand. Ward, who drafted the document, did not want it to circulate among the towns, fearing, as he put it in a letter to Winthrop, that it "will too much exauctorate [exaggerate] the power of" the General Court to "prostrate matters in that manner." Ward doubted that "it be of God to interest the inferiour sort in that which should be reserved inter optimates penes quos est sancire leges."[33] He surely sensed that Winthrop felt the same way.

Yet in one major respect the governor welcomed the reworking of authority in Massachusetts Bay. When a few English aristocrats let him know they were interested in coming to New England, Winthrop signaled through an intermediary that their rank did not entitle them to high political office in Massachusetts. He entrusted Cotton with the task of delivering this news, and Cotton did what was expected of him, telling Lord Saye and Sele that, as with Jethro and Moses, so in Massachusetts "the rule that directeth the choice of supreame governors" restricted the colonists to the "righteous" who feared God. Cotton turned aside Saye and Sele's complaint that, by tying the status of freeman to church membership, the colonists had drawn "all things under the determination of the church." When Saye and Sele and other Puritan grandees founded the colony of Providence Island in the Caribbean, they moved in a direction antithetical to the road being taken in Massachusetts. As Winthrop recorded their intentions in a journal entry of 1640, they "declared themselves much against" the "form of government" in Massachusetts, "and for a meer aristocratie, and an hereditary magistracy to be settled upon some great persons." The relief he felt that nothing of this kind had come to pass in Massachusetts is palpable. Observing that Providence Island failed to attract "goodly men" because such people wanted a framework of government that allowed them to "make choice of themselves" for "governours," Winthrop implicitly indicated his own preference for a system based on consent, elections, and other limits on executive authority, with no excesses of aristocratic privilege of the kind he had witnessed in England. In a political culture given to rhetorical exaggeration, he may have sounded more conservative than he really was.[34]

II

As THESE struggles were unfolding in Massachusetts, four other colonies were creating, or in one instance revising, their forms of government. Probably in explicit counterpoint to the disputes in Massachusetts, the colonies of Plymouth, Connecticut, and the towns that came together in 1647 to form Rhode Island omitted most of the powers of office Winthrop and his fellow magistrates were claiming as distinctly theirs. Beginning afresh, with no charter as point of reference and, in Plymouth, no gentry with expectations of leadership, the people in these other colonies located political authority in the freemen, and in officers only by delegation. For some of the colonists in Rhode Island, the master term for their system was "democracy," the category that Winthrop and many others in contemporary England found so alarming.

That word was not used in Connecticut when delegates from the three towns of Wethersfield, Hartford, and Windsor agreed in 1638 on a set of Fundamental Orders.[35] But the men who ratified the Orders were of the same mind as the Rhode Islanders in other ways. Both groups of settlers started out in Massachusetts, and both included people who objected to Winthrop's understanding of governance, in particular the group that, independently of the Massachusetts Bay Company, had founded Dorchester in 1630. When Israel Stoughton of Dorchester was censured by the General Court for objecting to the negative voice and barred from holding office for three years, "many" of his fellow townsmen appealed to the court to reverse the penalty. By 1636, a majority of Dorchester families had departed for the Connecticut River Valley, settling in a place they named Windsor.[36] The people who abandoned Newtown (Cambridge) and founded Hartford also had a bone to pick with Winthrop. After he was turned out of the governorship in 1634, one of his successors was John Haynes, a Newtowner. Thomas Hooker, who began his New World ministry in Newtown and resumed it in Hartford, would remain at odds with Winthrop over the meaning of consent, authority, and office.

Early on, the people who arrived in the Connecticut River Valley made do with the expedient—arranged by the Massachusetts government—of delegating certain responsibilities to eight men drawn from all three towns.[37] Once the Pequot War (May–June 1637) had ended and its costs were being levied on the towns, state-making got under way in earnest. The core premise embodied in the Fundamental Orders concerned the locus and scope of authority. Instead of differentiating magistrate from deputy or freeman, the Orders began with the provision that authority rested with the General Court as a whole. Two court sessions a year were specified, the first for the purpose of electing officers, the second for enacting legislation. With a watchful eye on England, where no Parliament had sat since 1629, the Orders allowed the freemen to call the Assembly into session if the governor and "major parte of the magistrates" refused to do so, specifying as well that any such session—with the governor presumably absent—"may proceed to do any act of power which any other General Court may." Moreover, only the Assembly could decide when to adjourn or to call a new election. The agitation in Massachusetts about rotation in office and accountability also left its mark upon the Orders, which specified that the person holding office as governor did so for one year at a time and could not stand for re-election. The same determination to shrink the powers of executive office led to provisions limiting the governor to administrative and judicial functions. Deputies (four from each town), magistrates, and governor were to meet as a single body and decide matters by majority vote. Other provisions described the procedures—drawn out and indirect—for nominating magistrates, though in the end both governor and magistrates were to be elected "by the vote of the country."[38]

The thinking of the men who drafted and ratified the Fundamental Orders cannot be recovered, for none of them wrote anything about principles and expectations. What is certain is that they wanted to protect the privileges of the towns against those of a general government, a policy that may explain why each town was assigned four deputies at a time when the Massachusetts towns had three, a number reduced to two a few years later. For a fuller understanding of the politics of statecraft in Connecticut, we must rely on two statements about civil government Hooker made in 1638, an "election sermon" he gave in the spring of 1638 and a lengthy letter he sent Winthrop in December, responding to one of his, now lost. In an earlier phase of these exchanges, Winthrop seems to have asserted that government should always be in the hands of the few rather than the many. In his December response, Hooker "fully assent[ed]" to the proposition that "the people should choose some from amongst them" and "referr matter of counsell to their counsellours." "Only the quaestion here growes," he noted, "what rule the Judge must have to iudge by" and "who those counsellors must be." Mindful of Winthrop's emphasis on judicial discretion that was being contested at the very moment Hooker and the Newtowners departed, he insisted that such discretion was *not* the right way for magistrates to proceed: "I must confesse I ever looked at it as a way which leads directly to tyranny." As for who should be involved in affairs of state, Hooker was resolute: "In matters of greater consequence, which concern the common good, a generall counsell chosen by all to transact businesses which concerne all, I conceive . . . [is] most sutable to rule and most safe." Contrary to Winthrop's preference for strong leadership by the few, Hooker concluded with an aphorism widely used in English politics: "In the multitude of counsellors ther is safety."[39]

The theme of the election sermon was sovereignty and, as befitted ministerial discourse, human liberty and power refracted through the overarching power of the Word. Hooker's opening "doctrine" was relatively bland: "The choice of public magistrates belongs unto the people, by God's own allowance." But the corollary was unequivocal, and in keeping with the spirit of the Fundamental Orders: "They who have power to appoint officers and magistrates, it is in their power, also, to set the bounds and limitations of the power and place unto which they call them." Then came an assertion about sovereignty—"the foundation of authority is laid . . . in the free consent of the people"—followed by an "exhortation" (a routine aspect of sermon structure) "to persuade us, as God hath given us liberty, to take it."[40]

Too much should not be read into these references to liberty and the people.[41] For Hooker, consent became legitimate and necessary when it was coupled with a willingness to obey the will of God and put the good of the "whole" before self-interest. This was how he glossed the maxim *salus populi suprema lex* in a treatise on church government he wrote in the mid-1640s. That he gave consent such importance in 1638 can be explained not only by the disputes in Massachusetts and England but, for him in particular, by the fact that the people who came with him to Connecticut were the very opposite of Winthrop's "common ranke" or "scumme." In what he wrote some years later about church government, a principal concern was to separate—very Winthrop-like—the authority of clerical "office" from the powers of decision-making among the laity. What church members delegated to the clergy was not in them intrinsically but only by another act of delegation, in this case Christ's.[42] Despite these qualifications, what he said in 1638 and would say some years later about the godly and their privileges in the opening pages of *A Survey of the Summe of Church-Discipline* (London, 1648) suggested that power flowed upward from the people to those who acted as their rulers. He did not write the Fundamental Orders, but the barriers it created against arbitrary rule were consistent with his sermon and letter of 1638.

Two years before the towns in Connecticut put together a colony-wide government, the freemen of New Plymouth revised and clarified the rules and structures of their system. With no patent or charter to guide them, the colonists who lived in Plymouth during the 1620s and early 1630s seem to have made do with the simplest of structures: an elected governor (who voted in these elections is unclear) and several "Assistants" functioning as a council and, less certainly, a General Court that encompassed a broader group of "freemen," but not deputies. A burst of town-founding in the mid-1630s put pressure on these arrangements. So did what was happening in nearby Massachusetts and faraway England, for in October 1636 the men who initiated a recasting of the government began by including all the freemen in twice-yearly meetings of a General Court and taking the first steps toward a system of "committees" from each town, a process completed in 1638. No one of Hooker's stature was on hand to articulate core principles, but the Plymouth colonists felt as strongly as he did that authority must be held in check by the rule of consent. The first act of the "whole body" that met in November 1636 was to say so in a way that looked back to the Magna Carta. In their words, "No imposition law or ordnance can be made or imposed upon us by ourselves or others at present or to come but such as shall be made or imposed by consent according to the free liberties of the State and Kingdome of England."[43] As in Massachusetts and Connecticut, a rule was put in place mandating annual elections, and although re-election of the governor was not precluded—William Bradford would hold that office almost every year between 1621 and 1657—he had only a "double vote" in meetings of a unicameral General Court. Otherwise, his duties were principally administrative. Meanwhile, all freemen were to meet once a year as a legislature, and another time for elections. Two years later, the freemen of the colony agreed to give up appearing annually at a court and to rely on deputies elected by each town, but they reserved the privilege of annulling any legislation when they gathered at the Court of Election.[44]

A decision of the Plymouth General Court in 1639 may explain why the freemen were so wary of a strong government. At a session that June, vigorous debate broke out over the distribution of colony lands in response to what some felt to be the excessive privileges of a tiny number of colonists, the "Undertakers" who in 1627 had agreed to pay off the colony's investors in exchange for grants of land and control of the fur trade. Now, with more towns being founded, the freemen wanted to take full control of how land was distributed. In what was clearly a compromise, the court raised a sum of money to buy out the Undertakers, agreeing, too, that "Purchasers or old Comers" could choose certain tracts of land for themselves. Once these steps were taken, "all the residue of the lands not formerly graunted forth either to plantations or particular persons" were to become the property "of the whole Body of the Freemen to be disposed of either by the whole Body or by such persons as shalbe by the whole Body of Freemen assigned and authorized." On this most crucial of questions, who should control the colony's one major economic resource, the freemen decided to entrust that authority to the largest group within the government.[45]

The four settlements that sprang up along the shores of Narragansett Bay and on Newport Island in the 1630s came together as a colony in 1647, after Roger Williams secured a charter from the

Long Parliament.[46] Naming themselves "Rhode Island and Providence Plantations," the parties to this coalition had a free hand to do as they pleased: no investors to repay, nothing in the charter to constrain their preferences for how they should be governed, no religious orthodoxy to uphold. Another circumstance was crucial—the making of colony government *followed* the creation of town governments, as it also did in Connecticut and New Haven. Some attitudes and decisions came easily to the people living in the four towns. Initially settling in Massachusetts, some of them had been forced out in the aftermath of the Antinomian Controversy. Twice marked by the struggles taking place in that colony, they were of a mind (as Roger Williams put it in a letter of 1636) to avoid "the face of Magistracie," that is, any sheltering of political office from direct dependence on the freemen and any coercion in matters of religion.[47]

First and foremost in their new frame of government, therefore, were assertions of majority rule and its corollary, that the freemen were delegating some of their authority to the men who held office in the new government. So a "Generall Court," formed by the two towns on Newport Island, Portsmouth and Newport, had already affirmed in 1641. Using the word "democratic" in a positive though limited sense, the dozen or so persons present "unanimously" declared that the "Government which this Bodie Politick doth attend unto in this Island . . . is a Democracie or Popular Government that is to say It is in the Powre of the Body of freemen . . . or major Part of them to make or Constitute Just Lawes." Earlier, the people who founded Providence had indicated their preference for majority rule and popular consent. Officers they would have, and a government empowered to regulate certain aspects of social and economic life, but only within sharp limits.[48]

The delegates who met in 1647 to spell out the colony-wide structure brought this expectation with them. It explains the decision to grant each town the right to send ten delegates or representatives to each session of the general government, thus ensuring the "multitude of counselors" Hooker desired in Connecticut. In similar fashion, the framework of government specified that laws affecting everyone were to originate locally; not until a draft version had circulated among the four towns would a statute come before the federation government to be ratified. Within that government, the "president" could not adjourn or dissolve the Assembly on his own, and everyone sat together in a unicameral body. According to a provision of the earliest code of laws, moreover, everyone who was "lawfully called" to office was enjoined against presuming "to do more or less, than those that had power to call him, did authorize him to do."[49]

Going well beyond Connecticut and Plymouth in guarding against any concentration of authority in the hands of a few, the delegates of 1647 were unique in using the same term to describe their new government that the Newport Islanders had embraced in 1641. Theirs, too, was a democracy, or, as they put it, "the due forme of government" in their colony "is Democratical, that is to say, a government held by the free and voluntary consent of all, or the greater part of the free inhabitants." The first of the statute laws was less original, for it reiterated much of what was said in the Petition of Right: calling for justice according to "known laws" and prohibiting any claims by the state to "lands or liberties" except by "the lawful judgment" of "peers" or a law enacted by the General Assembly. As a whole, however, the assertions and practices of 1647 stood at the other extreme from what Winthrop and his allies had sought for Massachusetts.[50]

Unique, too, was the clarity of Roger Williams' understanding of sovereignty. "I infer," he declared in *The Bloudy Tenent of Persecution* (London, 1644), "as before has been touched, that the Soveraigne, originall, and foundation of civill power lies in the people, (whom they must needs meane by the civill power distinct from the government set up.) And if so, that a People may erect and establish what forme of Government seemes to them most meete." "It is evident," he went on to argue, "that such Governments as are by them erected and established, have no more power, nor for no longer time, then the civill power or people consenting and agreeing shall betrust them with." Via this reasoning, consent acquired a stronger significance than it had for Winthrop or possibly for Hooker. Williams returned to its importance in *The Bloudy Tenent Yet More Bloudy*

(London, 1652), arguing in an aphoristic manner that "the People" were the "originall of all free Power and Government."[51]

Because he wrote the earlier of these books while he was living in London (1643–44), Williams may have borrowed this language from critics of the monarchy. Had he read or otherwise absorbed Henry Parker's *Observations upon Some of His Majesties Late Answers and Expresses* (1642), in which Parker asserted that "Power is originally inherent in the people" and in "princes" it is "but secondary and derivative . . . , the fountaine and efficient cause [is] the people"? Parker's was a daring argument at the time he made it (anonymously) on behalf of the radicals in Parliament, but by 1644 the civil war between king and Parliament had made something akin to it a practical necessity if Parliament was to levy taxes and conduct foreign policy. Whatever the influences on Williams' thinking, and wherever it took shape—in the 1640s he was most intent on guarding liberty of conscience from the civil state—his was probably one voice among many in Rhode Island when the decision was made to embrace the term "democracy" and emphasize so strongly the local sources of political authority.[52]

The making of New Haven Colony government happened several years after the founding of the *town* of New Haven in 1638. Initially it was the only place of settlement west of Saybrook, at the mouth of the Connecticut River. But in 1643, after other groups had settled along the coast, the political leaders of the town drew five of these nearby communities into a colony organized around a General Court consisting of a governor, magistrates, and deputies (two per town). Politically, New Haven was distinctive in four respects: it never gained a charter from Parliament, despite attempts to do so; its courts dispensed with formal juries; no rotation in office was required of the governor; and the status of freeman was confined to church members. The last of these became contentious in the 1650s.[53] Not long thereafter, in 1665, the colony had to concede its independence after the leaders of Connecticut secured a charter from the Crown that included all of its territory. In the history of state-making in early New England, the real significance of New

Haven lies in the attempt of town and colony to implement godly rule, a story told in Chapter Three.

III

WITH STATE-MAKING more or less completed by the mid-1640s, what could the colonists take for granted as principle and practice? What had become customary as ways of governance? In list form, these would have included the following:

• Certain "liberties" were "fundamental," secured for all time in a written code or by general consensus;

• One of these fundamentals reiterated a point in the Petition of Right, that the state could not take someone's property without the consent of that person's representatives. Particular to the colonists' situation was a related principle, that colony lands be distributed with broad-based consent;[54]

• Another "fundamental law of a people or Common wealth" was the "libertie to Exercise Imediate choise of theire owne Governors," a rule in Massachusetts after 1634 and in the other colonies as they came into being. From this "constant libertie" it followed that freemen may "discharge . . . all the general Officers" of a colony at the annual day of election;[55]

• Elections for deputies, magistrates, and governor happened annually or, as sometimes occurred in the 1630s, semi-annually;

• Two or more sessions of assemblies or general courts were to meet every year;

• In Connecticut, the Fundamental Orders empowered freemen or deputies to summon a session on their own, and a 1641 Massachusetts statute stipulated that the General Court controlled its own adjournment;

• The authority to specify the duties of officers and the "bounds" of their office rested with a general court, as did the authority to legislate;

• Rotation in the office of governor was encouraged in Massachusetts and, in Connecticut, made mandatory, but not observed in New Haven or, for the most part, in Plymouth;

• Majority rule prevailed unless, as in Massachusetts, a "negative voice" was conceded to magistrates and (after 1644) the deputies as well. In 1645, the Connecticut Assembly also introduced the negative voice for magistrates, and majority rule was denied in New Haven Colony.[56] Majority rule implied popular sovereignty, the negative voice a sovereignty divided between office (authority) and the people's representatives.

These practices and policies stand in sharp contrast to what the Puritan grandees who founded Providence Island in the Caribbean put in place. Forgoing an assembly or general court, the organizers of the venture entrusted a single man with the offices of governor and "Captain general," made him the "chief administrative, judicial, and military officer," and assigned him an "absolute veto" over the small group of persons, none of them elected, who formed a council.[57] As telling as this is, the better comparison may be with the workings of the English government before 1640 and the accomplishments of the Long Parliament. By the close of the 1630s, the colonists had eliminated all aspects of royal rule and its adjuncts: no king with far-reaching powers of appointment, a veto over any measures passed by Parliament, and authority to call into being or dismiss that body at his discretion; no privileged role in politics for men of aristocratic rank; no equivalent of the bishops who sat in Parliament. As for the Long Parliament, the radicals who, under the leadership of John Pym, persuaded that divided and frequently reluctant body to assert itself secured a Triennial Act requiring the king (or others) to summon a new Parliament within three years after the current body was dissolved, and another act forbidding the prorogation or dissolution of the Long Parliament itself without that body's consent. Certain courts were abolished, bishops excluded from the House of Lords, and certain levies or taxes declared illegal—all told, a "poor return for seven or eight months' effort" on the part of a parliament supposedly united in the cause of reform and a king disposed to accept some changes in how he ruled.[58] More daring steps followed as relations with the king worsened. The Nineteen Propositions presented to him in June 1642 gave Parliament the right to approve the appointment of privy councilors and tied the king's authority to the "advise and consent of the major part" of that group. But Charles would have none of this.[59]

By the end of 1642, with a civil war to fight, Parliament was asserting its powers to tax and raise armies, and it called into being an assembly of divines, most of them sympathetic to Presbyterianism, to determine the future of the Church of England. But the Long Parliament never produced a coherent description of sovereignty.[60] On its behalf, Parker and others argued for parliamentary sovereignty, a theory premised on denying the king a "negative voice"; others advocated a "mixed" structure in which "king in Parliament" was the locus of authority. Ambiguity and contradiction persisted, notably around the concept of representation and the meaning of "the people."[61] Never did the Long Parliament doubt that a monarchy with considerable powers of governance, an aristocracy with distinctive privileges, and a comprehensive church tied in key respects to the state would persist; as Parker pointed out in his *Observations,* the ideal government consisted of king and Parliament working together, with the people present through their representatives in the House of Commons. Any substantial empowering of the people at the expense of the gentry was not the way to go. Alienated though they became, Parliament and king found it difficult to free themselves from assumptions that John Pym voiced in 1640 as crisis loomed: the king possessed a "great prerogative" and could "do no wrong."[62]

Consequential in 1640s England—though disregarded after 1660, when Charles II assumed the throne from which his father had been removed—the reforms enacted by the Long Parliament fell significantly short of what the colonists had accomplished. Remarkably (and never adequately acknowledged), their program was nearly as robust as the gold standard of radicalism during the English Revolution, the demands of the Levellers and the army spelled out in the "Heads of the Proposals" offered by the army (July–August 1647), the "Agreement of the People" (October 1647), and associated documents. Fiercely hostile to the Long Parliament for remaining in session some seven years after its members were elected, dismayed by its indifference to broader reform, and critical of the relationship between social rank and political power, the Levellers called for elections to Parliament every year (though they compromised on biennial elections in a subsequent manifesto), seats in the Commons reapportioned to eliminate the "very unequal" system then in place, and popular sovereignty, with the House of Commons as its instrument or locus but enriched with a recognition that it checked the authority of both kings and Parliament, either of which could lapse into tyranny. As explained in "The Case of the Army," a tract influenced by Leveller ideas, "all power is originally and essentially in the whole body of the people of this Nation, and . . . their free choice or consent by their Representors is the only originall or foundation of all just government." Monarchy would persist, however, as would a revised House of Lords or a Council of State, with Commons effectively a unicameral legislature depending on the manifesto. What had no counterpart among the colonists were complaints about social and economic injustices and assertions of liberty of conscience; the Levellers wanted to dismantle a state church empowered to regulate belief and practice. Nor were the colonists as intent on expanding the franchise (freemanship), although the Levellers' more daring recommendations, which approached universal male suffrage, were watered down as they negotiated with the army. On the other hand, the Levellers' indictment of the English legal system was fully in keeping with reforms the colonists would undertake (Chapter Four).[63]

In the event, the Leveller program was never adopted—not by the Long Parliament, which refused all suggestions that it dissolve, nor by the commonwealth and protectorate when Oliver Cromwell was head of state, though he practiced a version of liberty of conscience. Politically, therefore, the accomplishments of the colonists became the fullest embodiment of the animus against arbitrary rule, monarchical authority, monopolies, and other forms of special privilege, and, on the side of state-building, the fullest realization of "fundamental liberties," the empowering of legislative representatives, and the principle of consent. That they found their way to this program owed much to circumstances: their reaction to Stuart rule, and the fact that no church, king, Parliament, or aristocracy could thwart their aspirations for civil government. In New England, the famous phrase of James I, "no bishops, no king," mutated into "no king, no strong central state"—and also, of course, no centralized church government. It made a difference, too, that state-building in three of the colonies arose after towns had been organized. Add to these transformations and practices the possibilities for participation and the shape of town governments (taken up in Chapter Two), the insistence on consent that made it necessary for all legislation on taxes, land, war, and other crucial matters to be voted on by the deputies in a General Court, the accountability of those in office, and the occasional expressions of something akin to popular sovereignty, and any characterization of colonial governments as oligarchic or authoritarian seems astonishingly at odds with what the colonists sought and accomplished.

At the time, some observers of events in the colonies sensed how much had changed. Writing to John Winthrop in August 1645, a colonist on his way to England asked that Winthrop share his wishes for "peace and prosperity" with others in Massachusetts, adding that unity and peace could "hardly be" accomplished in a place where "government remaines so popular." "Popular" was probably a reference to the frequency of elections, the consequence being, as the letter writer put it, that leaders were so "tosse[d] and tumble[d]" they could not "mannage the affayres of the country." Two months earlier, another correspondent expressed his sympathy for Winthrop in the aftermath of an attempt by the townspeople of Hingham to have him censured, noting that "experience every day every where proves it that there is noe stabilitie in the arm off Flesh especially in the common people."[64] To these perceptions could be added a multitude of complaints by English Presbyterians and moderate Congregationalists that the colonists had veered into the troubled waters of "popular" or "democratic" government in their churches. A grumpy

Winthrop shared some of these worries, none of which should be taken at face value, given the prevalence of rhetorical excess. Nonetheless, they communicate something of the flavor of governance in a society in which some dared to embrace the term "democracy," a word even the Levellers chose to avoid.

CHAPTER TWO

LAND, TAXES, AND PARTICIPATION

The Making of Town Governments

A s COLONY governments were forming, the colonists were busy devising rules and structures for the towns in which they lived. This, too, was a politics that aroused strong feelings, for the business of each town was deciding how land should be distributed. People watched and worried as this process unfolded, for the well-being of every family depended on having enough land. People also worried because the process could disrupt or strengthen social peace. Of conflict there would soon be plenty, once towns began to assign lots, map their boundaries, and require households to fence in gardens and planting lands: boundaries remained inexact, fences unfinished, and people sought more or different bits of land than what they had been assigned. Townspeople tried to head off disputes by appointing fence viewers, ordering pigs ringed, and arranging for town clerks to record grants or sales of land. Good fences made for good neighbors. So did good records, as the townspeople of Guilford, in Connecticut, recognized in asking the town clerk to keep careful track of sales and exchanges for "the better promotion of peace." The townspeople of Dedham, in Masssachusetts, tried something else, an agreement to "stand fully satisfyed with out Complayning or disquiet howsoever" as allocations of land were made. Peace of certain kinds there was, but litigation also flourished.[1]

The importance of land was the reason why so many people left the vicinity of Boston soon after arriving in New England, going from places such as Dorchester and Newtown (Cambridge) to the Connecticut River Valley (1635–36), from Salem to Providence (1635–36), from Lynn (where the soil was exceptionally poor) to Plymouth Colony (1637) and Southampton, Long Island (1640), from Watertown to Sudbury (1638), and, as William Bradford lamented in *Of Plimoth Plantation,* from decaying Plymouth to nearby Duxbury, Scituate, Sandwich, Taunton, and Yarmouth. Land was at the center of the making of town governments and the reason why, with few exceptions, those governments entrusted key decisions about its distribution to general meetings. Another aspect of town politics concerned taxes: Who would decide how the property of each household would be assessed ("rated") and establish each town's annual expenses? As was forcefully demonstrated in the Watertown protest of 1632 against a levy enacted by John Winthrop and the handful of assistants, people wanted a voice in deciding how they were taxed.

Beginning with decision-making about land and taxes, the men in every town had many opportunities for making their opinions felt. The governance of towns, and, to an even greater extent, the governance of local congregations, was deeply participatory. So was civil society as a whole, for the colonists brought with them a cluster of assumptions and practices that abetted popular involvement in everyday politics: an appetite for news, a confidence in sharing their opinions with local leaders, a facility for writing and reading, the custom of distributing handwritten texts to influence political decision-making, the experience of resisting (usually by ignoring) the rules of the Church of England, and the habit of using petitions to complain of grievances. Licensed to speak out in congregations and towns by the principle of consent, the colonists supplemented this principle with other rules that were less scripted. Sanctioned, encouraged, and seized upon in unpredictable ways, participation became an integral aspect of civil and religious life in early New England.

One other version of their English experience weighed upon the colonists. They had learned how to deflect orders that came from above in the towns and counties of their former homeland. There few wanted to march off to fight distant wars; there scores of parish churches had ignored the rules of the state church. Local inertia and the laxness of administrative structures meant that English towns and counties rarely accomplished what Parliament, church, and monarchy expected of them. Militias went untrained or unarmed, penalties for certain crimes were softened, the canons of the church flouted. Wanting a similar freedom to do as they pleased in their New World towns, the colonists brought with them a wariness of orders emanating from magistrates and General Courts.

A fuller description of town governments follows, and this chapter concludes with an inventory of the possibilities for participation.

I

THE ECONOMIC significance of town business fed the immense interest people showed in how power would be shared in their communities. Every town began with an extraordinary asset, the reserves of land it was charged with distributing to townspeople or holding in "common" for current use and future disposal.[2] Households needed several kinds of land—pasture for cattle, a house lot for a garden and orchard, meadow for growing hay, fields for planting grains—and in any of these forms, the quality could vary from one patch to the next. Other bread-and-butter issues also put pressure on local governance. Once land became theirs, townspeople fell to work building fences to protect gardens and orchards from voracious pigs and cattle and constructing roads to get their surplus grain and cattle to a market.[3] And they were cutting down a great many trees for wood to heat their houses, so many that some towns were running short by the mid-1630s, and many more would do so in the 1640s. Hence the rapid enacting of rules designed to conserve the local supply.[4] Meanwhile, there was a minister to pay and a meetinghouse to construct and maintain. Colony governments also needed money and set each town a quota to raise by taxing property. In Massachusetts, these levies fluctuated from one year to the next, spiking whenever the threat of war with Indians or a hostile English government prompted the General Court to summon the militia or rebuild and staff the ever-decaying fort in Boston Harbor.[5]

Starting afresh, and with traditional hierarchies in disarray, the colonists put together a form of government designed to distribute land in ways that satisfied most people. There was near-universal agreement that the surest means of meeting this goal was to refer decision-making to as many townspeople as possible and, concurrently, to keep local officers on a short leash. In the town of Sudbury, "every major issue was discussed in open town meetings," 132 of them "in the first fifteen years," with "more than 650 orders" adopted by the town during this same period. A few towns handed the task of distributing land to the congregation and its leaders—Dorchester at the beginning of the 1630s, Guilford in the early 1640s—almost certainly in the hope that lay saints and ministers would do the right thing.[6] Far more common were decisions of the kind made in Plymouth, Providence, and Portsmouth, Rhode Island. In Plymouth, the entire group of householders was involved in governance until 1649. In newly founded Providence (1636), the "masters of Families" were meeting every "fort night" without any "Magistracie" on hand. As late as the mid-1640s, Portsmouth was holding monthly meetings.[7]

This practice quickly gave way to a system that divided town business between general meetings and a small group of officers known as "townsmen" or "select men." Each town had to decide how many selectmen to have, some agreeing to use as few as four, others opting for seven or more. In 1638, the Ipswich town meeting fixed the number at seven, but the town raised it a year later to nine, possibly reasoning that there was greater safety in numbers. Almost universally, town meetings marked the transition to selectmen by limiting what these officers could do and singling out the division of land as the business of the entire community. The Hartford town meeting was unusually specific in ruling that, on their own, townsmen could not admit newcomers, levy fees or taxes with one exception (the expenses of herding cattle), change the location of roads, or make land grants except "an Ackre or Two at most to anny Inhabetant and that in case of present necessitye"—that is, helping someone in distress. A few years later, the same town meeting reminded everyone that grants of land must be made with "the knowledg and

Consent of the whole and If anny such Devesions shalbe made to be voyd and of noe effect." The Springfield, Massachusetts, town meeting continued to insist that "the giving out of the land belongs to the Towne" to decide, not to the selectmen. Annually, when electing their selectmen, some townspeople put on record that these officers were "under the same rest[r]a[i]ntes as the former townsemen had and wer under." The townspeople of Woburn, Massachusetts, ruled in the mid-1640s that the selectmen must meet "once a month, at the least," keep adequate records of "all orders," and inform the "public" of all "disbursements and disposal of the town's stock and land" at the close of each year. Portsmouth required its officers to report quarterly to the townspeople, who could alter or repeal any of their actions, rules a nineteenth-century historian of early Rhode Island characterized as indicating a "jealousy of delegated power."[8]

These ways of constraining town officers were accompanied by measures to ensure transparency and accountability. Townspeople remained nervous about delegating power to the few, as evidenced by the practice of appointing an additional group of men to work alongside or separate from the selectmen in making "rates" (assessments) or divisions of land; for example, Hartford added no fewer than ten to the group of townsmen in 1640 to decide a particular division of common lands.[9] Downriver on the Connecticut shore, the Guilford town meeting combined three versions of accountability, ordering that all selectmen should "bee yearly chosen," requiring them to make "no lawes nor orders . . . but before all the planters, then and there inhabiting and residing" had "due warning and notice of their meeting," and specifically allowing for "weighty objections" that must "be duly attended . . . and . . . satisfyingly removed." Springfield introduced a similar provision in 1646, allowing "orders and conclusions" of the selectmen to remain "in force" on the condition of their being "openly published, before the generality of the Towne after a lecture or at any training day, or any other publique meetinge," and specifying a seven-day period for protests before "silence" served to "confirm and establish" the selectmen's orders.[10]

Amid such efforts, a complicating circumstance was the lively market in land that sprang up almost at once. The emergence of a land market had everything to do with a restlessness registered in a rate of migration in and out of towns that surprised everyone.[11] A market linked to this pace of change made many of the colonists uneasy, for they tied their hopes for social peace to a policy of controlling who came into their communities. Wanting a "homogeneous spirit and people" and knowing from their English years that, if the "better part" were a minority in a town, "violence" between them and the "rudest" would erupt,[12] local people tried various means of keeping such people out. Nor did towns want anyone too disabled by age or illness, and therefore unable to support him- or herself. Hence a widespread determination to curtail the workings of the land market. As early as 1635 in Ipswich, the possibility that "doubtfull persons" given to "drinking and pilferinge" would arrive prompted the decision "to be very considerate in disposal of lootts and admission of people" in order to have "lesse of Satans kingdome" and "more" of Christ's. Moved by the same anxiety, the townsmen of New London voted in 1648 that "no persons or person shall have admittance . . . except the parties or partie shall bring some testimonie from the magestrates or Elders of the place that they com[e] from or from some neighbor plantation and some good Christians, what their carriage is or have been."[13] Newly incorporated Lancaster, Massachusetts, followed suit in 1653, voting to exclude "any excomunicat or otherwise prophane and scandalus" persons from residency.[14]

Another way of limiting the consequences of the land market was to regulate who sold what to whom. Almost universally, towns introduced rules and regulations to this end. At a "general meeting" in Boston in 1635, the townspeople specified that "none shall sell their houses or allotments to any new comers, but with the consent and allowance of those that are appointed Allotters," adding that newcomers must be "such as may be likely to be received members of the Congregation." Braintree opted in late 1641 for a rule that "noe inhabitant shall sell or dispose of any house or land to any that is not received an inhabitant . . . without it be first offered unto the men that are appointed to dispose of the towns affairs." If this provision failed, the selectmen were to sell "only to such as the town's men shall approve." Dedham had already introduced similar rules in 1636, and the earliest recorded votes in Hartford (c. 1636) and Wethersfield (in or near 1640) required anyone who left within four years to give up his land to the town, or sell it to someone approved by the town (Hartford), or to other townspeople (Wethersfield). Springfield spelled out a complicated set of options at the January 1639 town meeting, all of them designed to give "the Plantation" a voice in sales of land.[15]

Rules of this kind, though deeply felt, were undercut by the benefits of a land market. Necessary if a town was to recruit more residents, especially anyone with badly needed capital or special skills,[16] an unregulated market was also a pragmatic means of settling debts and distributing property after someone's death. Even better, it enabled townspeople to consolidate the scattered bits of land they were acquiring in successive distributions, or to buy more of the kinds they needed.[17] Attempts at regulation persisted, but markets became a fact of everyday life.

In and of itself, the market could not answer a key question, the status of people who arrived in a town after house lots and meadow had initially been allocated. Should these newcomers have the same rights and privileges as the founders? At the founding moment it was relatively easy to decide who could participate in the assigning of lands. Every householder who was present received something, and, of great consequence for the future, acquired the privilege of grazing cattle on the town's common lands, the right to harvest timber, and a share of subsequent divisions or distributions. Significantly, these privileges were never tied to church membership, not even in New Haven town, where a special rule ensured that all inhabitants (or "planters") "have right to their proper Inheritances, and doe and shall enjoy all other Civil liberties and priviledges," one of these being an appropriate share in future distributions of land, a position consistent with John Davenport's insistence that people in this category possess every "Civil right or Liberty that is due unto them as Inhabitants and Planters, as if none should have Lots in due proportion with other men . . . but only Church-members."[18] But should latecomers or children of the first planters also have the same rights or liberties? Every town had to debate this question, and everywhere the answer at the outset was a qualified no, mixed in with some concessions.[19]

Thus arose the category of "admitted inhabitant" as a means of incorporating people who arrived from England and elsewhere in the colonies. "Admitted" meant that such people had been approved and accepted as residents, usually after a town meeting voted to do so. Even when "admitted freely as planters" and guaranteed the same "Civil liberties and privileges" (except, it seems, freemanship) that the "free Burgesses" had, as New Haven wrote into its laws in the 1640s, they were probably denied automatic rights to future divisions of land. A complicating circumstance was demographic, the ever-growing presence of young people, some with parents in the town, but others, as in Providence, apparently arriving on their own. In that town, the "young men" pressed for a full share of privileges that initially the "Howse holders" had denied them. As Roger Williams informed Winthrop in 1636, they were "discontented with their estate, and seek the Freedome of Vote allso, and aequalitie etc."—wanting the vote *in town meeting*, because it would give them a voice in how future distributions were managed.[20] Late-founded Lancaster tried to close some of these doors by fixing the number of families entitled to share in the town lands at thirty-five. But nothing worked to keep the population static. "Admitted inhabitant" remained a kind of halfway status, with towns insisting that people in this category pay taxes on the same basis as everyone else, and sometimes allowing them to attend town meetings. But they rarely gained the crucial privilege of participating equally in future distributions.[21]

When townspeople got around to distributing town lands, an immediate question concerned what system of farming they would practice, "open field" or closed, or a mixture of the two. Coming as they did from different regions of England, each with its long-established customs, townspeople could not take for granted which system would prevail.[22] Everywhere, however, people wanted to acquire the right kinds and qualities of land. Thousands of acres were theirs, but some types of land always seemed in short supply or deficient; as was said of the land assigned to New London, it lacked "meadow sufficient for even a small plantation," and a group of people pondering whether to move to Woburn decided not to do so because their "minds were much for medow, and their judgments short in what they saw."[23] Given these expectations and constraints, debate arose about how to reconcile a set of principles or values the colonists brought with them. The first, and in most situations the dominant, value went by the name of "due proportion" or proportionality. Crudely translated, this rule dictated that those with more, especially more shares in a land corporation, should receive more. In point of fact, the rule was remarkably complex. On the one hand, it was a means of acknowledging hierarchies of wealth: families or householders of greater "estates" would receive more than those beneath them. But there were anomalies to consider, like the size of someone's family and the status of the men who were ministers or lay elders and deacons in the local congregation. Should they not be singled out as well? And what about the leaders in civil affairs, or laypeople with much-needed skills?

Working through these possibilities became a major task of town meetings. Early on, the townspeople of Watertown decided to take into account "the number of persons in family, the number of beasts, by which a man is fit to occupy the land assigned to him . . . and eminent respect (in this case may be given to men of eminent quality and descent) in assigning unto them more large and honourable accommodations in regard of their disbursements to public charges." The townspeople in Dedham were similarly detailed, spelling out "generall rules" beginning with "[1:] the number of persons is on [sic] considerable rule . . . yet not the only rule and it was concluded that servants should be referred to mens estates [i.e., not counted as members of a family]. 2: According to mens estates: 3 According to mens Ranke and Quallitie and desert and usefullnes either in Church or Common Weale: 4 that men of useful trades may have materials to improve the same be encouraged by have land as nere home as may be convenient." As a sidebar to these principles, the town also agreed that some land should be set aside to support a "free school" and the church.[24]

No evidence survives of how, in light of such rules, a town meeting or selectmen debated which family got what. But the results are telling. Instead of ranking every householder in a strict hierarchy, towns opted for ratios and categories that greatly simplified the task of apportioning any division of land and, sometimes, of deciding how many cattle a person could graze on the town commons. Guilford established four different categories. So did Rowley and nearby Andover, Massachusetts. Rowley's is a near-perfect example of a simplified proportionality. Founded in 1639 around Ezekiel Rogers, an experienced minister who arrived in the colony in 1638 accompanied by a small group of men who paid eight hundred pounds to clear a swath of land of competing claims, the town began by allocating house lots, then turned to distributing other land in small amounts (what someone could realistically prepare for planting). Rogers and one other person received the largest quantity (six acres), three received four, twenty-two got two, twenty-eight received one and a half, and a single person, one. These categories had nothing to do with church membership, for the great majority of the early settlers had entered the church and become freemen by the early 1640s (at a minimum, forty-one out of fifty-four). A few years later, Andover slotted most men into one of four sizes of home lots—four, five, six, and seven acres—and gave two men twenty acres each. With no minister yet on hand, the men who arranged the ranking favored several artisans as well as the one magistrate in their midst.[25] Dedham, Guilford, Hartford, Haverhill, Ipswich, Northampton, Salem, Springfield, Sudbury, Watertown, and Windsor all acted in more or less the same manner, late-founded Northampton noting that it did so "according to theire estates or eminent qualifications, as in other townes of this jurisdiction." Everywhere, special circumstances mattered; in Dedham, John Allin, not yet elected and ordained as the town minister but soon to be so, received the largest grant in the opening round of distribution.[26]

The multiple ways of calculating proportionality were made

more complicated by another rule or custom. In town after town, people agreed that anyone in need, or who had been left at a disadvantage as land was handed out, deserved special consideration. Accepting this rule was made easier by an ethics of mutuality that some towns and all congregations professed, an ethics abetted by the core principle of English poor relief, the responsibility of each town or jurisdiction to look after its own. No one in New England wanted to re-create the vagrants and idle poor seemingly omnipresent in England and everywhere a strain on local taxes. Handing out land was a practical means of keeping poverty at bay and caring for the disadvantaged.[27]

That towns should assist those in need was the message Edward Johnson wove into *The Wonder-Working Providence of Sions Saviour in New England* (completed in 1651 or early 1652 and published in London in 1654), a layman's history filled with brief sketches of each town in Massachusetts. Johnson was one of the seven men who secured the grant of land that became the town of Woburn, where he would live for the rest of his life. It was clearly pleasing to him that, in making grants and admitting inhabitants, the seven organizers "refused not men for their poverty, but according to their ability were helpful to the poorest sort, in building their houses, and distributed to them land accordingly; the poorest had six or seven acres of Medow, and twenty five of Upland, or thereabouts." The organizers had also taken geography into account, giving larger house lots to families whose principal lands were far from the meetinghouse and smaller ones to families with farms nearby.[28]

Elsewhere, too, special grants of land were repeatedly made to ne'er-do-wells or people experiencing some misfortune. Thus, in Dedham, the town acted on petitions pleading for adjustments on the grounds of need and, at one point, ruled that those who "nowe have the worst" land would do better in the next division. In the early 1650s, the selectmen were charged with arranging the disposal of a particular meadow "for the supplye of them that are most in want." Springfield empowered three men in 1644 to "dispose" of a particular patch of land "to whom they shall Judge most to be in need." In some towns, explicit provision was also made for "inhabitants," usually, as in Dedham, by assigning them a place on the scale of proportionality, though never at the top or the middle. In Guilford, the town placed its hopes for fairness on the principle that "the poorest planter" would receive "accommodation suitable of [what] hee desire." The town also mandated that everyone receive "equal proportion for quality and goodness"—that is, a proportional share of the better lands.[29]

In this as in other entries, the term "equal" crept into the language of decision-making about land. (It did as well about taxes and other social practices—a topic I return to in Chapter Four.) Almost certainly this term had various consequences. Depending on the context, it could mean giving some people equal shares or, as in Dedham, equal rights "to all undevided land." The Hartford entry to this effect implied a serious intention of being fair and possibly something more. Realizing that the rule of proportion had been accidentally distorted in one division, some "having more then is . . . their due," the town meeting added ten men to work alongside the selectmen in correcting things so that all "shalbe Just and Equall."[30] The initial grants in Providence were house lots of equal size; the most famous resident of the town, Roger Williams, though never an effective local leader, remained convinced that there should be "Equallitie . . . in Land." Where "equal" may have actually meant *equal* was in Lancaster, where, as noted in the town records, the house lots were "Laid out for the most part Equally to Rich and poore." The town did so for reasons both utilitarian and ethical: equality prevented "the Towne from Scatering to farr" and was done "out of Charitie and Respect to men of meaner estate." This sentence in the records also gave a much grander meaning to equality, describing it as "the Rule of God" and noting that, in future divisions of land, it would remain a goal—albeit a goal carried out "according to mens estates." Here equality and proportionality met and became entwined in an artful compromise.[31]

That town meetings agreed as much as they did on the rules for dividing up land does not mean that the process was conflict-free. True, the colonists were "accomplishing a virtual social revolution" by making it possible for "each adult male" to receive "some land, free and clear"—every adult male in this context meaning the earliest residents of a town. In the English communities from which they came, a substantial share of families would have been "landless laborers," and others, tenants.[32] But the tense moments were many as town meetings debated what was fair, allotters assigned portions, and surveyors laid out boundaries as best they could. These moments left their traces in votes to refer decision-making to a special group, to redo a particular division, or to declare an extra dividend of land, and probably in votes against or for particular selectmen. By the late 1640s, the "young men" in every town may have been the most likely to protest that their needs were not being met by systems based on proportionality, and the newcomers labeled as "admitted inhabitants" may have been perennially restless. In these early decades, the more privileged—the wealthier, the ministers—ended up with much more land than others in their towns. But a worst-case scenario of church members pushing aside those who were not, and the better-off abusing the system for their own benefit, seems not to have happened, and in towns such as Watertown and New Haven was contested or explicitly prohibited. There and elsewhere, the ethical rules of fairness and equality were constantly in view, if not always effective.[33]

One town where open conflict occurred was Boston. Constrained by its seaside location and the rivers that formed its boundaries, the town had little land of the better kinds to give away until it began to expand into adjacent areas or encouraged people to purchase tracts outside the town proper. The constant arrival of newcomers who stayed on the peninsula was another complication, as was the presence of men of substantial wealth and high status, some of them investors in the Massachusetts Bay Company. Early on, these men did well by themselves, so well that protests arose around the possibility (and reality) that "the richer men would give the poorer sort no great proportion of land." When the "Inhabitants" met in late 1635 to choose seven men to act as allotters, the "generality" (as one historian has termed them) spurned several of the leading men in the town in favor of "one of the Elders, and a Deacon, and the rest of the infearior sorte," as Winthrop noted in his journal.

The triumph of the generality was short-lived, however, for Winthrop and his allies persuaded the townspeople to annul the results and hold another election. Meanwhile, the town meeting agreed on the familiar expedient of forbidding the sale of land to persons who were not approved by a group of allotters and forbidding, too, outright grants to anyone unlikely to become a member of the church. Conflict persisted, with "the poorer sort" (a group that included people devastated by the inflationary pressures of the late 1630s) never feeling that their needs were adequately met. A "clamorous" town meeting in 1642 voted to reclaim the authority to allocate lands from the selectmen, a policy reversed six weeks later. In the earlier vote, the rule was established that in the next division "a greater Proportion" would go "to them that have had lesse then their due, and the lesse to them that have had more, and proportionably to them that have had none." This was as near as any town came to using a major allocation in behalf of social justice. But for reasons that remain unclear, nothing of the sort actually happened. The important families in Boston—Winthrop's being one of them—made out extremely well thanks to special grants from the General Court, town divisions, and their own investments. A middling group did all right, but many others ended up with small holdings.[34]

Second only to land and how it was apportioned was the question of how taxes would be levied. The Stuart kings, and especially Charles, had tried to solve their economic difficulties by imposing special levies, a policy Parliaments of the 1620s had repeatedly called into question. There was little chance of this happening in New England, if only because royal governance was extraordinarily expensive and wasteful—royal favorites with their hands in the till, a navy to maintain, castles to keep up. Spared the situation of the king and his policies, though well aware of what he was doing, the colonists had learned another lesson from their English years that would affect what they did in New England. Taxation in England favored the privileged few, the county leaders, sheriffs, and borough oligarchies responsible for collecting the sums voted by Parliament or demanded by the king. In each county or borough, someone had to decide how property would be valued and what amounts each corporation or person had, the next step being to fix a "rate" or tax on these valuations that would yield the necessary amount. Acting out of self-interest, county leaders lightened their own valuations and shifted much of the burden to others. It was unethical to do so, but the king wanted his money, and the county lieutenants and sheriffs who owed their offices to the Crown could do as they pleased. The rules of the game in England were arbitrary and unfair, favoring the few and abusing the many.[35]

The colonists wanted fairness and got it, although not without debate about the best safeguards, and not without making the position of the local constable, the person responsible for collecting from each household, the least desirable office in town government. What made their task a little easier than in England was that several forms of taxation disappeared—for example, tithes and a "poor rate" assessed by church wardens. What made their task challenging were the words the colonists associated with taxation. One of these was "just," a term the townspeople of Salem employed in ordering the constables to establish a "just" valuation of everyone's estate.[36] In this context, the term undoubtedly meant that all those with property would be taxed impartially, with valuations arrived at using a single set of figures for what cattle and land were worth, and with all subject to the same rate of taxation, paying more or less only in relation to how much property they owned. This was the rule the leaders of New Haven Colony bound themselves by, wording it as "rateing all men impartially according to their accommodations within the libertyes of this plantation," and tacking on another significant word, "equity." This order was in keeping with the colony's code of laws, which mandated a "single rate" for everyone obliged to pay taxes. In Plymouth Colony, the government was to behave in the same manner as New Haven's, but the language of the statute detailing how it was to do so—"without partiality"—specified that the freemen were not to be taxed at a different rate (heavier, perhaps?) than others. Hence the concluding words of the statute, that "the levy be equall."[37]

Equality, equitability, impartiality: such were the values each town and colony tried to follow in the yearly exercise of setting rates and collecting tax monies. The immediate difficulty in doing so was valuing cattle and land. Everyone knew from experience that this was an uncertain process made much worse in the 1630s and early 1640s by the boom-and-bust cycle that unfolded—boom during the closing years of the 1630s, as newcomers used the cash they had brought with them from England to buy supplies at inflated prices from the people whose land was producing a surplus, and bust when immigration suddenly ceased in 1640. Yet on such decisions depended not only the evaluation of each household's worth but also the quantity of grain or other goods someone had to provide the constable to satisfy the rate. Because the Massachusetts General Court levied taxes almost as soon as Winthrop and the few assistants began to govern, the court had to find its way through these difficulties before the towns did. In May 1634, the court arrogated to itself the sole "power to rayse moneyes and taxes," a power it relied on the towns to implement, allowing them to assess each person's "estate" but to exclude the "number of his persons." In 1638, the court made it clear that "every inhabitant in any towne" had to pay his share of "all common charges"—a measure designed to remove any difference between "admitted inhabitants" and those with full privileges—and, as deflation struck in 1640, the court advised towns to appoint a "committee" to value livestock "under their worth rather then above their worth." As early as 1633, the court was fixing the value of corn, and continued to do so throughout the 1640s, intervening again in late 1646 to avert "complaints, by reason of unequall rates . . . occasioned thorough the want of one generall rule and way of rateing throughout the country," and also to clarify who was required to pay taxes. The New Haven government enacted a similar rule to ensure fairness in setting rates, as did Connecticut.[38]

These attempts at valuations undoubtedly helped the men who had to decide the size of each estate and appraise the corn and livestock people were using to pay their rates. Still, it remained a challenge to persuade everyone that the process was fair. To defuse suspicions, some towns appointed a special group of "assessors" or "prizers" to do the work of rating. Most towns may also have allowed anyone who felt aggrieved or, because of other circumstances, unable to pay the rate, to ask for an abatement. Together with the principle of fairness, the rule of mutual good was also put to the test each time a town meeting decided a rate. In keeping with their social ethics, the men of Woburn voted in 1644 to give public notice of the rates "to the end, that men may shew their grevance if any bee; and mutual love and agreement may be continued, by takeing off the burden from the opressed."[39] The strongest sign of foot-dragging on taxes was the difficulty of recruiting persons to serve as town constable. Generally speaking, the men named to this office were not on the same social or economic level as most of the selectmen or the lay officers of the local church. But their most striking characteristic is their dislike of the post. No one in Windsor cared to hold the office more than one year at a time, and the same hesitation can be discerned elsewhere, persisting even after towns voted to fine anyone who turned the job down.[40]

With taxes, the colonists found their way to procedures free of the abuses of privilege and corruption that marked the English system. Either as principle or as practice, privilege had given way to rules aligned with fairness, equity, and justice. These were rules that worked in practice, for complaints of unfairness seem few until we reach 1651, when, as Edward Johnson remarked in a cryptic note, "Under the pretence of being unequally rated, many men murmure exceedingly, and withdraw their shoulders from the support of Government." He may have been referring to agitation in Massachusetts about merchants who, because much of their wealth was not "visible in lands, corne, catle," were being undertaxed, despite owning goods "of great vallew." Two years later, Stamford, Connecticut, was another site of agitation when a group in the town declared "they will paye no rates to . . . common charges" to protest their exclusion from the franchise and the colony's inaction against the Dutch in New Netherland.[41]

In certain ways, the workings of the land market and the policies of town meetings resembled the workings of colony governments. A virtual "revolution" had been wrought in how land was owned and

distributed and taxes were levied. Town meetings limited the authority of local officers in ways that mirrored the attempts to curtail
"magistratical" authority, and once local voting for officers and
deputies was opened up to virtually all adult men (a step described
in the next section of this chapter), town meetings became remarkably inclusive. As David Grayson Allen has pointed out, towns in
New England differed from their English counterparts in "the peculiar ease with which government by consent" emerged and took
hold. Another difference may have been the possibility of prevent-
ing local lands from being "engrossed into one hand," a preference
the townspeople of Guilford entered into the town records in 1643.
This said, it was also the case that the methods of apportioning land
were consistent with an understanding of wealth, status, and authority as unevenly distributed, with some having more and getting
more, and others having less and getting less. In most towns, a local
gentry had formed by the mid-1640s, and in most, the motor that
drove the political process was (as the ministers would rapidly begin
to lament) a craving for more or different kinds of land. Yet the
entire system held these differences together, aided in doing so by a
social ethics of publicity and fairness, the possibility of moving elsewhere, and a vigorous culture of participation, to which we now
turn.[42]

II

THE DOORWAYS to participation in early New England were several, and many were the ways in which the privilege, right, and
obligation of doing so were practiced. Of the places where participation was encouraged and expected, the most active were congregations, town meetings, courtrooms, and sessions of a General Court.
Governments authorized people to petition for favors on behalf of a
person or a policy, and the colonists did so frequently, using petitions to voice local grievances, weigh in on disputes, seek personal
favors, and everything in between. Handwritten texts were another
means of expressing religious and political opinion; the "book" in
which Israel Stoughton criticized the "negative voice" in 1634 was

followed by many more in which churches, towns, and people asserted themselves. Everywhere, people passed on news or rumors about affairs of state at home and abroad. The formal privilege of voting in elections was important at certain moments, though its place in a history of participation was secondary to speech, scribal publication, petitions, and venues of public debate.

Meanwhile, civil governments and churches were making some forms of participation mandatory, or nearly so. At a moment when their authority seemed dangerously fragile, the leaders of the "pilgrim" community preparing to land at Plymouth in 1620 secured the assent of most of the men on board the *Mayflower* to a "compact" binding the signers to "all due submission and obedience" to laws and "offices."[43] The Massachusetts government resorted to oath-taking for the same reason, as did Parliament in 1643, when it called on all Englishmen to join in a "solemn League and covenant." As these episodes indicate, participation was both imposed and voluntary. An aspect of social privilege and status on the one hand, on the other it was associated with the more egalitarian marker of church membership. Women as a group had few explicit privileges, and servants fewer still until their indentures ended. Denoting obligation or obedience in some situations, in many others the possibilities for participation beckoned toward popular politics.[44]

As is true today, people were not of one mind about the benefits of participation. Some were indifferent, turning up for town meetings only when they were aroused by a particular issue and doing their best to avoid local office-holding.[45] As is also true today, everyday modes of participation were played out in private. Little is known, for example, of the consultations that took place as someone facing death made a will, or those of executors as they finalized the distribution of an estate, though these decisions mattered greatly.[46] Court records capture some aspects of the "lively networks of local exchange" that brought debtors and creditors (and heads of households were frequently both) face-to-face, but negotiations about marriage remain almost invisible.[47] Officially silent and submissive and never included in the category of freeman, women offered petitions in keeping with long-standing English custom, served as executors of wills, participated in mixed and single-sex meetings to discuss their ministers' sermons, were willed books by fathers who took for granted their literacy, joined congregations earlier than their husbands, spoke up in churches when someone was being disciplined, and as widows or *femmes soles* managed households and the property attached to them. Everywhere, they were active in local economies through the crafts they commanded. Everywhere as well, they were recognized as having their own opinions. "I would knowe how farr the wives doe Consent or dissent from thear Husbands or whether thay be as resolut and obstinate peremptory as thay," John Cotton wondered of those who departed his congregation in 1638 and went to Rhode Island. That women would do both is writ large in all kinds of records.[48]

Always, the rules of the game differentiated between the acceptable and the unacceptable. As in England, courts intervened to punish some who spoke out, petitioned, circulated handwritten texts, or resorted to booksellers in London to publish a heterodox book. Yet the restrictions on who could do or say what coexisted with three countervailing assumptions and practices. The first was the rule of consent that figured in all descriptions of legitimate authority, with concepts of covenant in the background. The second was the "traditional political structure" of governance in Tudor-Stuart England, which made room for a "wide degree of participation in local government . . . by men of humble status." Villagers made "by-laws about such matters as gleaning or the use of commons," juries weighed the evidence in civil and criminal disputes, and local offices proliferated, all of them contributing to an everyday experience of majority rule and a broadly inclusive civil society.[49] The colonists brought these traditions with them, as they also did a third, the workings of voluntary religion within the Puritan movement. After 1558, when Mary Tudor's policy of returning the Church of England to Catholicism ended with her death, the godly could celebrate the heroism of the hundreds of men and women of ordinary status who, as Protestant martyrs, demonstrated the vigor of unofficial religion. Militant Protestantism emerged from beneath in mid-sixteenth-century Scotland in the same manner, constructed, like its English counterpart, out of the determination of thousands of people to obtain preaching and worship of a certain kind.

This determination passed intact to New England, where it acquired an even greater force within the form of church government known as the Congregational Way. Well before they immigrated, most of the colonists had become versed in the repertory of private meetings, conventicles, and fast days that sustained those who affiliated with the godly. The textures of this training are strikingly apparent in lay "relations" of religious experience made by men and women in Thomas Shepard's congregation, in John Winthrop's affiliations during his English years, and in autobiographical remarks by John Brock, who came to New England in the late 1630s. Looking back on their English years, Shepard's parishioners recalled deciding what minister to hear or consult, what books to read, what choices they faced in everyday life as they tried to avoid "sin," and why they decided to come to New England. "Wanting [lacking] company of saints," John Trumbull rejoiced after he reorganized his social life to be in the presence of the godly. Mary Angier had known both aspects of the religious geography of England, the "powerful ministry" of a famous minister and "a place of more ignorance," until, at her husband's urging, she agreed to participate in the exodus to New England, which she regarded as rich in "public means" of grace. In the Stour Valley, where John Winthrop lived until he immigrated, every aspect of voluntary religion was woven into his quest for religious knowledge. As John Brock remembered his youth in 1630s England, the emphasis fell on "going by Night and in by Ways to hear good Ministers" and deciding to leave England when "Persecutors" became "daily more odious in their Ways." Fashioned out of many such experiences, assumptions about free choice or "Liberty" (a favorite word of Brock's) fed the making of civil and religious society in New England.[50]

Such testimonies make visible the networks that sidestepped the regulatory powers of church and civil state. One of these linked colleges at Cambridge and Oxford with towns, villages, and patrons seeking someone to appoint as parish minister or lecturer. Shepard benefited from this network. After completing his training at Cambridge, he spent several months in Thomas Weld's house in a de facto apprenticeship that enabled him to consult with local "worthies" about where he should work as a minister. Looking back on the years he subsequently spent in Earle's Colne, Shepard was grateful for being set "in the midst of the best ministry in the country [county] by whose monthly fasts and conferences I found much of God." Another, overlapping network relied on word of mouth among ordinary people to transmit news of preachers worth traveling to hear, a practice known as "gadding." Manuscript sermons, treatises, and news flowed through these same networks, which is how "some got copies" of a letter of John Cotton's, and how the fervent lay Puritan Nehemiah Wallington, who lived in London, obtained a description of the wreck of the *Angel Gabriel* off the coast of Maine in 1635.[51]

In turn, the Congregational Way licensed new versions of participation: the men who were members electing a minister[52] and voting on candidates for membership; the deacons collecting gifts for purposes of charity; the elders intervening to rebuke the wayward; and, from time to time, collective acts of admonishment and excommunication, a list that must also include the devotional practices that, as reported by a minister in 1638, found the people of his congregation "searchinge the scriptures and comparinge place with place, others singeinge, others conferringe." As this description implies, congregations provided a space where laypeople talked over matters of theology and the merits of their minister or errant clergy elsewhere. Hearing of Roger Williams' "Errors in Doctrine," the congregation in Boston collectively assented to a compilation of these doctrines and dispatched them to the attention of Williams and the "erring" lay members of the Salem church.[53]

An unusually intense dispute over theology in 1636 and 1637 fueled an explosion of text-making and frank criticism. The Antinomian Controversy originated within the Boston congregation. Winthrop was present when his fellow church members assailed one of their ministers, John Wilson, for complaining to the magistrates about how he was being treated, "all the congregation" except Winthrop and "one or two others" reproaching him "with much bitterness." Meanwhile, the congregation was exchanging statements of theology with the church in nearby Cambridge. Some laypeople spoke out on their own, as Stephen Greensmith, a timber merchant in Boston, did, saying that "all the ministers . . . did teach a covenant of works." By the time the controversy came to a close, some twenty-five texts had been published, all of them handwritten.[54] Several years later, the congregation in Dorchester watched and listened as the town's two ministers, Richard Mather and Jonathan Burr, argued with each other about grace and works, each man publishing his views in a handwritten text. Sometimes a single layman challenged the assertions of his minister, as Thomas Stoughton did in Windsor around 1650, when he disputed the proper interpretation of the Sabbath. In nearby Wethersfield, Connecticut, in the early 1640s, one faction drafted a critique of Henry Smith, the town minister, and sent copies to neighboring congregations. In other congregations and towns, infant baptism and church membership flared up as divisive issues.[55]

Every congregation was also the epicenter of agitation about its "liberties," chiefly the privilege of selecting its own minister. The congregation in Salem fought back in 1635, when the Massachusetts government requested that it not appoint Williams its "teacher," calling on "other Churches to admonishe the magistrates" for the "haynous sinne" of rejecting a petition about acquiring more land, as the court had done to punish the church. A few years later, the same congregation objected to the government's suggestion that its minister Hugh Peter return to England to represent the interests of the colony (he went anyway), complaining so loudly that "the agitation of this business was soon about the country."[56] In 1638, the townspeople of Dedham played the trump card of congregational privileges after being told they could not organize a congregation without the magistrates' approval. Three years later, the Body of Liberties consolidated the two possibilities of autonomy and supervision in a single sentence: "Every Church hath free libertie of Election and ordination of all their officers . . . provided they be able, pious and orthodox," a formula leaving open the possibility that local groups and the civil state would clash, as they did in Malden,

Massachusetts, when the church ordained Marmaduke Matthews in 1651 despite being told not to do so by the government, supporting him even though he admitted using questionable language in his sermons. Called to account by the General Court, the church alluded to "our laws" in remonstrating that churches were entitled to "ordain their own officers." Matthews acknowledged some of his mistakes but warned against the "magistrates' power in matters of religion." By now his congregation was fully engaged in the controversy, as evidenced by the willingness of thirty-six *women* members of the church to sign a petition to the court asking that he continue his ministry.[57]

In 1652, it was the turn of other Massachusetts congregations to complain of interference. Second Church, Boston, newly organized and precarious, voted to install a layman who was already serving as its minister, a vote Michael Powell accepted "upon these terms, that . . . the magistrates and ministers did approve and consent thereunto." The Massachusetts General Court demurred on the grounds that Powell lacked the "learning" expected of a minister (he was not a college graduate), and the Suffolk County Court enjoined the congregation from calling and ordaining him to office. With, it seems, broad support from outside Second Church, Powell objected that, were "civil authority so disposed," a church could end up without any officers, adding that he felt it his moral duty to become the congregation's minister. In the event, he settled for the office of elder (unusually, receiving a stipend from the church for doing so) alongside a better-qualified man who was ordained in 1654. Robert Pike of Salisbury, Massachusetts, outraged by an order of the court prohibiting two men from preaching in his town church, publicly declared that those behind this order "did break their oath to the country, for it is against the liberty of the country, both civil and ecclesiastical." Fined and disenfranchised, Pike had the satisfaction of knowing that large numbers of townsmen in his own and four nearby towns signed petitions asking the court to relieve his sentence, which it eventually did.[58]

Meanwhile, congregations were making scores of decisions about whom to admit as members and whether to admonish or excommunicate the erring and wayward. Although Thomas Hooker complained of lay members' "curious inquisitions and niceties" as they scrutinized prospective members, most of this decision-making was uncontroversial.[59] Nonetheless, some colonists were angered by the refusal to open local congregations to everyone who had been a member of the Church of England. When Mary Oliver was turned away from the Salem congregation in the late 1630s, she "openly" pleaded "her right" at a public lecture day to take part in the Lord's Supper on the grounds that "all that dwell in the same town, and will profess their faith in Christ Jesus, ought to be received to the sacraments there."[60] Others shared her thinking, and a few churches may have been broadly inclusive. But it was church discipline, a practice that involved both men and women church members, that proved especially contentious and divisive. When the church in Scituate voted in 1635 to excommunicate a member for wanting to marry "a woman of scandalous carriage" and lying about his intentions, a leading lay member "did not consent," and two others walked out in protest.[61] Conflict flared in Wenham as well. As the give-and-take over someone's misdeeds became intense, men and women contested one another's testimony, voted with their feet by staying away, and loudly criticized those who judged them.[62]

Wenham was an unusually active congregation, for John Fiske, the minister, sought its advice on a wide range of questions. Meeting for this purpose after the Sunday service in November 1644, the group agreed on the procedures to be used in admitting new members, debated whether to hold a day of thanksgiving, and discussed what to do about "members of other churches" who asked to participate in the Lord's Supper. So it went Sunday after Sunday, keeping Fiske busy incorporating long swaths of argument (some of which may have circulated in handwritten copies) into the church records. This, too, was a congregation that took its privileges seriously. When the Massachusetts General Court solicited responses to the newly drafted *A Platforme of Church Discipline* (1649), much "agitation and debate" arose "touching some expressions" in the *Platforme* and an accompanying document, the Westminster Confession. After voting its "assent" to both, the congregation carefully specified that "this our assent extends not itself to every particular circumstance in every chapter and section in the said platform." Early and late, the congregation was suspicious of any rules or practices that seemed "an impeachment of the church's liberty."[63] At mid-century, Samuel Stone, the minister in Hartford, described the workings of church government as "a speaking aristocracy in face of a silent democracy." This was not how governance functioned in Stone's own congregation or in Fiske's. On the contrary: empowered by the Congregational Way, laymen (and, less visibly, laywomen) remained politically active.[64]

Some of these situations or privileges were unique to congregations, but others like them were widely available to the colonists. The Body of Liberties granted every freeman in Massachusetts the privilege of "full freedome" to "give any advise, vote, verdict, or sentence in any Court, Counsell, or Civill Assembly . . . So it be done orderly and inofensively for the manner." The document also endorsed much broader forms of participation. Liberty No. 12 authorized "every man whether Inhabitant or Forreiner, *free or not free*," the privilege of coming "to any publique Court, Councel, or Towne meeting, and either by speech or writeing to move any lawfull, seasonable, and materiall question . . . whereof that meeting hath proper cognizance, so it be done in convenient time, due order, and respective manner." The Plymouth government had already offered every man in the colony, *freeman or not,* the same privilege. Thus did freedom of speech become partly sanctioned, as did the sharing of handwritten statements.[65]

To be sure, speech and writing were regarded as dangerous, and as Philip Round has pointed out, gossip or "village speech" functioned outside of (or in "dialogic" relationship with) officially sanctioned patterns of discourse. Hence the insistence in Liberty No. 12 on "due order, and respective manner," lest either of these practices threaten the stability of state and church.

One after another, the English monarchs in the late sixteenth and early seventeenth centuries had regulated what printers and booksellers could publish, punishing writers who criticized the king's person or any royal policies, enforcing laws against "seditious libel," denying freedom of speech except in places like the House of Commons, and attempting to control what passed as news, for in principle any information about the king's affairs fell within the confines of secrecy. These measures were justified as necessary to sustain the authority of the Crown; to do otherwise, to allow ordinary people to debate "what lords, what bishops, what councillors . . . [judge] most meet for a commonwealth," was to encourage factionalism. In the judgment of contemporaries, it was a short distance from such disorder to something far worse, the unhinging of lawful authority, or sedition. The same concern about sedition, blasphemy, and the capacity of speech to disrupt social peace existed among the colonists and passed into statute law.[66]

Contentious speech and writing and the transmission of news happened anyway.[67] By the 1620s, and possibly two or three decades beforehand, networks of communication were doing this work in England. Severe though they were, prosecutions for seditious libel failed to stem the flow of unsigned, unauthorized, and insult-laden texts. Everyone seemed to know what was happening at court and during the sessions of Parliament, in part because a lively trade in handwritten "separates" informed interested readers of what was being said and done. Popular speech was uncontrollable and printing almost so, for printers and booksellers frequently sidestepped the process of licensing. Even if not printed, a sermon as daring as Thomas Hooker's *Danger of Desertion,* finally issued by a bookseller ten years after he gave it on the eve of quitting his English ministry, circulated in handwritten copies and by word of mouth.[68]

These experiences and expectations traveled with the colonists. Some were already familiar with conventicles or private meetings, where discussion happened with a certain freedom, as it surely did in a New World meeting held in the Boston home of Anne Hutchinson. So many women attended—according to a hostile observer, some "fifty, sixty, or eighty at once"—to listen as Hutchinson commented on the sermons these women were hearing that the civil government became alarmed. Her meetings came to an abrupt halt in 1637, but the Body of Liberties guaranteed the right of laypeople to meet in this manner, as some continued to do for the rest of the century.[69] Unlicensed printing and the practice of penning libels did not recur among the colonists in the early decades; to have something printed, dissidents such as Roger Williams, Samuel Gorton, and, at the beginning of the 1650s, William Pynchon relied on the London trade. But in the 1630s, Williams was airing his criticism of church and state in Massachusetts in handwritten texts. Many others in the 1630s and 1640s also turned to scribal publication as their means of participating in political debate.[70]

One way or another, information, rumor, and written texts circulated widely. They did so in part because men and women in New England were remarkably literate in the sense of knowing how to read. The laws requiring parents to teach their children this skill couched such instruction as a means of inducing obedience, but literacy was always and everywhere a two-edged sword. The letters reaching John Winthrop, the notations in his journal, and local records show such texts and comments passing from pulpit to congregation, from deputies to town meeting and vice versa, from ministers to magistrates, from General Courts to every town, from one dissident to another, from New England to England, and, most strikingly, from "people" to deputies, magistrates, ministers, and governor.[71] Once again, the Antinomian Controversy is a case in point, for it shattered every rule of decorum. Winthrop himself stirred the pot of news, rumor, and opinion by drafting a description of a "monster birth" and sending copies to others in New England. Word spread that Cotton's colleagues had turned against him; in Plymouth Colony, the church in Scituate celebrated a day of thanksgiving in October 1637 for the "Reconciliation betwixt Mr. Cotton, and the other ministers," and the "victory over the pequots." Because the controversy called into question the legitimacy of the ministers stigmatized as "legall" preachers, the synod that met in September 1637 to resolve matters of theology became an experiment in participation. Making its sessions available to everyone, friend or critic, the clerical organizers of the synod gave "liberty . . . to any of the Countrey to come in and heare, (it being appointed, in great part, for the satisfaction of the people) and a place was appointed for all the Opinionists to come in, and take liberty of speech (onely due order observed) as much as any of our selves had, and as freely." Thomas Weld, the source of this story, reckoned that the openness of the synod played a significant role in quelling discontent.[72] The risk an ethics of openness and transparency ran was worth taking if such an ethics strengthened or restored the authority of governance.

At still other moments, towns and colony governments opted for broad-based participation. Realizing that the tense debate in 1637 over a law empowering the magistrates to turn away immigrants sympathetic to the antinomians had left the losers in that struggle "obstinate and irreconcilable," the Massachusetts government arranged for a public reading of the three texts generated by the debate, two defending the law and a third, by Henry Vane, criticizing it. From time to time, the government allowed an indiscriminate array of people to attend sessions of the General Court, as happened in March 1637, when, with the court deliberating what to do about John Wheelwright's inflammatory fast-day sermon, "the doores" were "set open for all that would to come in (and there was a great Assembly)"; in 1643, when "a great assembly" listened to the government's objections to the religious radical Samuel Gorton; and again in 1645, when the attempted impeachment of Winthrop reached its climax with his "little speech on liberty."[73] Laws in draft or final form were shared in the same manner. Early on, the Connecticut government ordered the colony clerk to send a copy of "all the penal laws or orders standing in force" to the "constables of every town," who in turn were to "publish the same within 4 dayes more, att some publique meeting in their severall Townes." It was also ordered that someone in each town write the laws into a "booke" and that, "once every yeare," the laws in force be read aloud.[74]

The Massachusetts government resorted to a similar openness during the drafting of the Body of Liberties. Winthrop's description of this process includes three references to "the people" wanting a code of laws, one of them to "all the people," which in context meant every adult man, whether freeman or not: "At length (to satisfy the people) it [the court] proceeded, and the two models [John

Cotton's and Nathaniel Ward's] were digested with divers alterations and additions, and abbreviated and sent to every town . . . to be considered of first by the magistrates and elders, and then to be published by the constables to all the people, that if any man should think fit, that any thing therein ought to be altered, he might acquaint some of the deputies therewith against the next court."[75] Here was a process that began with hierarchy—magistrates and elders—and broadened out to become remarkably comprehensive. This same sequence unfolded for printed books of laws, with colony governments ordering large quantities and distributing them to as many households as possible, a procedure wholly different from how law books were produced and distributed in England. Thus, in 1648, the Cambridge printer produced six hundred copies of the *Lawes and Liberties,* and in 1656, the leaders of New Haven imported five hundred copies of the London-printed *New-Haven's Settling in New-England and some Lawes for Government.*[76]

Encouraged to participate but also risking censure, many of the colonists made their opinions felt whether the government wanted them to or not. Rumor and the sharing of news figured in this process, as did public meetings, published texts, and sermons. John Eliot, the minister in Roxbury, used his pulpit in late 1636 to criticize "the magistrates for proceedinge" in the war against the Pequots "without the Consent of the people," and a nervous Winthrop noted that "the people beganne to take occasion to murmure against us for it." When the colony was roiled in the early 1640s by the disputed ownership of a stray sow, Winthrop himself wrote and "published" (meaning, almost certainly, distributed in handwritten copies) "A breaviate of the Case betwene Richard Sheareman pl[aintiff] by petition and Capt. Robert Keaine [sic]," which marshaled the arguments in Keayne's favor. Before he did so, Elizabeth Sherman, who claimed ownership of the sow, was telling people in Boston that Keayne, a wealthy and much-disliked merchant, had "killed" it, whereupon, as Winthrop noted in his journal, "the noise hereof [was] . . . spread about the town." Juries and the General Court weighed in, with "much contention," and a new element, the "clamours" of a young man who befriended Goodwife Sherman, prompted "great expectations in the country" that the court would reverse itself and punish Keayne. More text-making followed in the summer of 1642, as the magistrates defended their negative voice, which became entangled with the case.[77]

A year later, tensions ran so high that Deputy Governor Thomas Dudley told a minister who disagreed with him, "Do you think to come with your eldership here to carry matters"? Meanwhile, the deputies were reporting that "their towns were not satisfied" with the outcome of the case, specifying the substantial fine imposed on Widow Sherman for defaming Keayne. In distant Casco, Maine, popular anger was alive and well in 1645, for someone complained "that the Court had doon great wrong to a pore woman about a sowe, and that none could have Justice from you [in Massachusetts] but such as were members of the Church." Citing nineteen witnesses against Keayne, the same person declared to others in the settlement that "they weere as good live in turkie as live under such a government."[78] The allusion to Turkey (the Ottoman Empire, not modern Turkey) implied an apocalyptic scenario of the end times, when the oppressed would rise up and overthrow all unjust kingdoms.

Rumor, gossip, and discontent among the colonists flourished anew around the Massachusetts government's efforts to aid Charles La Tour, a French colonizer locked in a contest with one of his countrymen for control of Acadia, a region in French Canada. To welcome a Catholic to Boston and visibly support him was too much for many. Once again, the colonists turned to rumor, sermons, and letters to voice their unhappiness with this policy. So Winthrop reported in his journal: "The rumor of these things soon spreading through the country, were diversely apprehended, not only by the common sort, but also by the elders, whereof some in their sermons spoke against their entertainment. . . . Divers also wrote to the governour, laying before him great dangers, others charging sin upon the conscience in all these proceedings." From Ipswich, where protests were centered, John Endecott reported that "the Countrie heereabouts is much troubled" by the leadership having "any thing to doe with theise Idolatrous French." Forced to defend himself,

Winthrop sent letters as far as New Haven in which "he layd downe divers reasons why the Massachusetts gave liberty to the Frenchmen." Dismayed by so much publicity and realizing that divisions within the court were abetting the flow of news, the General Court set up a special committee in 1644 "to consider of and to drawe upp an order to prevent the members of this howse from discloseinge any of the private buisnesses thereof abroad, as alsoe to drawe upp an order for the preventeinge of falce rumors which are to[o] frequently spread within this jurisdiction." A year later, the court made it a crime to tell lies, including any in the form of "false newes or reports" that damaged the commonwealth.[79]

This was to close the barn door after most of the cows had escaped. Across the Atlantic, the Long Parliament was dealing with a similar situation, for the collapse of licensing and censorship in 1641 prompted a surge of unrestrained printing and speech. The Massachusetts government was never so overwhelmed, although it, too, was unable to shut down the channels of rumor, gossip, and sermons. Like the Long Parliament, it used its powers to punish some of the people who criticized ministry and magistrates, doing so with fines, whippings, brandings, and the spectacle of public apologies. So did the Connecticut General Court; in a typical reaction, it ordered Henry Smith's critics in Wethersfield to recant their criticism.[80] These efforts at coercion may have lowered the volume and visibility of dissent—though whether this actually happened is unclear—but came nowhere close to eliminating it. The persistence of dissent was a function of the contraries built into Puritanism, the culture of participation the colonists brought with them, and the capacity of local interests to withstand central governments. One example must suffice, the crackdown in 1643 on the "wealthy tanner" Nathaniel Briscoe of Watertown for circulating a handwritten "book" in which he objected to a tax being levied in his town to pay the minister's salary. Briscoe apologized and probably paid the fine levied on him, but in 1647 he became one of the town selectmen. A few who spoke out, and especially the women who did so, were effectively silenced, but not someone of Briscoe's local standing.[81]

Another important site of participation was the courtroom. A single case could precipitate an outpouring of testimony, as happened in Springfield in 1650 and 1651, when thirty-nine people, eleven of them women, described the behavior of a wife and husband accused of witchcraft.[82] In New as in old England, the exercise of justice relied almost entirely on the willingness of ordinary people "to serve as witnesses, sureties and prisoner guards" and to detect and report breaches of the law. With no police available to investigate or arrest people for misdeeds, courts had to assume that suspects, accusers, and witnesses would turn up. During the nearly thirty-year period from 1638 to 1665, a grand total of four suspects avoided the hearings they had been warned to attend in New Haven Town and Colony; another four attempted to escape and were apprehended before doing so.[83] Not that people were necessarily terrified of what courts would do: the courtroom was a place where negotiations unfolded between magistrates and local people, some as plaintiffs and defendants, others as witnesses and members of a jury. As a historian of English law and local administration has pointed out, justices of the peace had to "meet the populace at least half way."[84] Usually, magistrates in early New England and their counterparts in early Stuart England treated justice not as an abstraction or an end in itself but as a means to the end of social peace. For this to happen, quarrels had to be resolved and penalties adjusted to fit personal circumstances. Mostly, local and county courts in Massachusetts dealt with everyday disputes and petty infractions of the rules: unpaid debts, estates awaiting distribution, fences left in bad repair, defamatory speech, theft, and the staples of local justice on both sides of the Atlantic—abuses of alcohol and sex outside of marriage.[85]

Nathaniel Hawthorne's *The Scarlet Letter* (1850) conveys a different impression of justice in early New England. The "grim rigidity" he imputes to the men and women wearing "sad-colored garments" who gather outside the Boston prison to observe, self-satisfied, the punishment of Hester Prynne embody an ethics of righteousness devoid of human sympathy or, as Hawthorne would have it, "heart." Hence Hester's exclusion from the community, a narrative theme consistent with Hawthorne's liberal Unitarian perspective.

He was right in one respect, but wrong—very wrong—in others. Judges and juries would have agreed that the purpose of justice was to uphold righteousness, or the moral law spelled out in the Ten Commandments and elsewhere in the Bible. The ideal of righteousness and therefore scriptural precedents figured in every colony code (even Rhode Island's)[86] and permeated the judicial system, including the rules of evidence. But every trial that took place within this framework turned on the guilty party's confessing his misdeeds. Confession, not punishment, was the crucial moment in this drama, the one sure and certain means of purging a person and a society of the taint of sin—and every breach of the moral law contaminated the entire community. Confession had a double significance: socially, it discharged some of the fear, anger, and feelings of revenge that accumulated around misdeeds; and theologically, it deflected God's anger at both person and culture. Justice within the framework of righteousness was about overcoming sin in people and communities, the same principle behind the practice of fast days and ceremonies of covenant renewal. Always, confession opened the way to reconciliation and restoration. The normative ethics in situations of this kind were summarized by a magistrate in New Haven who told a defendant, "[You had] best speak the trueth, for if [you] shall hide or cover it, it will encrease both your sin and punishment and therefore [you are] wished to confess [your] sinne and give glory to God, and to remember what Solomon says, he that hideth his sin shall not prosper." So the people on trial in New Haven were repeatedly told. Almost as repeatedly, they obliged, at which point the court frequently dispensed with or reduced the usual penalties.[87]

Adultery was certainly a sin, and John Cotton included it in a list of capital laws he prepared in the 1630s. Other crimes deemed capital included witchcraft, blasphemy, and rebellion against parents. Ratified in the Body of Liberties, these provisions, which other colonies also put into their codes, seem the perfect example of Puritan severity. Yet, with the exception of a man and woman executed in Massachusetts for adultery in 1644, and five persons (four women and one man) who had died as witches by 1650, these laws were never enforced.[88] When the Rump Parliament was overcome with a

fit of moral zeal and made adultery a capital crime in 1650, the outcome was the same. Such laws were more show than tell, more about
declaring than doing, as though what God really wanted was a public assertion of righteousness. Instead of confirming, they contradict
the premise that Puritans "put the full machinery of the state behind
the enforcement of sexual morality."[89] Courts did want people not
to work on Sundays, again with righteousness in mind. But few
such actions were penalized: three by one Connecticut court over
a fifteen-year period (out of seventy-eight penalties for various
crimes), four by the Court of Assistants in Massachusetts (out of
455), and none in Plymouth. As for family government and the
ethics of patriarchy, courts did even less.[90] Parents could not tell
their children whom to marry, and although women deemed "las-
civious" were sometimes whipped, and those who became pregnant
out of marriage were publicly rebuked or shamed, together with the
men who got them pregnant, most of these people went on to marry
and settle down.[91] For all of its bluster about righteousness, the legal
system in the colonies was surprisingly flexible and only intermittently severe, with juries and magistrates looking the other way
rather than enforcing statutes to their hilt.[92]

There remain two key aspects of participation: the practice of
petitioning and the franchise. Both deserve more attention than is
given to them here—especially petitioning, which awaits its historian. Petitions were a routine feature of English political culture, a
means of voicing "every conceivable grievance . . . to all extant seats
of authority." As James I was traveling from Scotland to London in
1604 to begin his new kingship, he was "bombarded with an assort-
ment of petitions" that prompted him to propose convening Parliament for the purpose of relieving "all grievances of our people."
Then and later, grievance was a flexible category that encompassed a
wide range of requests. Every Parliament in the early seventeenth
century faced the challenge of sorting through and acting on the
petitions it received, as did the Council of State convened in late
1653 during the Protectorate of Oliver Cromwell, which found itself
swamped with a backlog of requests. By this time, petitions had also
become a means of mobilizing popular support; a petition in 1640

to Charles I asking for a new Parliament and signed by twelve peers was immediately printed and distributed, as would happen with many others, including petitions initiated by the Levellers.[93] No printed petitions circulated in New England, but in Massachusetts the colonists petitioned the General Court so frequently that it created a separate committee to sort through them; as a stopgap measure, the court voted in 1644 not to consider any during the first three days of a session. Locally, people brought their problems and requests to town governments. To a greater extent than for any other aspect of participation, petitioning was widely available to the colonists without reference to social rank, wealth, gender, or church membership.[94]

The fifty or so petitions that came before the General Court in 1645, and the smaller number presented in the same year to the Connecticut government—where, as in Massachusetts, freemen and others were guaranteed the privilege of petitioning—encompassed a broad range of matters, most of them local: someone wanting permission to sell wine and beer in his town, a debtor asking for an extension on settling up, a group of people seeking approval of a new town or complaining of a decision the government had made. Frequently, people sought relief from a fine or other punishment, as Sarah Gosse did in 1640 when she pleaded her husband's "distemper of spirit" as the reason he had "abuse[d] . . . his tongue." Remarking that the twenty-pound fine was "very prejudiciall unto myselfe and children," she had the support of the Watertown minister and other leading figures in the town. Four years later, Peter Bulkeley, the senior minister in Concord, was the lead petitioner in a similar case, a man named Martin fined for "speeches uttered against the church-covenant" but now experiencing "great decay of his estate" with its consequences for his family. As happened quite often, the court released Gosse from his fine and probably did so for Martin. Common wisdom among the people of Massachusetts ran strongly in favor of petitioning as a means of getting relief of one kind or another, a wisdom voiced by Robert Keayne when he decided not to trouble "the Court with any petitions for remission or abasement" of a fine levied on him for "oppression," even though he was "advised by many friends" that the court "would be willing to embrace such an occasion to undo what was then done in a hurry."[95] Towns were also vigorous petitioners and counterpetitioners, usually around grants of land or boundaries. Necessarily, some petitions went unanswered. Fifty-seven men in Ipswich warned in 1637 of the harm that would come to their town if a leading local resident, John Winthrop, Jr., were to become captain of the fort in Boston Harbor, but Winthrop soon moved elsewhere anyway.[96]

As General Courts surely recognized, a favorable response reaffirmed the fundamental fairness of the process, fair because so many people—men and women, rich, middling, and those in distress—resorted to the practice, and fair because the courts acted positively on so many. Petitioning presumed the obligation of a government to relieve people of their troubles and attend to the welfare of communities. These were the intentions of a good king and, no less so, of every colony government in New England. Acting fairly strengthened the legitimacy of those in power. But it did so only if the process resulted in genuine quid pro quos—a town got extra land, inheritors of an estate received what they expected, widows were granted the economic security of a license to sell wine. By the mid-1640s, the process was also enabling groups of people to propose or challenge a particular policy. A Massachusetts statute of 1644 denying any rights to Baptists drew a quiet protest from a group of men who asked that the law be abrogated or changed. Several months later, in May 1646, the court received a petition signed by seventy-seven men in support of the law. Here, in a situation of divisiveness, the second petition—which some members of the court may have solicited—gave additional legitimacy to a law.[97] Whatever form the practice took, petitioning became a key aspect of the culture of participation in New England, an effective means of linking deputies, magistrates, ministers, and local officials with the day-to-day needs of the colonists.

Some petitions were different in kind and consequences. The Petition of Right of 1628 denied the legitimacy of several policies of Charles I, beginning with the forced loans he was exacting. Nine years later, in Massachusetts, a group of men handed the Massachusetts General Court a "petition and remonstrance" complaining of the censure of John Wheelwright.[98] Their petition opened with gestures of humility and deference, the signers representing themselves as "humbly beseech[ing]" the redress of the government's decision, and pledging their "due submission." But they were also certain that the court had acted unjustly. Insisting that Wheelwright had said nothing to warrant the verdict of sedition the court had recently voted, the petitioners suggested that the hand of Satan was visible in the General Court's decision; it was "the old method of Satan" to have "raised up such calumnies against the faithfull Prophets of God." To this strong language they added the warning that acts of injustice would provoke a righteous God to punish the colony.[99]

As David Zaret has pointed out in his study of petitioning in early Stuart England, the legitimacy of the practice was always fragile. Petitioning was licit if, and only if, those who did so voiced a deference to Crown or Parliament conveyed through expressions of humility and loyalty in the boilerplate with which the typical petition began. Humility was also in keeping with the recognition that petitioners were availing themselves of a privilege, not a right. Additionally, it signaled that the person or people submitting the petition were not acting as a "faction"—that is, not contesting the authority of the government. Gestures of this kind marked petitions of "grace" that in essence begged those in power for some favor.[100]

Charles I had objected to the Petition of Right, and the Massachusetts government spurned the petition and remonstrance of 1637, doing so forcefully in November, when it characterized the document as a "seditious libel" and punished everyone whose name was on it. Responding to the remonstrance of 1637 (or possibly to a similar document that no longer survives), Winthrop rebuked the three Boston church members responsible for the text, telling them that they "broke the bounds" of their "calling" when they questioned the verdict of the General Court and called on "the bodye of the people" to join in their protest. Making such an appeal was seditious in and of itself, for a popular uprising would "overthrow the foundation of our Com[mon]w[ealth]."

Seven years later, the court was almost as hostile to the eighty-one men in the town of Hingham who complained to the court of having "their libertyes . . . infringed" when Winthrop and others in the government intervened to overturn a local election of militia officers. Outraged that the deputies had accepted the petition before the magistrates had considered it, and deeply angered by the accusations against him, Winthrop characterized the document as "a mutinous and seditious practice" and transposed the event into an assault on authority in general. His fellow magistrates mostly agreed with him and, after much back-and-forth, the court fined the leaders of the protest, though with a substantial minority of the deputies dissenting. Peter Hobart, the minister in Hingham, who was one of those fined, complained that the court had violated his right to petition: "He could never knowe wherefore he was fined, except it were for Petitioning," an outspokenness that drew another fine from the court for "speeches" that "tended to sedition and contempt of Authoritye."[101]

Nor did other groups fare any better. When several men, chief among them Robert Child, submitted "A Remonstrance and Petition" in May 1646 asking for fundamental changes in the structure of church and commonwealth and threatening to inform Parliament that the people of Massachusetts were being denied the customary "liberties of Englishmen," they were heavily fined and imprisoned, and their papers seized, actions the court took in response not to the petition itself but to the group's political agenda, a distinction Edward Winslow labored to sustain in a tract he wrote for an English audience.[102] As already noted, in the early 1650s the court rapped the townspeople of Malden on the knuckles, and a year later punished the towns and people who supported Michael Powell. The agitation in Wethersfield about the tenure of Henry Smith, the town minister, also involved a petition that initially the government was willing to entertain. But the episode concluded with the government's ordering that the leaders of the protest enact a public apology. In such situations, leaders invoked the ethics of obedience, or, as Winthrop put it in his response of 1637 or 1638, the obligation of "every soule to be subject to the higher powers."[103]

Yet to focus on these episodes as though they demonstrate the authoritarianism of the regime is to overlook the fact that petition-ing was endorsed by the Massachusetts General Court. Strikingly, the court said so in the very midst of the Antinomian Controversy. After penalizing the men who participated in the "seditious libel" about Wheelwright, the court entered on its records this statement: "It is not therefore the intent of this Court to restraine the free use of any way of God, by petition, or other private advertizment, nor the free use of any lawfull publike meanes, where private shall not pre-vaile, for the reformation of any . . . failing in any Court, or mem-ber of the same."[104] Four years later, in 1641 the court renewed its commitment to the "free use" of petitions, embedding the right to do so in Liberty No. 12 of the Body of Liberties. Warranted but also vulnerable to being named a seditious libel, petitioning unfolded amid persistent tensions about popular participation and popular politics. That governments endorsed it at moments of intense con-flict is strong evidence of the everyday assumption that the practice was a basic right or liberty.

The final aspect, and possibly the most puzzling to understand, is the question of who could vote. In the 1960s and 1970s, several historians attempted to quantify the percentage of men admitted as "freemen" in the colonies of Massachusetts, New Haven, and Ply-mouth, freemen being the only ones who could vote in colony elec-tions for governor, magistrates, and deputies. Problems with the data stood in the way of hard-and-fast answers, but a rough consen-sus emerged that something like 50 percent of adult males—in some towns as many as 65 or 70 percent, and in others possibly as low as 40 percent—had become freemen by 1647 in Massachusetts, though the figures would slowly decline in later decades. In Plymouth, New Haven Town, Connecticut, and Rhode Island, the percentages were possibly more robust in the 1640s.[105] These findings destroyed a cru-cial premise of the "oligarchic" paradigm, that the few ruled the many thanks to severe restrictions on who could vote for governor and magistrates. (Gender was never taken into account in this debate.) Before these findings became available, the sole authority was a much-repeated mid-nineteenth-century guesstimate that a mere 20 or 25 percent of men became freemen in Massachusetts.[106]

Once the Pandora's box of voters and voting was opened, it became evident that voting also occurred in other settings—local congregations, of course, but also militia companies and town meetings. Voting in militias for some of their officers was unusually inclusive, for military training was required of all men aged sixteen and older, and in Massachusetts the government expressly waived the distinction between freeman and nonfreeman for such elections, though requiring approval by higher authority of the men chosen as officers.[107] As for towns, the same government decided in 1635 that no one but freemen could vote in town affairs. Within certain limits, this privilege was extended to nonfreemen in 1647, an important step that some in the government had proposed as early as 1644, and that may already have occurred in New Haven; in Plymouth, householders had been able to vote in town and colony elections well before this. All such laws were moot in one respect, for every careful study of governance in Massachusetts towns has turned up evidence of much broader participation, some of it informal or in contradiction of official rules. In 1638, for example, as central government was coming into being in Connecticut, it was ordered that "admitted inhabitants in the severall Townes" were to vote in the election of deputies. Such language suggests that town leaders looked the other way or, more likely, recognized that anxieties about decisions on land and taxes were more easily relieved if town meetings were inclusive.[108] Towns were already admitting men to the status of "inhabitant" or "commoner" and giving them a variety of privileges, mostly economic but possibly including informal participation in town meetings, something Guilford specifically mandated in 1643.[109] Thus, in Hartford, anyone (meaning, almost certainly, any adult man) with a grievance could present his case at those sessions. Generalized references to "the town," implying an informal inclusiveness, had their parallel in statements at the colony level that "the said inhabitants" or "whole body" should assemble, or that no law could be "made or imposed" unless it had the "consent" of all "freeborne subjects of the State of England," as the Plymouth government declared in 1636.[110]

Considered together, the confusion about or indifference to

clear-cut categories, the documented reluctance of the "many" qual-ified men in Massachusetts who refused to take up the status of free-man, the tentatively inclusive language in town records, and the absence of protests from nonfreemen until much later in the century suggest that access to voting cannot be neatly categorized as either democratic or oligarchic. We do better if we regard it as a flexible privilege that, from one town to the next, could be modulated in different ways. It is also clear, however, that no group in New En-gland wanted suffrage to be as close to universal (for men) as some within the Leveller movement were advocating in late-1640s En-gland. Among the colonists, as among English Puritans of moderate or theocratic leanings, suffrage was deemed a privilege available to those who supported godly government and a righteous social order. Always, voting was represented as an act of conscience or moral obligation, not as a civil right.[111]

A mixture of rules and informal practices, with local flexibility on how to proceed—such was also the situation of voters and voting in early-seventeenth-century England, where long-standing laws connected voting with the privileges of social rank and property, a practice the Levellers vigorously protested.[112] But the more impor-tant continuity may have concerned the significance of voting in local and colony-wide elections. In New England as in old, voting was not a matter of taking sides. Most of the time in most colonies, freemen were presented with a single list of the persons standing for election as magistrates (assistants). The persistent re-election of the same person as governor in Plymouth, New Haven, Connecticut (where two men exchanged the post on a rotating basis), and Mas-sachusetts demonstrates a preference for agreement or consensus. Continuity was also the norm in most towns, with a small group of men constantly re-elected.[113] Rarely was voting an instrument for deciding contests about policy and legislation, the role it would assume in the nineteenth century, when national and state elections became organized around political parties that competed for power. No parties existed in the colonies. Voting mattered in the general election of 1634 in Massachusetts, when Winthrop was turned out of office, and again in 1637, when he returned as governor. Contests were more common in towns, showing up in the turnover of select-men. But here as well, the continuity in the tenure of town officers is striking, especially after 1640. Within the culture of participation the colonists brought with them, to vote was to consent or, in the language of the time, to link the "interest" of the people with those who held office. Hence the limitation of the franchise to church members—a rationale described more fully in Chapter Three—and allowing "inhabitants" to participate in town meetings. To take this step was not to install an oligarchy or a narrow elite in any of the ordinary meanings of those terms, but to empower as many right-minded men as was possible.[114]

If the story of "oligarchy" falters in the face of this evidence, so does the story of "democracy," for it ignores the moral, cultural, and social parameters of voting and, more generally, of participation. The most important constraint on who could vote was the require-ment of religious affiliation. An express condition of the franchise in Massachusetts and New Haven Colony and, in a much weakened form, evoked in Connecticut and Plymouth, this rule made sense in the context of the colonists' hopes for godly rule. Nonetheless, the cup is more than half full, for the colonists sharply curtailed the roles that property and rank played in England in determining who could vote. Nor did any group in the colonies have an influence over local elections comparable to the role of county gentry and aristo-crats in the English system. Hence the complaints of Lord Saye and Sele about democracy in Massachusetts: almost a decade before any of the Levellers were beginning their assault on social, religious, and political privilege, Saye and Sele realized that the colonists were con-structing a different kind of public life from what had been the norm in Stuart England.

CHAPTER THREE

GODLY RULE

Empowering the Saints

Explicating the book of Revelation to a lecture-day audience in Boston, John Cotton urged the colonists to "raise up" their "hearts in holy thankfulnesse to God" that they had been "delivered" from the "great beast" of Roman Catholicism. The central theme of his sermon series on Revelation was power, just and unjust, limited and unlimited: the unjust and virtually unlimited power asserted by the Papacy over churches, civil societies, and the consciences of Christians, as contrasted with the "simplicity" of the apostolic or "primitive" church, its leaders exercising limited authority, its communities enjoying a cluster of "liberties," and the churches as a whole renouncing any role in civil government.[1]

Appropriate to an exegesis of Revelation, Cotton sketched a politics of authority rooted in a broader story of "warre" between the saints and the forces allied with the Antichrist and Satan. In his telling of this story, conflict had broken out in the fourth century, when, despite the seeming triumph of Christianity under Constantine, the true saints had fled into the "wilderness." For centuries thereafter, a saving remnant had undergone great sacrifice and suffering. This struggle held two lessons: first, that a lust for power arising out of human sinfulness was always and everywhere directed against the saints, and, second, that the day was coming when, as prophesied in Revelation, Daniel, and Isaiah, the tyranny associated with the Antichrist would give way to a church liberated from such abuse and accepting Christ as its sole head.[2]

The people listening to these lectures also heard him say that in

New England ministers and people had collaborated to restore the form of church government practiced by the earliest Christians—that is, not "nationall" or "Diocesan" but "congregational." Warranted by the New Testament, the Congregational Way (as Cotton and others named the New England system) eliminated the abuses of power that had infiltrated Christianity, doing so by the simple steps of allowing every congregation the privilege of self-rule and giving every minister the same rank. All unlawful and corrupting hierarchies thus dispensed with, the saints could look ahead in time as well as back, for the Congregational Way betokened the emergence of the fuller "libertie" Christ had promised those who were participating in the "first Resurrection," the long-awaited moment when churches would cast off "Idolatry and Superstition." Using slightly different language, a lay colonist declared in 1638 that the "endes of Comminge into these westerne partes" were "to establish the lord Jesus in his Kingly Throne as much as in us lies here in his churches and to maynteine the Common Cause of his gospel with our lives and estates." So it also seemed to an Englishman who sympathized with the colonists; evoking the New Jerusalem of Revelation 21, he wrote one of the Winthrops that "the harts of all Gods people here are all bent toward your Syon."[3] For him as for many of the colonists, the church stood at the heart of their project of reform.

During the same period when Cotton was delivering his lectures on Revelation (1639–41), others in England were voicing similar hopes for reform within the framework of apocalyptic prophecy. Before 1641, the possibilities for doing so publicly were few, for the regime of Charles I had ordered the book trades not to publish any commentaries on Revelation. When Thomas Goodwin predicted the coming "reign" of the "saints" and the overthrow of the Antichrist, he was living in exile in the Netherlands, and English readers had to wait for a posthumous printing of his sermons on Revelation. Ephraim Huit's explication of the book of Daniel, completed in 1632, was not printed until 1643, four years after Huit had immigrated to New England.[4] Speculation on the signs of the times persisted in private letters, as when an English correspondent of one of the colonists identified Swedish King Gustavus Adolphus, whose army was contending against Catholic forces on the Continent, as "an instrument for the fall of Antichrist." The Scottish Covenanters who revolted against Charles I in 1638 were more daring. Inserting themselves into the scenario in Revelation of the Antichrist "assaulting our Christian liberty," they likened their cause to Christ's "hunting and pursuing the beast," to them both sign and symbol of the king's mistaken policies.[5]

With the calling of the Long Parliament (1640) and the collapse of state censorship in 1641 came the possibility of full-throated apocalypticism premised on the assertion in Daniel 2:44 that "the God of heaven will set up a kingdom which shall never be destroyed." This way of thinking animated the London-printed *A Glimpse of Sions Glory* (1641), an exultant evocation of "Babylon's destruction" at the hands of the new Parliament and of the possibilities for yet greater reform: "The work of the day [is] to give God no rest till he sets up Jerusalem in the praise of the whole world."[6] Everywhere in 1640s England, similar themes were being voiced—in fast-day sermons to Parliament, in a 1642 pamphlet summing up a Revelation-based critique of the Church of England fashioned by a minister who died in 1607, in preaching by laymen and -women who claimed the sanction of the Holy Spirit.[7] In the early 1650s, these hopes for change animated the "Fifth Monarchy," a group so named because of their argument that the four kingdoms (Daniel 2) were giving way to the kingdom of Christ. In a characteristic voicing of Fifth Monarchy themes, the former colonist William Aspinwall declared in 1656, "The Power of Civil-Government is laid upon the shoulders of Jesus Christ, the MESSIAH, the Son of David, and to him it doth of right belong."[8] Throughout these decades, the tides of speculation about the fall of the Antichrist and the coming kingdom waxed and waned, exciting some, alienating others, and recognized by friend and foe alike as potentially a means of turning ordinary forms of authority upside down.

The colonists acted on these expectations of reform well before anyone in England and Scotland could do so. The central hopes were two: first, to transfer power to the "saints" in keeping with Daniel's vision (Daniel 7:18) that "the saints of the Most High shall take the kingdom and possess the kingdom for ever," and, second, to remodel church *and commonwealth* so that Christ was truly "king" and all policies, practices, and structures were aligned with his commands. As Henry Vane, Jr., insisted in 1637, a society ruled by Christ was one in which "whatsoever is done in word or deed, in church or common-wealth, must be done in the name of the Lord Jesus Christ."[9] These assertions formed the substance of godly rule, a far-reaching program of reform that encompassed church, state, and civil society. Never adequately acknowledged in the scholarship on early New England,[10] the themes and principles of godly rule animated a cluster of manifestos that date from the mid- and late 1630s: a "Model of Church and Civil Power" drafted by a group of ministers in 1635; Cotton's *Abstract of the Lawes,* written in 1635 or 1636; John Wheelwright's fast-day sermon of January 1637; John Davenport's *A Discourse About Civil Government in a New Planta-tion Whose Design Is Religion,* printed in 1663 but dating from 1638 or 1639; a collectively authored "Epistle Written by the Elders of the Churches in New-England," dating from the end of the 1630s; Cotton's sermons on Revelation; and portions of Richard Mather's *Church-Government and Church-Covenant Discussed,* written in the late 1630s and printed in London in 1643. John Eliot's *The Christian Commonwealth: Or, The Civil Policy of The Rising Kingdom of Jesus Christ,* dating from 1651 and printed in London in 1659, was a belated addition to this series.

By this time, too, the layman Edward Johnson had written *The Wonder-Working Providence of Sions Saviour in New England* (London, 1654), a history informed by Johnson's apocalyptic assertion that New England was "the place where the Lord will create a new Heaven, and a new Earth in, new Churches, and a new Common-wealth together."[11] Former colonists were publishing similar mani-festos in England during these years—Hugh Peter in *Good Work for a Good Magistrate* (London, 1651); Vane in several works, although most contentiously in *A Healing Question Propounded* (1656);[12] and Aspinwall in *The Legislative Power Is Christ's Peculiar Prerogative* (London, 1656) and other brief books and pamphlets. Many others in New England sympathized with the apocalyptically inflected anti-popery that accompanied arguments for godly rule, as when the Massachusetts magistrate John Endecott despoiled "the kinges Coulours" in 1634 because the Cross of St. George was "a superstitious thinge and a relique of Antichriste." In his own distinctive manner, Roger Williams was also performing variations on the theme of "long[ing] for the bright Appearance of the Lord Jesus to consume the Man of Sinn."[13]

Godly rule was about liberty and being liberated, but it was also about obligation and obedience, for true liberty meant subordinating self-interest to the will of Christ, as made evident in the Bible. Scripture was normative, providing rules or patterns for all of society. So the ministers and laymen attempting godly rule in New Haven declared in 1639: "The Scripturs do holde forth a perfect rule for the direction and government of all men in all dueties which they are to performe to God and men as well in the government of families and commonwealths as in matters of the church."[14] A dozen years later, John Eliot reiterated this premise in *The Christian Commonwealth.* Addressing an English audience, Eliot called on his former countrymen to acknowledge that "the Lord Jesus will bring down all people, to be ruled by the Institutions, Laws, and Directions of the Word of God; not only in Church-Government and Administrations, but also in the Government and Administration of all affairs in the Commonwealth."[15] To undertake godly rule was to cast off every corrupt form of authority and install structures and practices mandated by a sovereign Christ.

As reformers on both sides of the Atlantic came to realize, putting godly rule into practice raised a host of questions. How were the saints, the saving remnant of true Christians, to be differentiated from all others who said they followed Christ? How in particular were the saints unlike the "carnal professors" and "lukewarm" Christians of Laodicea (Revelation 3:16) evoked in Puritan critiques of the Church of England? What authority were saints to have within a remodeled church, and would giving them a central role in a "Christian commonwealth" threaten the participation of others, to the point of producing a new kind of tyranny? Would a liberated church depend on the cooperation of the civil state, in keeping with magisterial Protestantism, or insist on protecting itself against the state? How would liberty of conscience function in a new-modeled society? And should the pace of reform be rapid or deliberate, of zeal overriding all obstacles or patient change? Underlying these questions was a principle of difference and its consequences: If the saints were truly different from the ungodly, how should that difference be incorporated into civil and religious institutions?[16]

These were questions that could only be answered politically, in the sense that any attempt to transform institutions as basic as church, state, and the law would raise some people up and displace others. Godly rule was political in challenging the power of vested interests. So the history of the English Reformation had abundantly demonstrated—cautious advances and sometimes retreats during the reign of Henry VIII, daring steps under Edward VI, caution once again under Elizabeth I and James I, and (in the eyes of many) retreat under Charles I. That the colonists could attempt godly rule so openly and with so much success was only possible because they were far removed from Charles I and the politics that impeded the accomplishing of godly rule in revolutionary England. Yet again, circumstances differentiated the unfolding of religious reform in New England from what happened in revolutionary England.

Much of this story follows, though some aspects of it are deferred to Chapters Four and Five.

I

GODLY RULE was rooted in an interpretive tradition dating from the sixteenth century. A backward glance at that tradition is necessary if we are to understand the policies and politics of godly rule among the colonists. They owed much of their thinking to English Protestants who, in the middle of the sixteenth century, used a mixture of prophecy and history to condemn Catholicism and justify the English Reformation.

Biblical prophecy was (and is) elusive to decipher, or, as people in the sixteenth and seventeenth centuries readily acknowledged, a matter of "mysteries" no one but God could fully comprehend.

What was *not* mysterious to sixteenth-century apologists for the English Reformation was the point around which Cotton built his sermons on the book of Revelation, that Roman Catholicism—more specifically, the Papacy—was an instrument of the Antichrist and therefore the antithesis of true Christianity. John Bale and John Foxe had set this argument in motion by the 1550s, whence it passed into the annotations of the Geneva Bible (1560).[17] To answer the Catholic taunt of where Protestants had been during the many centuries before the Reformation, Bale constructed a theory of two churches, the one false although encompassing most of Christendom, the other true although tiny and ever imperiled, the saints who fled into the wilderness (Revelation 12:6). According to his scheme, the coming of the Reformation signified that the faithful few were finally on the verge of victory, the moment when the "Beast" of Revelation 13 (the Antichrist; the Papacy) would be slain.[18] Nebuchadnezzar's dream (Daniel 2) could be glossed as telling a similar story of saints who suffered under a series of kings or empires (likened to four beasts) for "a time, two times, and half a time," until, at long last, they became free to rule the fifth and final kingdom.

In the wake of Foxe and Bale, mainstream English Protestantism thrived on evocations of the tyranny of Rome and the warfare under way between the Antichrist and the saints. Thus a bishop of the church could declare in 1608, "The Church of Rome is the whore of Babylon, the see of Antichrist, the mother of all fornications and abominations, being also . . . dyed red with the blood of the Saints, and of the Martyrs of Jesus."[19] A story line so widely used to defend the coming of Protestantism to England and Scotland was worth repeating by a king, as James VI of Scotland (and future James I of England) did in *An Fruitfull Meditation . . . on the Twentieth Chapter of Revelation* (1588). Aware that English Protestants were asserting the divine source of kingship to justify Henry VIII's break with Rome, James employed the framework of apocalypticism to enhance the role of kings as protectors of true religion.[20] Foxe supported the same argument, with Elizabeth I playing the role of Christian prince. Writing in the immediate aftermath of the reign of Mary Tudor, whose brief rule (1553–58) brought about a restoration of Catholicism, Foxe likened his new queen to the Emperor Constantine, crediting her "true . . . and imperial crown" with making it possible for "the brightnesse of God's word" to be "set up again to confound the dark and false-vizored Kingdom of Antichrist." Foxe also reiterated the story of near-miraculous persistence by a saving remnant of Christians. In them the "primitive" purity of the early church was sustained until, with the coming of the Reformation, their fidelity to Christ expanded into the cause of Protestantism.[21]

But whether kings and bishops were instruments of the reformation to come was already being questioned by Bale, who suggested that the "saints" would play a greater role than "magistrates, princes, bishops, established power in general" in the struggle against the Antichrist.[22] By the 1570s, a few English Protestants were also arguing that the office of bishop was "unlawful" and insisting that episcopacy (the form of church government in England) was an instrument of Antichristian tyranny. John Field and Thomas Wilcox said so in *An Admonition to the Parliament* (1572), as did "Separatists" who withdrew from the Church of England because it was "unlawful." For them as for Field and Wilcox, the state church had yet to disengage itself from Rome. Too many aspects of Catholicism remained, like "set" or "stinted" prayer and certain sacramental practices. In their judgment, the Church of England also deviated from the practice of the early churches in refusing to purge itself of "hypocrites" who fell woefully short of being sincere Christians. Separatists called for replacing comprehensive parishes with congregations consisting only of "the worthiest, were they never so few."[23] To support this line of argument, Separatists modified the customary dating of early church history. Contrary to Foxe, they argued that the church began its long slide into corruption and tyranny with Constantine. The "Pilgrims" who founded New World Plymouth in 1620 placed the story of their particular struggles within this narrative, insisting, as William Bradford said in *Of Plimoth Plantation,* that the ancient "hatred against the holy discipline of Christ in His church hath continued to this day," as proved by the

English bishops' persecution of "all zealous professors in the land . . . if they would not submit to . . . popish trash." For Bradford and his fellow colonists, both Papacy and English bishops were "the very voice of antichrist."[24]

The colonists adopted most of this version of the past themselves, thanks to the influence of an English minister John Cotton described as a man blessed with a "Prophetical spirit" and the "most serviceable . . . of all that have written" on Revelation.[25] Thomas Brightman lived quietly as a minister in England until his death in 1607. Two years later, a Frankfurt bookseller issued Brightman's lengthy exegesis of Revelation, *Apocalypsis Apocalypseos.* Translated into English as *A Revelation of the Revelation* and printed in Amsterdam in 1615 and 1635, it received its first London printing in 1644. A primitivist who imagined restoring the church to its initial purity, Brightman added two new features to the framework of apocalypticism. Before him, English Protestants and Christian theologians in general had regarded the thousand-year reign of Christ (the millennium) forecast in Revelation as having already occurred. Brightman agreed, but he also argued that something akin to the millennium, a "Middle Advent" or "Brightness of his Coming," lay ahead, a period of time when the Christian church would increasingly liberate itself from Catholicism.[26] Brightman backed this argument by aligning the visions and numerologies of Daniel and John of Patmos with recent history. According to his calculations, Rome (or Babylon) would collapse at the end of the seventeenth century. In his wake, other English students of apocalyptic prophecy agreed that the rule of the saints would happen before the end of the century, or shortly thereafter. Brightman thus taught his contemporaries to look for signs that the grand scenario of Revelation, the war between the saints and the Antichrist, was hastening to its close in their lifetimes.

With this "millenarianism," Brightman altered the trajectory of the apocalyptic tradition and the hopes for godly rule. He did so as well by rejecting John Foxe's emphasis on the Christian prince or emperor as the prime maker of godly rule, and by arguing that a new kind of church would arise, a purified community he likened to the "Philadelphia" of Revelation 1. Brightman praised Elizabeth, but he also identified the Church of England with "luke-warm" Laodicea, neither "hot" nor "cold," and therefore in danger of being rejected by Christ. What made the Church of England another Laodicea was its failure to eliminate all vestiges of Catholicism. Reiterating a persistent complaint of Puritan-minded reformers, Brightman described the church as an unhealthy mixture of the true and the false. For him the way forward lay in emulating the Reformed churches of the Netherlands and Scotland, which had no bishops and used the tool of discipline to exclude the indifferent and the profane. Such churches and only such churches were in keeping with the Philadelphia extolled in Revelation. Because Elizabeth had rejected this demand and abetted the harsh treatment of Separatists, Brightman would write of the "men called Christian Princes" that "they exercised the savage cruelty of the Heathen under that name." Much more strongly than Foxe, he emphasized the role of fugitive groups like the Waldensians in preserving and transmitting true Christianity. In his thinking, the hopes for reformation lay with a "godly" people.[27]

Ever malleable, the dream described in Daniel and the beasts, seals, vials, trumpets, and numerology of Revelation continued to attract interpreters in the early decades of the seventeenth century. Some of them disagreed with Brightman's politics and defended the Church of England, but followed him in aligning time past, time present, and time future in attempting to specify when Christ's spiritual kingdom would be restored.[28] Always, other frameworks were intertwined with apocalypticism, notably the Old Testament theme of a vengeful God punishing a people that persisted in sinfulness and idolatry. A commonplace of English preaching, the assertion that God would abandon those who sinned, even a people as favored as the English had been, was evoked in 1629 by Thomas Hooker, soon to become an exile in the Netherlands. Warning the townspeople whom he served, "You that have enjoyed great means, the Lord will proceed more heavily against you than against others when he begins to execute his wrath," he quoted the famous warning (Revelation 2:5), "I will come unto thee quickly, and remove thy candlestick out of his place." That England was growing unsafe, and that carrying the church into a "wildernesse" would "helpe on the cominge of the fullnesse of the Gentiles," was one of the reasons cited in 1629 by a group of London merchants and East Anglian gentry for planting a colony in New England. That the Church of England was increasingly burdened with "grievous corruptions" to the point of a "willfull rejection of Reformation" was, as Richard Mather remarked soon after reaching Massachusetts, another sign that the candlesticks of Revelation were vanishing and that England was akin to Laodicea.[29] In these years as well, although especially after 1640, apocalyptic prophecy was sometimes combined with an emphasis upon the liberating power of the Holy Spirit. Construed as "light," the Spirit was replacing the darkness of false doctrine and Antichristian corruption with an expanded understanding of what was true—a "new light" that would guide the fashioning of worship, church, and piety.[30]

This cluster of themes informed the experiments in godly rule the colonists would initiate in the 1630s. Cotton was the most important spokesman for this program, the Cotton who wrote John Davenport, then in exile in the Netherlands, that "the Order of the Churches and of the Comonwealth was so settled" in New England, "by common Consent, that it brought to his mind, the New Heaven and New Earth, wherein dwells Righteousness"; who evoked Brightman in foreseeing a "second resurrection" that would bring about a thorough transformation of the church; and who provided a time line for the overthrow of the Antichrist, which he foresaw happening in the 1650s.[31] This was also the Cotton who, faced with choosing between a patient, drawn-out process of reform and immediate action, urged the colonists to "goe fast whom the Spirit of God drives," calling on them not to "give rest . . . till in Family, Church, and Common-wealth we have set a patterne of holiness to those that shall succeed us."[32] Relying on the idiom of covenant he had already used in *Gods Promise to His Plantations* (London, 1630), he informed the colonists in June 1636 that they had taken "Christ for [their] king, and priest, and prophet." Doing so bound them to "reform both church and commonwealth" in accordance with the "moral laws, and statutes, and judgments, unto all which [God] doth require obedience."[33]

Cotton translated this language into a specific program. Spelled out in biblical commentaries, a brief description of the true church he wrote in or around 1635, *The True Constitution of a Particular Visible Church* (London, 1642), and several treatises he wrote in the early 1640s, this program was premised on his assertion that the one and only form of church warranted by the Word was "congregational."[34] Almost without exception, his colleagues in the ministry agreed with him, as did the great majority of the colonists. Some of them had already started down this path in 1629, when the colonists in Salem organized such a church. Thereafter, the people who dispersed across New England fashioned dozens of autonomous, covenanted congregations. Where the records are unusually ample, as they are for the newly founded town of Dedham, this process began when the townspeople agreed to organize a "particular visible" fellowship of "a certaine number of visible saints," based in Dedham as it was elsewhere on "a mutual . . . profession of the covenant of grace." At once, this procedure dispensed with bishops and any other authority beyond the local congregation. Of equal significance, Cotton and his colleagues also agreed that Christ had given the "power of the keys," or direct authority in congregational governance (Matthew 18:17), to the laymen of each congregation. Daringly, the ministers in New England insisted that such a group was entitled to choose and dismiss its own clergy. Not the rite of ordination as performed by bishops in the Church of England, or approval by some outside authority, but a local election bestowed office and legitimacy on church leaders.[35]

For Cotton and his colleagues, these steps were a means of eliminating arbitrary, unbounded power. Warning that where "transcendent power is given," it "will certainly over-run those that give it, and those that receive it," Cotton underscored the corollary, "that all power that is on earth be limited." In the new order of the Congregational Way, sovereignty rested with Christ and secondarily with the saints, by delegation. Contradicting the contempt for popular rule voiced by the leadership of the Church of England and, in the 1640s, by many Presbyterians, Cotton celebrated the empowering of ordinary people in their guise as saints. So did Roger Williams in the early 1630s, when he was ministering to the church in Salem. "However it hath been the Praelates plea, the people are weak giddie and rash, and therefore shold not enjoy such liberties," he wrote in 1635, New Englanders acknowledged that their church members had "a wisdom greater than theirs." Richard Mather made the same point. Responding to a group of English ministers who complained that the Congregational Way gave far too much authority to "illiterate" people, Mather altered the meaning of literacy by locating it in the "hearts" of those who "have learned the Doctrine of the holy Scripture in the fundamentall points thereof." How could anyone "reproach as illiterate or unworthy" the people covenanted together in congregations, he asked, for they were singularly wise in spiritual affairs.[36]

Thomas Hooker also rebuked the Scots and English Presbyterians for being so conservative in their estimation of the people. Citing Brightman, he argued in *A Survey of the Summe of Church-Discipline* (1648) that "these are the times when people shall be fitted" to receive and practice far greater privileges of governance. Like Mather before him, he deployed this apocalypticism to subvert long-lasting tropes that stigmatized "the people" as ignorant and unskillful and therefore "not fit to share" in church governance. In the new day that was dawning, God was making His people "fit" to do all that He wished. Hooker hymned the reversals forecast in biblical prophecy. Those of low rank or status were now raised up, for "the Lord hath promised: To take away the vail from all faces in the mountain, the weak shall be as David, and David as an Angel of God. The light of the Moon shall be as the Sun." At a later point in the *Survey*, he connected his argument to the maxim *salus populi suprema lex*, interpreting it to mean that all acts of authority in a congregation must rest on "mutuall and free consent."[37]

Other practices followed from this remodeling of authority, some of them aligned with the motif of opening up the church to the free movement of the Holy Spirit. Reasoning that the Spirit worked through laypeople as well as ministers, Cotton justified allowing laymen (but not laywomen) to prophesy once a minister finished his sermon. He warranted asking questions of a minister during the service and endorsed the critique of "set" prayer Field and Wilcox had voiced in *An Admonition to the Parliament* and Separatists had reiterated. No set prayer, no liturgy, and, to the astonishment of moderates in England, no fixed stipends or tithes as a means of extracting money from church members. Shortly after he arrived in Massachusetts, Cotton was extolling voluntary contributions as most in keeping with primitive Christianity. In *Church-Government and Church-Covenant,* Mather turned to Revelation to justify the same practice, stigmatizing "stinted" maintenance on the grounds that no such practice was "appointed by Christ our Lord" in the early days of the church. For him the villain was Constantine, who "brought settled endowments into the Church," a practice Mather regarded as "poison."[38]

By the mid-1630s, another major piece of the Congregational Way was in place, construing church membership as limited to "visible saints" capable of describing the "work of grace" they had experienced. Starting afresh, as it were, the colonists were free to enact (in the words of the English Congregationalist John Owen) the long-sought "separation and sequestration" of the godly "from the world and men of the world," the same ambition voiced in Goodwin's explication of Revelation and *A Glimpse of Sions Glory,* which celebrated the possibility that "hypocrites shall be discovered and cast out of the Church." As Mather phrased it, congregations could finally rid themselves of the "Doggs and Swine" who "have no right . . . to the priviledges of the Church." For Cotton, the key point was that churches in New England could ask in all seriousness, "What manner of men hath God appointed, to be received as Brethren and members of his Church"? For him the answer was obvious: not the promiscuous multitude, but the godly. In *The True Constitution,* he was specific about the criteria to use: "Such as are called of God out of this world to the fellowship of Christ (1) and do willingly offer and joyne themselves, first to the Lord (2) and then to the Church (3) by confession of their sins (4) by profession of their faith (5) and by taking or laying hold of his Covenant (6)."[39] Amplified in what rapidly became known as a "relation" of the "work of grace," these expectations transformed membership from something more or less mandatory, as it was in the parish system of the Church of England and most versions of Presbyterianism, into something voluntary and selective. For biblical warrant, he and his fellow ministers had Revelation 21:27, "But nothing unclean shall enter it, nor any one who practices abomination or falsehood, but only those who are written in the Lamb's book of life," though the deeper warrant may have been the social experience of the colonists in their homeland of cohabiting with the "wicked" and "rudest." At long last, the faithful few, the saving remnant of authentic Christians, were coming into their own.[40]

Saints empowered, saints differentiated from hypocrites and the ungodly—these were extraordinary steps to take. When the ministers turned to the question of church and state, the outcome was almost as remarkable. The great lesson their English years taught the colonists was the mistake of allowing the state to assert its authority over doctrine, the selection of ministers, and the disciplining of church members. This lesson was registered in Brightman's hesitation to endorse the concept of the Christian prince or emperor, a staple of sixteenth-century Reformed "political theology" but a concept discounted in *An Admonition to the Parliament* and Separatist manifestos.[41] That Cotton shared some of this reluctance is apparent from his suggestion that the Emperor Constantine had initiated the corruption of the church. To follow out the logic of this point of view was to imagine the saints as always and everywhere a persecuted remnant. Hence another thesis of his lectures: never let the church assert any authority over the civil state, and never let the civil state dictate matters of doctrine or polity to the church. The troubled history of the Puritan movement, with its demands for change persistently thwarted by unsympathetic monarchs, confirmed the merits of these twin principles. Were further sanction needed, John Calvin (and before him, Martin Luther) had insisted on differentiating the "spiritual" kingdom of the church from the "temporal" kingdom of the civil state. Cotton was reiterating a commonplace of the Reformed tradition, therefore, when he declared, "The Church of Christ doth not use the Arme of Secular Power to compel men to the Faith . . . for this is to be done by Spirituall weapons, whereby Christians are to be exhorted, not compelled."[42]

His colleagues had already made the same point in "A Model of Church and Civil Power,"[43] a text organized around the question "how the Civill State and the Church may dispence their severall Governments without infringement and impeachment of the power and honour of the One or the Other, and what bounds and limits the Lord hath set betweene both the Administrations." Opening with an assertion of the differences between the spiritual and the civil spheres, the "Model" spelled out its consequences. Primary among these was the obligation to establish "that forme of Church Government only, of which Christ hath given them a pattern in his Word." The corollary to this was that the church accepts no one "but Christ" as its head and maker of its rules, followed by a list of those rules: congregations choose their minister, admit people to membership, and perform acts of "discipline" without ever involving the civil state. On the other hand, "Churches as Churches, have no power (though as members of the Commonweale they may have power) of erecting or altering formes of Civil Government, electing of Civil officers, [or] inflicting Civill punishments," a list that also included a ban on ministers' holding civil office. At one stroke, therefore, the colonists dispensed with the role of English kings and queens as head of the church and the powers suited to that role.[44]

These principles were codified in the Massachusetts Body of Liberties, a text leavened with the ethos of godly rule. In Liberty No. 95, "A Declaration of the Liberties the Lord Jesus Hath Given to the Churches," one provision granted any group of colonists "full liberty to gather . . . into a Church Estaite." Others described the steps a church could take on its own, like selecting officers and admitting, dismissing, and disciplining ministers and members. These measures culminated in a general rule restricting the power of the civil state: "No Injunctions are to be put upon any Church, Church officers or member in point of Doctrine, worship or Discipline, whether for substance or circumstance besides the Institutions of the lord."[45] Similar rules—or, if not specific rules, similar expectations—prevailed in all the orthodox colonies. Collectively, these rules upended the ideal of the confessional state that for centuries had animated Catholicism and continued to animate the Church of England in the early seventeenth century. It is telling that, in their determination to protect the saints from an abusive civil state, the ministers reversed an argument made famous by James I and much reiterated by supporters of the Church of England. James warned in 1604 that if bishops were eliminated, as some Puritans were demanding, the office of kingship would immediately become vulnerable. John Cotton repudiated this argument in a 1636 letter to the English aristocrat Lord Saye and Sele. Citing the late-sixteenth-century Puritan leader Thomas Cartwright, Cotton insisted, "It is better that the commonwealth be fashioned to the setting forth of Gods house, which is his church: than to accommodate the church frame to the civill state."[46]

Curtailing the reach of the civil state was also a means of guarding liberty of conscience. The colonists were indebted to Catholic and Protestant casuistry for the premise that conscience was a "natural" capacity in everyone for discerning divine truth and accepting the guidance of the moral law. Conscience was infallible in registering the difference between right and wrong. When someone erred by choosing the immoral or the proscribed, anguish of conscience became God's way of imposing "just judgement against sinners." It followed that conscience could function only if its "liberty" was respected, a liberty construed as freedom from coercion by either civil state or church.[47] Consistent with this teaching, Cotton could say in all sincerity in the 1630s, "It is not lawfull to persecute any for Conscience sake Rightly informed; for in persecuting such, Christ himselfe is persecuted in them," and Hooker could remark in the *Survey,* "Outward constraint and violence, is crosse utterly to the Government of Christ in his Church," the underlying point being that the church could only impose "spiritual censures." Knowing of these statements, Roger Williams conceded that his orthodox opponents were opposed to punishing "secret sinnes in the Soule." With the martyrs evoked in Revelation always in mind, Cotton would declare that the Christian church "doth not persecute, but is persecuted."[48]

This determination to preserve the church from unjust or coercive authority, or from exercising the wrong kinds of power, coexisted with a positive role for the civil state in matters of religion. Despite their reluctance to embrace the figure of the Christian prince,[49] Cotton and his fellow ministers did so on the basis of Old and New Testament passages (Isaiah 49:23; 1 Timothy 2:1–2) representing kings as "nursing fathers" of the covenant with God, forceful opponents of "idolatry," and upholders of the "outward peace" that God preferred. Unlike Williams, they continued to believe that saints and the fallen world were both encompassed within the reign of God. Proof of God's comprehensive reign, and a sufficient reason for authorizing the civil state to act in matters of religion, was the fact that some parts of Mosaic law were "everlasting." Hence the dual responsibility of the Christian prince or magistrate: first and foremost, to protect the church from heretics and other enemies, and, second, to enforce those laws that were "perpetuall." In *An Apologie of the Churches in New-England for Church-Covenant* (written c. 1637, published in London in 1643), Richard Mather evoked the latter rationale in proposing that the "Christian Prince doth but his dutie when he doth not tolerate within his Dominions any open Idolatry, or the open worship of false Gods by baptized persons, but suppresseth the same."[50]

Excluded in order to safeguard liberty of conscience, coercion became legitimate when Christians went astray. That conscience *would inevitably mislead* became, for both the colonists and John Calvin, warrant for the civil state to override its freedom. As Cotton insisted in his lectures on Revelation, and again in the mid-1640s in debating Williams, a conscience hardened against the truth betrayed its very reason for being. Once this happened, the civil magistrate was entitled to punish blasphemy, sedition, and idolatry, the three crimes Cotton singled out as extreme violations of God's law. Reminding Williams that the colonists had classified these three as civil, not religious crimes, he underscored the point that the true church could only use spiritual weapons against them.[51] By the mid-

1640s, however, a stronger interpretation of magistracy and its powers had re-emerged alongside Cotton's Luther-like evocation of the
church as ever persecuted, with Hooker arguing in the *Survey* that
civil officers could "compel Ecclesiastical persons to do, what they
ought in their office." Yet, as late as 1649, the chapter on church and
state in *A Platforme of Church Discipline*, a quasi-official summary of
church order, acknowledged a role for godly magistrates only after
several sections emphasized the church's independence. What Cotton said in his Revelation sermons about unjust power provoked a
long-lasting uneasiness among the colonists about some aspects of
magisterial Protestantism and, especially, the tradition of the Christian prince.[52]

Always mindful of how things had gone wrong in the history of
the Christian church, and determined to prevent another Constantine from emerging in their midst, the advocates of godly rule
insisted on one other rule affecting church and state, that officers of
the state came under the "watch" of the church and could be cen-
sored ("disciplined") for any misdeeds they committed. Effectively,
the ministers and laypeople who supported this rule were saying
that, in a worst-case situation, the church could bar civil magistrates
from the Lord's Supper and their children from baptism. No English monarch had acknowledged the church's right to do so, and
when Archbishop Edmund Grindal reminded Elizabeth I that she
was "a mortal creature" and should respect the spiritual authority of
the church, she responded by suspending him from all powers of
office. Nor was the Long Parliament especially welcoming of such a
rule when it was proposed by the Westminster Assembly as part of a
new Directory of Worship.[53] Only in New England, although not as
easily as Cotton and his colleagues would have hoped, was it incorporated into the Body of Liberties.[54]

By 1641, the advocates of godly rule had accomplished most of
what they sought. The surest testimony to the breadth of their program was the dismay it aroused among English and Scottish Presbyterians and, no less telling, the inability of the Long Parliament to
terminate the abuses of privilege and power—lay patronage of
church "livings," for one—that hampered the Church of England.

The colonists had done much more than implant a system of church government that, before 1635, had been attempted only by exiles in the Netherlands or fugitive groups of Separatists in England. In and of itself, this was astonishing. They had gotten rid of tithes and ecclesiastical courts (as did the Long Parliament), and barred their clergy from holding civil office. Written law codified the distinction between church and state and permitted congregations to discipline church members no matter what their status. And, as was noted in the previous chapter, civil and criminal law had been aligned with Scripture as part of a broader process of legal reform that no English Parliament was able to accomplish, despite attempts at doing so. In his Revelation sermons, Cotton could rightly celebrate a fundamental reworking of authority that some Puritans had long imagined. Here in New England, he told the audience for his lecture sermons, "the Lord hath given us to enjoy Churches, and Congregational Assemblies by his Covenant, to worship him in all his holy Ordinances; . . . he hath given us to look for no Laws but his word, and no rules nor forms of worship, but such as he hath set down in his word; no platforms of Doctrine, but such as are held forth in the word of the Prophets and Apostles."[55]

It was tempting and, for leaders such as Cotton, Davenport, and Eliot, imperative to expand the scope of godly rule to the structure and practices of civil governance. Tempting but also fraught with uncertainties: Scripture was much less explicit about civil government than it was about the polity of churches, and a civil government confined to the saints would risk alienating any who failed to become church members. But among the colonists—as in England, with the Fifth Monarchists—some were determined to take the crucial step of empowering the saints. If "a kingdom and dominion of the Church, or of Christ and the Saints, is to be expected upon earth," as a small group of English radicals argued in 1649 on the basis of Daniel, Isaiah, and Revelation, it followed that church members and *only* church members should "have voice in elections." Underlying this argument was the assumption, central to apocalyptic readings of Christian history, that existing structures must be overturned and "the ungodly" cast out of their places of power.[56] In April 1631, well before arguments of this kind were being voiced in England, the Massachusetts government voted to limit the status of freeman to men who were church members, doing so soon after granting the franchise to 116 men, some of whom had not yet joined a local congregation. Several years later, the ministers in the colony drafted a rationale for this rule and its corollary, that anyone holding office in the commonwealth must also be a church member. Citing, among other verses, Proverbs 29:2 ("When the Righteous rule, the people rejoice"), the "Model" of 1635 gave two reasons for requiring "that all free men elected, be only Church-members": the risk that those outside the church would choose "others besides Church members" to govern, and "the pattern of Israel, where none had power to choose but only Israel, or such as were joined to the people of God."[57]

Some months later, Cotton defended the Massachusetts law in his response to Saye and Sele, who had written to Winthrop and others asking for civil privileges consistent with his rank. Undoubtedly at Winthrop's urging, Cotton described the law as "a divine ordinance," citing Exodus 18:21 ("Moreover, provide thou among all the people men of courage, fearing God . . . and appoint such over them to be rulers"), and explaining "that none are so fit to be trusted with the liberties of the commonwealth as church members." The very breadth of those "liberties" among the colonists—Cotton instanced the role of the freemen in choosing magistrates and in making and repealing laws—gave the practice its importance. Were it not for the Massachusetts law, he pointed out, the colonists might end up being ruled by someone hostile to the saints, a warning based on what was happening in England. Ephraim Huit had made the same point in his commentary on Daniel, with the situation in 1630s England in mind: "The Professors of God and men of the world can never hartily love one another."[58]

The other colony where this rule was adopted was New Haven. A year after settling along the Connecticut shore, the informal leaders of the *town,* all of whom had been members of the same church in London under John Davenport's ministry, convened some seventy men—almost certainly the entire number of "free planters" in their community—to "consult about settling civill Government according to God." As narrated in the town records, someone opened the meeting by reminding everyone "of the busines whereabout they met (viz.) for the establishment of such civill order as might be most p[leas]ing unto God." It was probably Davenport who framed the initial question to be discussed: "Whether the Scripturs doe holde forth a perfect rule for the direction and government of all men in all dueties . . . as well as in the government of famylyes and commonwealths as in matters of the church," to which everyone "assented . . . by holding up of hands." Harking back to a "covenant" made the previous year in which the "free planters" had committed themselves to "be ordered by those rules which the scripture holds forth to us," the group reaffirmed its obligation to these rules. Once this and other gestures of assent had occurred, Davenport reminded everyone that, hereafter in New Haven, church membership would be required of all officers and "free burgesses" or freemen. After responding to a solitary expression of dissent, he called for the group to vote on this proposition, whereupon (as noted in the town records) "it was agreed unto."[59]

Possibly in response to the one dissenter, Davenport drafted a fuller rationale for limiting civic participation to church members, the manuscript printed in 1663 as *A Discourse About Civil Government in a New Plantation Whose Design Is Religion*.[60] Here he employed the category of "interest" to justify connecting church membership and civil privileges. A staple of English political philosophy, interest was a way of analyzing which groups would be loyal supporters of the state, the answer being: those who had a stake in its policies.[61] Davenport and other advocates of godly rule were asking a narrower version of this question, how to ensure that civil government in New England would uphold a broad program of "righteousness." The interest Davenport wanted to safeguard was religious and, especially, ecclesiastical, for he knew that the decision to establish a gathered church in the town could become divisive. Limiting the franchise to church members would forestall the two great threats to a system of gathered churches, a civil state that "compel[led]" a congregation to "receive into fellowship unsuitable ones" or a state that imposed "Ordinances of men" in the practice of worship. From his point of view, the English state and the Church of England had made both of these mistakes.[62]

Elsewhere, this rule gained some support, though none in the Rhode Island towns, and only in a weakened form in Connecticut, where church membership was required of governors. Urged on by their minister Henry Whitfield, the townspeople of Guilford voted in 1643 that "only such planters, as are also members of the church here, shall be, and bee called freemen, and that such freemen only shall have power to elect magistrates, Deputies and all other officers."[63] Once New Haven fashioned a colony-wide government, the same rule came to prevail in other nearby towns. Ultimately of limited significance in New England, this aspect of godly rule was briefly influential in English politics during the early 1650s, when a handful of Fifth Monarchists began to urge a similar policy on Oliver Cromwell. Needing a new Parliament, Cromwell and the army officers on whom he was relying decided in early 1653 to choose its members on their own, though soliciting some recommendations from gathered (Independent, Baptist) ministers and congregations. Addressing the men who met in July 1653—the only Parliament to sit during the 1640s and 1650s without being elected—Cromwell evoked the principle of godly rule, confessing that he "never looked to see such a Day as this . . . when Jesus Christ should be so owned as He is, this day, in this Work." In the same speech he justified the process of selection on the grounds of "interest," noting that otherwise his government might have fallen "into the hands of wicked men and enemies! I am sure, God would not have it so." With Hosea 11:12, "Judah yet ruleth with God, and is faithful with the Saints," as his text, he urged the new parliamentarians to regard themselves as "truly . . . called by God . . . to rule with Him, and for Him," asking them also to remember that they must "be faithful with the Saints who have been instrumental to your call."[64]

The Barebones Parliament of 1653 was short-lived, and the impasse in which radical advocates of godly rule found themselves pushed a handful of Fifth Monarchists toward revolutionary violence in 1657, and again in 1661.[65] Also short-lived was a singular experiment, this one in New England. In the backwash of the Antinomian Controversy, a handful of people disaffected with the Massachusetts government founded Aquidneck, on Newport Island. The group included William Coddington, a man of wealth and an investor in the Massachusetts Bay Company who got himself exiled for protesting the treatment of John Wheelwright. Joining with William Aspinwall, William Hutchinson, and others in a covenant in 1638, Coddington and this group promised "to submit our persons, lives and estates unto our Lord Jesus Christ, the King of Kings and Lord of Lords, and to all those perfect and most absolute laws of his given us in his holy word of truth, to be guided and judged thereby." The community's version of godly rule centered on reclaiming the role of judge (with life tenure) that Coddington found in the Old Testament. Agreeing in early 1639 to attempt such a government, the "Body" of inhabitants also acknowledged a parallel principle, "that the Judge together with the Elders shall Rule and Governe according to the Generall rule of the word of God, when they have no Particular rule from God's word by the Body proscribed as a direction unto them in the case." Almost as soon as this attempt at theocratic governance was under way, however, local rivalries brought the experiment to an end.[66]

One other New England community seemed uniquely suited to godly rule—the Indians who, in very small numbers, were converting to Christianity. Encouraged by the execution of Charles I in January 1649 to assume that the end times were approaching, John Eliot, the minister in Roxbury, Massachusetts, who took the lead in reaching out to local Indians, wondered if the men he was converting to Christianity could organize their "praying towns" along biblical lines. Eliot sketched his thinking in a manuscript he wrote at the beginning of the 1650s, around the time he helped bring Natick, the first of the praying towns, into being. Eliot imagined a republican government with Christ as its sole monarch, an assertion that embarrassed the Massachusetts government when the manuscript was belatedly published in London in 1659. *The Christian Commonwealth* drew on Exodus 18:21–22 for its scheme of self-governing groups organized in tens, fifties, and hundreds to thousands, each presided over by rulers. As Eliot remarked in his treatise, he favored this Old Testament scheme because it aligned the Indian communities with the earliest system of government practiced by the people of God. At the time he wrote the treatise, Eliot was looking to England as the place where Christ would return to rule, but in August 1651 he read from Exodus 18 to the group of Indians gathered in Natick on the day they chose their rulers. Unlike Cotton, Davenport, and some Fifth Monarchists, Eliot was silent about church membership as a condition of the franchise, almost certainly because no Indian church yet existed. Unique in turning back so emphatically to the Old Testament, he had the bad luck of having his preference for a republic made public in England just as the monarchy was being restored.[67]

II

So much accomplished, so much reason for celebration: as a layman wrote John Winthrop in January 1647, "Is not government in church and Common weale (according to gods owne rules) that new heaven and earth promised, in the fullnes accomplished when the Jewes come in; and the first fruites begun in this poore New Engl[and?]"[68] Yet, by the mid-1640s, the program of godly rule was beginning to falter. Church membership and the category of saint were at the heart of its difficulties. Both were under siege in the late 1630s, English critics insisting that the standards for membership within the Congregational Way were excluding too many good Christians, and some in New England itself arguing exactly the opposite. The Antinomian Controversy that erupted unexpectedly in Massachusetts in 1636 over the relationship between sanctification and free grace turned in part on differing opinions about the criteria for deciding who was a visible saint. Once again, Cotton was at the center of this agitation. In sermons of the mid-1630s, he was complaining that the colonists were too inclined to credit "secret Prayer, Family Exercises, Conscience of Sabbaths . . . [and] Frequenting of Sermons," all of which he and his ally Anne Hutchinson stigmatized as "duties" and mere "reformation," in contrast with the transformations worked by the Holy Spirit; as Cotton remarked pointedly in his Salem sermon of 1636, "Reformation is no assurance that God hath made an everlasting covenant with us." In that sermon he linked these complaints to the process of admitting church members. Others did so more explicitly, for a synod that met in September 1637 to resolve the controversy cited three "errours" growing out of Cotton's critique of duties and the emphasis he was giving the "Seale of the [Holy] Spirit." Error No. 24 took dead aim at the latter and its implications for deciding who qualified for church membership, rejecting as mistaken the argument that "He that hath the seale of the Spirit may certainly judge of any person, whether he be elected or no." Another error concerned the opinion that "Such as see any grace of God in themselves, before they have the assurance of Gods love sealed to them are not to be received members of Churches," and a third, the assertion—consistent with Cotton's critique of duties—maintained, "The Church in admitting members is not to looke to holinesse of life, or Testimony of the same."[69]

To a minister befriended by Cotton and Hutchinson, the confusion about who was rightly a saint and who was not warranted returning to the book of Revelation. In the fast-day sermon John Wheelwright preached in Boston in January 1637, he evoked the apocalyptic struggle between the true followers of Christ, the "elect," and those who wanted to put "a false Christ . . . in true Christs roome." For him the "warfare" between the true and the false revolved around the acute difference between free grace and righteous behavior, or "sanctification." This was not some distant warfare but, as Wheelwight repeatedly emphasized, a struggle happening right before him as he preached. Adhering to the inner logic of apocalypticism, he numbered the true saints in New England as a small minority surrounded by "hypocrites" whose outward appearance as saints masked their antagonism to Christ. Again in keeping with that logic, Wheelwright imagined the true saints as suffering, martyrlike, until their day of triumph came. Then they would have "power over the Nations, and they shall breake them in peeces as shivered with a rod of iron; and what rod of iron is this, but the word of the Lord." Hutchinson told a variant of this story in her testimony before the General Court in November 1637. Evoking Daniel's miraculous rescue from the lion's den (Daniel 6), she prophesied that persecutors in high places would be laid low and she herself saved as Daniel was.[70]

Here was godly rule run amok, saints set against saints in scenes of argument and insult, with "Antinomians" turning the rhetoric of anti-popery against the ministers they disliked.[71] Here was the fundamental premise of godly rule, the difference between the saints and the worldly, turned into an assault on the very saints who held power! If we must strain to interpret the winners of this conflict as proto-democratic, it is even more of a strain to imagine Wheelwright and Hutchinson trusting the votes and voices of a heterogeneous multitude. Well before the failure of the Barebones Parliament, the colonists thus faced the problems Cromwell found intractable, divisions among the saints themselves, the intransigence of the few who claimed the authority of the Holy Spirit, and the uncertain legitimacy of a civil government that owed its authority to church members.

Should godly rule be modified to protect church and state against these dynamics? What safeguards could be introduced to prevent contentious saints from overthrowing their ministers, as nearly happened in the Boston congregation in 1636? To these questions, events and trends of the 1640s added another: Would some version of toleration be introduced, and the program of state-enforced righteousness be curtailed? No one in 1630s New England could have foreseen the shift in opinion that prompted some English Puritans and especially some Congregationalists to come out in favor of a fuller liberty of conscience. Wholly unexpected, indeed astonishing, this turn of events was brought home to the colonists when, as Winthrop put it in his journal, some of "the most godly and orthodoxe" in England wrote in 1645 to protest the anti-Baptist laws enacted by the Massachusetts General Court in November 1644, and again a year later, when "some of Boston, who came lately from England," objected on the grounds of "Liberty" to the calling of the synod charged with preparing *A Platforme of Church Discipline*. Simultaneously, the Massachusetts authorities learned that an order had emerged from the Long Parliament allowing "Libertye of Conscience" in Bermuda and the West Indies.[72] Similar currents were apparent in Plymouth Colony, where magisterial Protestantism had never really taken hold. To Edward Winslow's amazement, in late 1645 a petition was presented to the Plymouth General Court urging it to "allow and maintaine full and free tollerance of religion to all men that would preserve the Civill peace, and submit unto Government." Unusually, the "all" encompassed "Turke, Jew Papist Arian Socinian Nicholaytan Familist or any other," or so Winslow alleged. Together with a handful of colony officers, he prevented the court from accepting the petition, and the Plymouth government did its best, not always successfully, to curtail dissent and, especially, outbursts of anti-clericalism, for another two decades. So did New Haven and Connecticut.[73]

From other quarters came a different challenge to godly rule, the complaint that gathered churches and a franchise restricted to men who were church members affronted the basic liberties of the English. So the petitioners associated with Dr. Robert Child alleged in 1646. Dipping into the grab bag of rhetoric available to everyone, Child and his co-petitioners assailed the workings of godly rule as "arbitrary" and tyrannical. Tone deaf to the category of interest as it was understood by Winthrop, Cotton, and Davenport, the group called on the English government to replace godly rule with the equivalent of a state church encompassing all of the colonists.[74] In England, some had another complaint. Socially conservative gentry in Parliament, always leery of godly rule because of its capacity to disrupt their privileges, resisted a set of rules drafted by the Westminster Assembly giving Presbyterian-style congregations the authority to excommunicate or exclude people deemed unfit. For these gentry, as for more daring reformers in England such as the poet John Milton, any system that empowered the clergy to supervise moral behavior was akin to tyranny, or, as Milton complained rhetorically in a poem of 1647 directed at English and Scottish Presbyterians, "New Presbyter is but Old Priest, writ large."[75]

How New England congregations and ministers responded to questions about membership and the meaning of visible saints is suggested in the case study of Cambridge that follows in Chapter Five. How ministers tried to reinforce their authority is described elsewhere,[76] though whether they had much success in doing so is questionable. Meanwhile, aspects of the program of righteousness, already compromised by the reluctance of civil courts to impose "the full penalties prescribed" by statute law, would gradually fade away, as would the more fervent hopes in both England and New England for a new Sion. Much of the program persisted in the colonies, however, in parts if not as a whole—the principles of congregational participation in church governance and church membership for adults as voluntary, and a curbing of the civil state's control of religion, something Puritans in England had pursued since the middle of the sixteenth century, without success.[77]

With toleration or liberty of conscience, we come to the parting of the ways between the colonists and the Levellers, who wanted the civil state to withdraw from the business of policing true religion. The Levellers never advocated any of the provisions of godly rule except, in their own fashion, the empowering of ordinary people and the weakening of unjust hierarchies. For the Levellers, the reform of civil society and social injustice was their alpha and omega; for the colonists, the reform of the church came first, with a civil society remade in the name of righteousness a close second. When the "magisterial" aspects of godly rule came under attack in the mid-1640s, at the very moment that on-the-ground sectarianism was exploding, the Long Parliament and the government of Massachusetts responded by reasserting state regulation of religion and tightening up the machinery of enforcement. Because they were critical of these attempts, the Levellers seem modern or proto-liberal, the colonists conservative and authoritarian.

But as the evidence amassed in this and the preceding chapter indicates, the colonists never re-created the alliance of church and state that, in sixteenth- and seventeenth-century England, relied on state-ordered executions, imprisonments, and mutilations in a vain attempt to create or sustain uniformity. Inheriting two versions of true religion—one centered on the handful of saints who fled into the wilderness in order to escape persecution, the other on the image of a new Israel uniting church and civil society against idolatry—the colonists favored the first of these when they devised the Congregational Way, although they incorporated elements of the second. Authority and order mattered, but so did empowering ordinary people in church governance and curtailing the capacity of the civil state to intervene in religious affairs. In this context, an outcry in 1638 against imposing civil penalties on anyone excommunicated from a congregation was immensely important. Thereafter, no single congregation could resort to the civil courts to enforce acts of discipline—which is what John Milton feared would happen if Presbyterians ran the Church of England. Meanwhile, any orthodoxy of practice within the Congregational Way was tempered by the discretion allowed each congregation in how it managed the business of admitting and disciplining members. Local religion thus re-emerged—always, however, in tension with attempts (often for the benefit of an English audience) at demonstrating uniformity.[78]

Saints empowered: such a proposition alarmed many in the seventeenth century, as it would if someone were to propose it today. But in early New England or, more narrowly, in Massachusetts and New Haven, what kinds of power did the "saints" crave or expect would become theirs? The evidence is telling: few men, if any, sought church membership in Massachusetts or New Haven in order to gain access to political or social power. Nor was so much at stake that the civil government supervised who became a church member. With latitude to admit whom they pleased, congregations singled out moral behavior and testimonies of "grace" as the criteria that enabled some to enter and others not. That, within a decade or so, married women were joining earlier than their husbands underscores the distance between membership and social power.

Any simple comparison of Levellers and colonists falters for another reason: the failure to acknowledge the mediating effects of social practice. The Levellers were never able to practice their ideas. The colonists were, and as happened throughout early-modern Europe, a rhetoric of uniformity and obedience mutated into several kinds of compromises that tempered state-imposed rules.[79] The absence of executions for adultery is a striking example. Not in any strict sense a compromise, the possibility of dispatching dissidents to Rhode Island or watching them go there independently spared the Massachusetts magistrates from taking harsher steps. As social policy, godly rule in civil society survived because of the realism of a John Davenport about rights to land apart from church membership, a point he made in *A Discourse* and implemented in New Haven. What made the entire system work was the many possibilities for participation it contained and, more tellingly, the capacity of churches and civil courts to practice reconciliation.

CHAPTER FOUR

AN EQUITABLE SOCIETY

Ethics, the Law, and Authority

THE HOPE that everyday life coincides with an ethics of love ("charity"), peace, and justice is as old as Christianity and as fresh as last Sunday's sermon in our twenty-first-century churches. So is the sentiment that the two are misaligned, the everyday world slipping further into disarray as people pursue false gods and revel in temporary satisfactions. It seemed this way in ancient Israel and, in the early sixteenth century, to Thomas More, who imagined a better way of living in *Utopia* (1516). In Shakespeare's England, "wonder" stories dramatized God's revenge on Sabbath-breakers, and in *The Pilgrim's Progress* (1678) John Bunyan described the temptations awaiting the Christian who ventured into the city of Vanity Fair. The allure of worldly things, but also the possibility of reawakening to divine instruction, became the theme of Anne Bradstreet's "Verses upon the Burning of our House," a poem she wrote in 1666 to record the sorrow she felt as a fire destroyed so much she cherished and her resolution to look toward "the home" God had promised the faithful. "Has not the wisest of men taught us this lesson," she wrote in one of her prose meditations, "that all is vanity and vexation of spirit[?]"[1]

That the ideal and the real would converge was another of the aspirations of the colonists, an aspiration shaped and strengthened by their hopes of carrying out a long-awaited "further reformation." Ministers and laypeople looked first to congregations as the place where love, mutuality, and righteousness would flourish, and second to civil society. Ever intent on translating values into action, the colonists devised specific practices for each of these communities. Alongside love, mutuality, and righteousness they placed another set of values summed up in the word "equity." Employed in a broad array of contexts, the concept of equity conveyed the colonists' hopes for justice and fairness in their social world.

Always, these hopes owed their buoyancy to the colonists' idealizing of the early church. Reading the apostolic letters and the Acts of the Apostles through the lens of their yearning to restore true religion, they resonated to Paul's advice to the Galatians to "do good unto all men, especially unto them who are of the household of faith" (Galatians 6:10) and the injunction in his second letter to the Corinthians that, amid a "great trial of affliction," Christians demonstrate "the abundance of their joy" in the "riches of their liberality." But among these counsels they may have preferred Paul's likening of the union between Christ and the church to "the most perfect and best proportioned body in the world," perfect because its parts were "united" and "mutually" participating "with each other." John Winthrop cited these and other passages in his "Charitie" discourse of 1630, moving from them to the moral injunction of Matthew 7:12, "whatsoever ye would that men should do to you," and the great commandment of "love among Christians" (Matthew 22:36–40).[2] Winthrop did not cite Paul's counsel to the Galatians to shun "adultery, fornication, uncleanness, . . . witchcraft, hatred, variance, emulations, wrath, strife, seditions, . . . envyings, murders," and "drunkenness" (Galatians 5:19–21), but the colonists transposed this instruction into their codes of law. Like so much else in the Bible, the communalism of the earliest Christians was powerfully relevant to a people freshly joined in covenant with God, the premise on which Winthrop constructed his "Charitie" discourse.[3]

Other sources reinforced and complemented the New Testament. Attending Church of England services in their homeland, the colonists had repeated Paul's adaptation of the Ten Commandments (Romans 13), a passage incorporated into the Book of Common Prayer. In that book they had also encountered injunctions to demonstrate "compassion" for the poor and abstain from the Eucharist if they felt "malice or envie" toward their neighbors. Catechisms reiterated the lesson of mutual obligation or reciprocity between inferiors and superiors, emphasizing as well the fifth commandment and the imperative to obey parents, kings, and other superiors. Injunctions against adultery (the seventh commandment) broadened out into a long list of offenses that no Christian should commit: rape, incest, sodomy, prostitution, the wearing of immodest apparel.[4] Few Sundays passed in parish churches without some reference to Scripture passages about fairness, generosity, and love of one's neighbors. Apart from Scripture and theological reflections extending far back into Catholicism, these themes owed much to Renaissance humanism and its emphasis on virtue. Humanism held out the hope of a widespread reformation of society if virtue were to prevail.[5]

In their English years, the colonists had also witnessed the workings of civil governments, parish churches, and ecclesiastical courts as they undertook to curtail social conflict and provide for the poor. Every king professed his devotion to the welfare of the people, and local governments intervened to make food available and dampen "oppression" at times of scarcity. Juries listened as magistrates charged them with responsibility for "the quiet of the good and correction of the bad, the stay of the rich and relief of the poor, the advancement of public profit and the restraint of injurious and private gain." This ethics passed intact to New England. When the New Haven government voted in 1640 "that justice be done between man and man, (because false weights and false measures are an abomination in the sight of the Lord,) that all measures for commerce, for buying and selling, should be made equal to the standard used at New Haven," it acted in keeping with a deep-seated assumption that fairness, not self-interest, should prevail in the world of commerce.[6]

One other context influenced the colonists' hopes for something better, the literature on colonization in the New World. The English promoters of such projects had been arguing since the beginning of the seventeenth century that the people who participated in these ventures would free themselves from the corruptions of the Old World. So the moderate Puritan minister and supporter of the

Massachusetts Bay Company John White suggested in *The Planters Plea* (1630). Enumerating both the problems and the benefits of colonization, White reasoned that founders of a new colony were much more likely to succeed if they practiced "justice and affection for the common good." In his reckoning, colonization also worked to curtail "coveteousness, fraud, and violence." Almost certainly, Winthrop had read *The Planters Plea,* which circulated in manuscript before being printed. Some of White's anxiety about the moral climate of England crept into the "Reasons to be Considered" Winthrop drafted in 1629, and some of White's counsel infused the ethics of community he pressed on the colonists he was charged with governing. Acknowledging in the "Reasons" that anyone going to New England would have to "endure . . . hardshippe," he recast this "objection" into the proposition that colonization was God's "meanes" to "bringe us to repent of our former Intemperance." For a parallel in Scripture, he reached back to the flight of the children of Israel into the wilderness to escape the "fleshpots of Egipt."[7]

Alongside the Congregational Way, godly rule, and a "due forme" of civil government, therefore, the goals of the colonists included a program of social ethics drawn from several sources. Thanks to their newfound freedom, they could realistically hope to close the gap between values and practice. No king stood in the way of Sabbatarianism, as Charles I had done. With the saints newly empowered in their congregations, the machinery of church discipline that seemed so feeble in the Church of England could finally become effective. Social peace also seemed within reach in the absence of their antagonists in England, the many people who scoffed at the godly and impeded their program. "Here the greater part are the better part, here . . . are none of the . . . sons of Belial knocking at our doors disturbing our sweet peace or threatening violence," a minister wrote his friends in England shortly after arriving in Massachusetts.[8] Within reach, too, was the possibility of reforming civil and criminal law to bring it into line with an ethics of fairness and equity.

High hopes, but all too soon, daunting challenges and disappointments of a kind that any reader of the Bible would have recognized. For a history of social practice, the question that matters is not whether "declension" set in but the workings of congregations, governments, and civil courts as instruments of a visionary ethics. If the saints began to falter and the ritual practices central to the possibilities for peace and mutuality weakened, could other means be found to sustain that ethics? Beginning with the practices adopted by congregations, and how the civil state intervened on behalf of peace and mutuality, this chapter turns to the concept of equity, reform of the law, and the complexities of "authority" as a principle of ethics.[9]

I

To BE ethical in the seventeenth century was to make yourself right with God and, as this was happening, to enter an unusual kind of time and space, a virtual "heaven," as Thomas Shepard told the people of Cambridge.[10] People experienced the difference. They knew what it was like to pass from ethics as aphorisms on a printed page or advice in a spoken sermon to ethics as embodied in everyday encounters. People revisited those encounters as we revisit certain novels and films that have affected us, returning to them to refresh their hopes for peace and the public good. To this end they created memorials in elegies and prose passages of situations in which someone labored for the good of the whole—William Brewster's tending the sick and dying the first winter at Plymouth, John Winthrop's working "with his owne hands" during the initial months he was in Massachusetts.[11]

These expectations were at their highest for the covenanted communities of the Congregational Way, spelled out in John Cotton's brief description (c. 1635) of the saints in fellowship. Like Winthrop before him, Cotton echoed Paul's counsel to the earliest Christian churches, calling on the saints to practice "brotherly love . . . and the fruits thereof, brotherly unity" and "brotherly equality." By unity he meant a congregation "perfectly joined together in one mind and one judgment . . . not provoking or envying one another . . . but forbearing and forgiving."[12] By equality he meant a version of the Golden Rule, Christians "preferring others before ourselves . . . and seeking one anothers welfare . . . and feeling their estates, as our owne," playing here on the double meaning of "estate" as worldly wealth and spiritual condition. Some thirty years later, Jonathan Mitchell, who succeeded Thomas Shepard in Cambridge, was unusually eloquent in evoking the same ethics of fellowship among the godly, asking his congregation to "consider how sweet is the Communion, Company and Converse of Gracious Saints here on earth; How do your hearts burn in Godly Conference (as Luk. 24.32)," and reminding them of the sensate "sweetness . . . you find therein; it may be you smell of their Company a good while after, your hearts are somewhat the more Savory for it." Together, Cotton and Mitchell implied that, within the social world of the colonists, church members were singularly privileged in being able to recoup apostolic practice. This was also Winthrop's assumption in the "Charitie" discourse, that "a difference" existed "between Christians and others" flowing from "the new birth" that true Christians experienced.[13]

The church as a fellowship of the saints was a church fashioned around a covenant. Every such covenant bound a congregation to ethical values and practices. In 1639, the founders of the congregation in Branford, Connecticut, agreed to "deny ourselves . . . all ungodliness and worldly lusts, and all corruptions and pollutions wherein in any sort we have walked," and, looking ahead, to "walk together . . . in all brotherly Love and holy Watchfulness to the mutual building up one another in Faythe and Love." Woburn's congregation affirmed a commitment to "mutual aid," adding a rejection of "the ordinate love and seeking after the things of the world." In Concord, the covenant opened with a backward glance at the "yoke and burdening of mens traditions" of the colonists' English years and the "precious liberty of his ordinances" they were enjoying in New England. Agreeing to subject themselves to Christ as king, the church members spoke with unusual realism about the possibility of "devour[ing] one of another" and giving way to "self-love." Hence the promise they made to "carefully avoid all oppression . . . and hard dealing, and [to] walk in peace, love, mercy, and equity, towards each other, doing to others as we would they should do to us." In 1647, the congregation in Windsor, Connecticut, renewed its commitment to "love, humility, wisdom, peacefulness, meekness, inoffensiveness, mercy, charity, spiritual helpfulness, watchfulness, chastity, justice, truth, self-denial," and mutual encouragement in the form of "counsel, admonition, comfort, oversight."[14] Covenants of this kind presumed the Old Testament theme of a people set apart from all others and the apocalyptic theme of the faithful few—that is, covenants were like a wall that God erected to protect His people from the dangers of the world. The very length of the Windsor covenant suggests something else, that world and church were not so easily kept apart. So first-century Christians had learned through sad experience. Were congregations in New England armed with a repertory of practices that would keep their walls intact?

Covenants were accompanied by specific social customs. As in the liturgy of the Church of England, so among the colonists, the ethics of love and mutuality shaped the meaning of the Lord's Supper. No one in New England needed a prayer book to learn the rule—possibly never written down, but widely familiar—that anyone wanting to participate in the sacrament should be at peace with his or her neighbors.[15] Discipline, the collective name for the procedures a congregation used to rebuke or exclude someone who had misbehaved, was another of these practices. Discipline resembled a courtroom trial, in which witnesses described a person's conduct and the congregation asked questions and finally voted on whether someone in their midst deserved admonition or excommunication. A kindred practice was the penitence expected of people who had been disciplined. Discipline as ritual was incomplete until someone voiced a "sorrow" for his misdeeds and sought forgiveness, which congregations gladly offered. For everyone, repentance and reconciliation were daunting obstacles to surmount.[16]

Unique to the saints, discipline as godly watch and regulation played a large role in the everyday life of the gathered churches in Boston, Roxbury, and elsewhere. A typical entry in the Boston church records noted that, having learned that "Robert Parker our brother" had engaged in "scandalous oppression of his wives children selling away their inheritance," the congregation voted to excommunicate him and, some months later, to receive him back into fellowship "upon profession of his repentance." John Eliot kept track of similar events in his Roxbury congregation. A servant who "had some weaknesses, but upon the churches admonition repented," a man expelled in the aftermath of the Antinomian Controversy for "proud and contemptuous cariage" who "returned and repented, and was reconciled to the church" after the "Lord awakened his heart"—these were deeply satisfying moments that demonstrated the power of the ritual process to preserve the congregation from behavior that "might corrupt" its purity.[17] In other cases, the outcome was a compromise that left some wondering if a person had truly repented; in still others, attempts at reconciliation failed. The Reading congregation readmitted a woman in the early 1650s in a spirit of "charity," though the evidence she presented fell "short of what they Judged needful." Compromise and ongoing conflict happened repeatedly in John Fiske's Wenham congregation and, from time to time, in Roxbury.[18]

As a counterweight to the possibility of conflict or factionalism as cases of discipline were decided, the Boston congregation set itself the goal of reaching unanimity. Doing so in early 1638, when the church debated what to do with Anne Hutchinson, was no easy matter. With members of her family present, including a son-in-law who openly declared himself dissatisfied with the recommendation that she be excommunicated, Shepard, on hand from nearby Cambridge to parse Hutchinson's theology, proposed to the hesitant that they could "show more love to her Soule" by making her "answer to theasse dayngerous and fearfull Errors." No longer Hutchinson's ally, Cotton added the warning that "naturall not religious Affection" was "evell" if it "hinder[ed] the Church in her proceeding." Eventually, the "whole Church" came around to accepting her punishment. Unlike many others, however, Hutchinson refused to play her part and give "Satisfaction" to the church, spurning the delegation that traveled all the way to Newport Island to seek her out for this purpose. A triumphal moment of congregational agreement from one perspective, Hutchinson's church trial also dramatized the tensions that accumulated around the process of church discipline and threatened its effectiveness.[19]

A congregation's repertory for sustaining peace, love, and mutuality extended beyond discipline and covenanting. Words mattered, as did fast days and ceremonies of covenant renewal when congregations relived the cycle of confession, repentance, and restoration at the core of Puritan spirituality. Confession was the most important means of cleansing a church—and, for that matter, the civil community—of animosity and repairing a fractured peace. It was common for church members to refer to one another as "sister" and "brother," a way of indicating fellowship (with overtones of equality) that Quakers would make more explicit by reverting to the personal pronouns "thee" and "thou" among themselves. Late in the century, William Morse, an elderly man in the Newbury church, drew on the expectations embedded in this language of sisterhood and brotherhood when he reminded some of his fellow members who had told tales of his wife's sharp tongue and witchlike behavior to a civil court that "being in church communion with us [they] should have spoken . . . like a Christian" about their grievances to the Morses directly. He was calling local saints to account for allowing the mutual trust presumed by the language of sister and brother to break down.[20]

Trust was tested in another aspect of congregational life, the attempts to care for people in need, whether sick or without sufficient resources of land and goods. No one proposed imitating the communism of some early Christian communities,[21] but congregations took seriously the task of sustaining the poor in their midst or, as was said in *A Platforme of Church Discipline,* of helping those "in necessitie." To this end, and with the early church as described in Acts 4:35 in mind, every congregation appointed two or three persons to the office of deacon to supervise such acts of mercy. Week after week, deacons collected free-will contributions to cover the salary of the minister and, several times a year, donations to pay for the bread and wine used for the Lord's Supper. Gifts were also needed for the church "stock," the fund on which the deacons relied to address situations of need.[22] Little evidence survives of how a church stock was actually used (for this, we must wait until Chapter Five), but gift-giving for the sake of helping others figured in wills that evoke other aspects of trust among the saints. Robert Keayne, the Boston merchant caught up in the dispute about a stray sow that fractured the Massachusetts General Court in the early 1640s, contributed a portion of his wealth to pay for improvements in the civic life of Boston and, in particular, to aid the town poor, noting in his lengthy, much-rewritten will that his practice as a Christian and church member had been to keep on hand a supply of "ready money" from which he could make loans "to any poor godly Christian or minister in need (besides what I give away)." Others in Boston and elsewhere were making similar if less sizable gifts, moved to do so by the principle of fellowship. A few examples must suffice. Some had little to give, like a man in Salem who left a goat for the use of the poor, specifying that, "the first years use," it was to benefit only "such as are godly," that is, church members. He also asked the town ministers to look after his young children. As a man in Windsor neared death in 1648, he asked that what was left after his debts were paid and his widow provided for be used for "the poore of the Church"; in this same year, another Windsor resident gave three pounds "to be distributed by the Deacons unto the poor," and a third man left fifty shillings to the "pore" of the "church." George Willys, an important merchant in Hartford, left "twenty Nobles to the poore of the Towne" and smaller amounts to the poor in three other communities, and in 1648 another Hartford resident gave the church sixty pounds, probably for the same purpose.[23]

Some wills document a less tangible but no less pregnant aspect of gift-giving, the personal support and, of great importance at certain moments in the life cycle, the trust on which people counted. Faced with the task of naming executors who would supervise the distribution of their lands, cattle, and household goods, people turned to their ministers, deacons, and elders to act as guardians and executors. Sarah Dillingham of Ipswich willed Nathaniel Ward, the town minister, five pounds, but the more telling language in her will was the request that he would "see this my will fulfilled in the bonds of Christian love." Another resident of Ipswich, a widower with underage children—always a situation that put extra pressure on how property was distributed—asked "our reverend and faithfull Teacher mr John Norton" to become one of the "overseers" of his will. A minister in Wethersfield entrusted his wife with the role of executor of his estate, but also asked "the Church . . . to take an oversight of" his four children, "that they may be brought up in the true feare of God, and to see that this my will be faithfully performed." In 1643, Samuel Hagborne of Roxbury "intreate[d] the Reverend and beloved Elders and deacons of our church . . . to be overseers, and I give them power to order all my estate, and guide my wife in all her wayes." Many also made gifts to ministers, George Willys doing so to "my loving friends" the two ministers in Hartford and two in nearby towns "as a token of my love," and Keayne to the senior minister in Boston, his "loving brother" John Wilson, "as a token of my love and thankfulness for all his kindness showed to me," adding other legacies to Cotton's widow, the ruling elders in Boston, and local ministers. Occasional references in church records call attention to such bonds of sentiment, an entry in Roxbury's noting that, when one of its deacons died in 1640, "the Pore of the church much bewail[ed] his losse." Of another deacon, who died in 1657 after holding multiple offices "of trust" in the town, the church records noted that he was "a man of peace, and very faithful. . . . The Lord gave him so much acceptance in the hearts of the people."[24] And in what may be a unique (and oddly Catholic) gesture of trusting fellowship, James Astwood of Boston asked in 1653 to have "my body buried at the feet of Mr. Cotton, as neere to him as I may, though not to hinder my betteres."[25]

Congregations may have been the epicenter of an ethics of mutual care and peace, but aspects of this ethics were also crucial to the workings of civil society. Hence the resort to covenants and, more commonly, to arbitration. The townspeople of Dedham entered into a covenant as intense as any congregation's in its evocation of mutuality, peace, and the collective good, telling themselves they would "walke in a peaceable conversation [behavior] with all meekenes of spirit for the edification of each other . . . and the mutuall encouragment unto all Temporall comforts in all things: seeking the good of each other out of all which may be derived true Peace." The townspeople also agreed to resolve disputes by arbitration. Knowing of the conflicts that had roiled a great many towns, the householders in late-founded Lancaster vowed that, "for the better preserving of peace and love, and yet to keep the Rules of Justice and Equity among ourselves," they would never "goe to Lawe one with an other in Actions of Debt or Damages . . . but to end all such Controversies among ourselves by arbitration or otherwise." Other towns and colony governments adopted the same practice, Providence crafting a series of procedural rules for doing so in 1640, and Wethersfield attempting it after the General Court urged this means of resolving a dispute about land.[26]

In these ways and, almost certainly, in others that are not captured in church and town records, the colonists inserted themselves into the lineage of true Christianity. Yet theirs was a precarious gesture, for they knew from Scripture and the history of the Christian church that many before them had failed, and although they may not have needed further warnings, the ministers reminded them repeatedly that, human sinfulness being what it was, they, too, would betray the ethics of mutuality and fellowship. The townspeople of Lancaster resorted to a more humdrum explanation of conflict, "the boylings, and breaking forth of some persons difficult to please," in a petition asking the government to let a local person handle small-scale disputes and asking, too, for a surveyor and an additional grant of land.[27] Every town had people of this kind, just as most had their peacemakers.

What cannot be measured with any precision and certainly not rendered in hard-and-fast numbers is how fully the normative values of peace, love, and mutuality were maintained. But certain tendencies are clear, especially a growing reliance on the civil state to step in and resolve conflicts. Gifts for the poor figured in only a small fraction of wills in two Massachusetts counties, Suffolk and Middlesex, and gifts on behalf of institutions were even fewer.[28] Congregations sustained the practice of discipline more vigorously within the first ten years of being founded, and less so thereafter, a transition linked to impossibly high hopes for the Congregational Way. Back in England, it had been easy (and conventional) for Puritans to attribute the ineffectiveness of church discipline to structural aspects of the Church of England and to assume that this laxness would disappear once the authority to admonish and excommunicate was placed in the hands of each local congregation. A preference for compromise as more conducive to social peace, together with the complicated hierarchies and kinship networks within New World towns and congregations, worked to undermine this assumption. The pressure on ruling elders to relax their scrutiny is registered in the complaint that those in this office were losing their "Lion-like courage" to pursue cases of discipline. The deeper pressures arising out of the recognition that peace was better served by gestures of reconciliation—the recognition that lay behind the widespread practice in civil courts of abating fines and other sentences—is registered in Robert Keayne's train of thought about the censuring he underwent in 1639 for overcharging. Still angered by what he felt was the unfairness of his congregation, he suggested that the reproof of sinners should "not hinder . . . a loving converse" or "acceptable partaking of the Lord's Supper."[29]

The broader question posed by Keayne's advice was whether church discipline could sustain peaceful fellowship among the saints. Keayne was suggesting an alternative to the high expectations evoked in church covenants and enforced by the process of communal discipline. Another possibility was to add more teeth to the process of involving the civil state. In 1638, the General Court passed a law imposing a range of civil penalties, from fines to banishment, on any person excommunicated from a congregation who did not repent and reconcile with his or her church within a period of six months, justifying the law by citing the "sad experience, that diverse persons, who have bene justly cast out of some of the churches, do prophanely contemne the same sacred and dreadfull ordinance, by presenting themselves overbouldly in other assemblies, and speaking lightly of their censures, to the great offence and greefe of Gods people." The immediate provocation may have been the intransigence of Anne Hutchinson and other antinomians who had moved to Rhode Island. A year later, the court repealed the law after Cotton denounced it in his Revelation sermons; when the magistrates raised the possibility of re-enacting it in 1644, the deputies demurred.[30]

What had gone wrong seems obvious. Discipline presumed a bounded, stable community, when in fact the disaffected or the dissident were finding it easy to move elsewhere and elude the pressures, formal or informal, to participate in the ritual process.[31] Discipline also presumed a sharp difference between the churched and the unchurched. This, too, the civil state was blurring. It did so in Massachusetts in 1638 by ordering every rate-payer in the colony to contribute to the maintenance (salary) of the local minister, and every adult to attend Sunday services. Each was at odds with the spirit of the Congregational Way—not surprisingly, John Cotton pleaded publicly for the practice of voluntary maintenance, which his church managed to sustain—for they moved congregations closer to parish-style churches, with every resident of a town involved one way or another. Together with a burst of legislation in the mid-1640s about "blasphemy" and other crimes, these measures enlarged the government's policing of religion in the name of a peace and order less inflected by the New Testament.[32]

As the court was taking these steps, fractures in political and social life were affecting certain ritual practices. A case in point was the annual election sermon in Massachusetts, an occasion for a minister to reflect broadly on principles and policies. Unexpectedly, in May 1642 a group of freemen and deputies claimed the privilege of choosing the person to preach this sermon. The man they chose, Ezekiel Rogers of Rowley, promptly urged the freemen to practice rotation in office at a moment when Winthrop was expecting re-election (which in fact happened). Thereafter, with magistrates and deputies frequently at odds, the custom became for them to alternate in choosing the annual speaker. By the 1670s, when factionalism in the colony was far greater than in the 1640s, deputies and magistrates were using this privilege to abet a partisan agenda; also by this decade, the tense relationship between deputies and magistrates had spilled over into the drafting of fast-day proclamations and arguments over who or what was to blame for "declension."[33]

Meanwhile, other aspects of ethical practice were tilting toward the civil state. Congregations had not been able to play a significant role in poor relief, and, as was quickly demonstrated, towns and colonies had much greater resources for doing so. An easy and, in all likelihood, effective means of caring for the poor and disabled was to grant them extra land or abate their taxes; by the close of the 1640s, towns were also letting the poor (mostly widows) support themselves by selling wine, beer, and spirits.[34] As for social peace, the abolition of ecclesiastical courts meant that the business of policing abuses of alcohol and sex fell to civil courts. Almost at once, moreover, these courts had become the place where disputes involving property were settled, defamatory speech was punished, and conflicts within congregations or towns were adjudicated. Colony governments were also reaping the benefits of another peacekeeping device, the careful recording of land grants, boundaries, and wills. In the opening pages of the town records of Southampton, Long Island, founded in 1640 by people from Lynn, it was noted that "the delayinge to lay out the bounds of towns and all such land within the said bowndes hath bene generally the ruine of townes in this country." Hindsight was foresight for these twice-seasoned immigrants, who, faced with deciding how to tax people's property, opted "for the most peaceable way." The same pragmatism prompted colony governments in Connecticut and Massachusetts to insist that every town appoint a clerk to keep track of grants or sales of land, wills, and related matters, and a law in Rhode Island mandating that, to prevent "needless suits in law," all bargains be "drawn up, in writing . . . in as few words, and as plain forms, and as easy to be understood as may be."[35] Litigation persisted, but in straightforward measures such as these, and a legal system to which everyone had easy access, lay long-term remedies for some versions of conflict.[36]

Thus were practices modified, and the premise of zealous, covenanted saints practicing fellowship drained of some of its everyday significance. During the 1650s, as Oliver Cromwell came to realize that all his critics could not be subsumed within the category of the Antichrist, he, too, would experience a discrepancy between social practice and apocalyptic hopes for purity and peace. The source of Cromwell's disappointment lay in the deep divisions that marked English culture and society in the 1650s and, more tellingly, the divisions that emerged among the godly. The colonists remained much more united than the English, in part because some kinds of conflict were muted by the capacity of towns and congregations to go their own way. Moreover, in the four orthodox colonies, civil courts and local magistrates continued to believe in state-imposed righteousness, a program undermined in Cromwell's England by the Protector's sympathy for liberty of conscience. Nonetheless, no ritual process or zealous magistracy could surmount the fragility of a program that depended on the "saints" to make it work.

Writing Winthrop in December 1638 to complain of undue interference by the Massachusetts government in the affairs of Connecticut, Thomas Hooker quoted back to him the language of "brotherly love" Winthrop had used in the "Charitie" discourse, noting how the "malice and hatred" of Satan against the saints could easily poison the "unity of the spirit and eat asunder the synewes of society the bond of peace." Hooker accused Winthrop and others in Massachusetts of hostility to the new settlements in Connecticut. The false reports they were spreading were, Hooker implied, akin to the "malice" of Satan and utterly at odds with the ethics of love. "Do these things argue Brotherly love," Hooker asked rhetorically, or flow from "pity" for "the necessityes of . . . brethren"?[37] Hooker had reason to complain, for the interests of Connecticut and Massachusetts were genuinely at odds. The newer colony wanted complete independence of the other; each was claiming the settlement at Springfield, with its lucrative access to the fur trade; and each wanted to reap the benefits of the Pequot War, which, as Hooker also pointed out, the Massachusetts government was blaming on Connecticut. Fractures of this kind were everywhere by the early 1640s—towns competing against towns for extra grants of land or for a favorable decision on boundaries, Essex County merchants arrayed against their Boston counterparts, colonists from one part of England contesting control of a town with those from elsewhere, or, as in Wethersfield, three different groups of settlers, each with its own expectations, making life difficult for the other two. Sharing so much in common, colonies, towns, churches, and people were also dogged by disagreement.[38]

Even so, ethics and practice were aligned more effectively than under any regime in England. By most measures, the colonists were observing the moral code concerning sex out of marriage and respecting civil courts and ministry; the rate of births out of wedlock subsided from its English levels, and anti-clericalism of the kind that ran wild in 1640s and 1650s England did so as well, probably because the much-hated system of tithes was scrapped and congregations were entrusted with the authority to select their own ministers.[39] Despite bursts of litigation and intracommunal conflict, people continued to admire their leaders—Winthrop most notably, but also Bradford in Plymouth, and Theophilus Eaton, the long-serving governor of New Haven—and the peacemakers in their midst, men such as Captain Richard Lord of New London, commemorated in verse after he died in 1662 for his works of mercy, an anonymous versifier asking, "Who can deny to poore he was reliefe and in composing paroxysmes was cheife," and Matthew Grant of Windsor, town clerk for decades, who, in his self-estimation, "never set out land to any man until I knew he had a grant to it from the Townes men and Townes approbation. . . . I can saye with a clear conscience, I have been carefull to doe nothing upon one mans desire."[40]

But the most remarkable accomplishment may have been the reworking of civil and criminal law, a process driven in part by another core value of the colonists, the principle of equity. A description of that term and, subsequently, of how the law was reformed, follows.

II

CHARITY, RIGHTEOUSNESS, and mutuality made their way into the social ethics of the colonists via Scripture and the weight of centuries of preaching and writing on these virtues. Arguably, equity had the same importance and some of the same sources. Arising out of a tangle of Greek and Latin words, making a brief appearance in Scripture,[41] and re-emerging to play a much stronger role in sixteenth- and seventeenth-century Reformed casuistry, the concept of equity became ubiquitous among the colonists, though it is largely unnoticed in modern scholarship. A first step toward recovering its history is to recognize that the word had become detached from its legal context—that is, the capacity of judges to modify or overrule the law as written in order to further the end of justice. Something of this meaning persisted among the colonists, but a more compelling context was Protestant casuistry. The Elizabethan theologian William Perkins was among those who transposed equity into an aspect of Christian ethics. In *A Treatise of Christian Equity*, he characterized it as "so excellent as the careful practice thereof is the marrow and strength of a commonweal; and where it is there cannot but be peace and contentment." For him, a well-regulated conscience was where equity as a principle of moral action resided. Equity also pointed beyond conscience to the fundamental nature of covenant. As expressed in Psalm 72, the covenant God made with His people was an instrument of justice. Indeed, the whole of the moral law was such an instrument, as binding on Christians as it had been on the people of Israel because of its perpetual "equity."[42]

Like so many other master words in the colonists' ethical vocabulary, "equity" had no single meaning. Kings used it to justify royal office and others to call such authority into question when a ruler was perceived as violating the moral law.[43] To grasp its overlays of meaning among the colonists, we must seek out some of the contexts in which it was used in New England. Property was one such context or situation. As the managers of the Massachusetts Bay Company were pondering the process of colonization, they sensed the importance of reassuring the remnant of an earlier attempt at founding a colony, the "Old Planters" on Cape Ann, that "wee seek not to make them slaves." To this end, the Company decided to guarantee their ownership of any land they had already begun to farm, and to make them further grants of land if these were "agreeable to equitie and good Conscience." A decade later, in 1640, Ezekiel Rogers, the testy minister of Rowley, was pressuring the Massachusetts General Court to grant the town an additional allotment. Angered by the court's reluctance to do so but realizing he had stepped out of line, Rogers apologized for his behavior and suggested a compromise, that he "propound the case to the elders for advice only about the equity of it." When the minister in Wethersfield, Henry Smith, offended some of the townspeople by fencing in a disputed plot of land, the Connecticut government dispatched two magistrates to the town "to settle the same as in equity and justice they shall see fitt, that peace and truth may be continued." In the context of the rivalry between Massachusetts and Connecticut for control of Springfield, Edward Hopkins of Connecticut argued against a tax that the Massachusetts government had levied, questioning "whither such an imposition be lawfull and regular, bottomed upon a foundation of equity and righteousness."[44]

Collectively, these statements presume that decisions about property and taxes must correspond to "fundamental" rights (as was said in 1657 of a case involving a tax someone had disputed) and a moral standard of the highest kind—that is, a moral standard recognized and regulated by "conscience." Hence the phrasing of the freeman's oath in Massachusetts, "as in equity I am bound" (i.e., as in conscience). Making this connection was to put equity on the same plane as justice and righteousness, words frequently joined with it in ethical discourse. The market in property, the making of rates, and the apportioning of land—all were subject to this value and its great guardian, conscience. Some of the consequences are suggested by a decision by a Dedham town meeting in 1656. Wrestling anew with what "permanent rule" to use in distributing land, the townspeople realized that proportionality, the one rule on which there was general agreement, "bore hardly on several poor persons" and, following the logic of "equity," allocated these men additional rights to land. As shown in Chapter Two, equity also guided decision-making about taxes. In keeping with the Levellers, for whom equity was a significant term, the colonists thus linked the word with fairness and equality.[45]

The meaning of "equal" remains something of a puzzle, though for most of the colonists it may have been closer to "impartial" than to "equal" in the sense of "alike" or "the same." For sure, we are not in 1789 France and the sloganeering around "*égalité*" (itself hopelessly ambiguous, then and ever since). On the other hand, neither the Levellers nor the colonists had anything in common with seventeenth-century champions of patriarchy and royalism such as Robert Filmer. When Thomas Hooker used "equity" in his December 1638 letter to Winthrop, where it appears three times, he was calling for an equality of power in the relationship between Connecticut and Massachusetts consistent with "that equity which is to be looked at in all combinations of free states." The two reiterations of the word that promptly follow have the same flavor: a "rule of equity" or the "bounds of equity" impinged on all acts of statecraft; those that did not coincide with this principle would neither "end differences" nor bring about social peace. When John Lilburne and other Levellers used the word, they resorted to strings of synonyms or associations, as when Lilburne conflated "Law, Justice, Equity and Conscience."[46]

A few other allusions to equity as a constraint on executive or state power are worth noting. The word appears in the very first of the 1641 Body of Liberties, which declares that life and property are protected from central state power "unlesse it be by virtue or equitie of some expresse law." Responding to Winthrop and his fellow magistrates in 1631, William Bradford of Plymouth offered to negotiate with the larger colony provided that the process was governed by "the rules of equitie." In John Davenport's election sermon of 1669, he argued that rulers must be "just" and (quoting Psalm 72) "judge with equity," the context implying that they must be impartial. In a letter of 1650, the Connecticut government defended a rate it was imposing on the grounds of its "equity," and in 1639, the same government asked that the procedures for laying out a new town be "most agreeable to equity and reason." In Nathaniel Ward's *The Simple Cobler of Aggawam,* a book he wrote after returning to London in the mid-1640s, he justified taking arms against the king on the grounds that "Equity is as due to People, as eminency to

Princes."[47] Elevated in these contexts to a standard by which to judge the legitimacy of state power, equity could take on populist overtones, as (surprisingly) it did with Ward.

Attached to specific practices but also a principle affecting all of governance, a magnet for other highly significant words but also used by itself, equity may best be understood as expressing strong hopes for even-handedness in a world where "unrighteousness and iniquity" were visibly present in the workings of English politics, civil society, ecclesiastical governance, and the law, each of which was aligned with structures of privilege and power.[48] In the program of the Levellers, "heightened [appeals to] equity and heightened radicalism work[ed] in tandem."[49] The same can be said of equity as a social and moral principle in New England. As a value that impinged on practice, equity acquired some of its force because it was divorced from assumptions about hierarchy or difference that lurked behind the principles of mutuality and peace; peace could be imposed from above, as could mutuality, and in schemes of godly rule, both depended on the saints. Free of such associations, equity was potentially areligious if not secular—tied to conscience in some versions of Protestant casuistry, but in most allusions to it in New England, entirely independent of godly rule and its category of saint. Expecting fairness and reason to prevail instead of stubborn custom or entrenched privilege did not turn the colonists into revolutionaries. But this attitude set them on a different course from many of their contemporaries. They wanted an equitable system of justice, and that is what they got.

III

WITHOUT ANY of the fanfare or controversy that surrounded the making of the Congregational Way, the colonists created a legal system remarkably different from its English counterpart. Publicly the organizers of the Massachusetts Bay Company said nothing about these changes as immigration was getting under way, and, with one exception, no one in the 1630s spelled out the reasons for doing so. Aside from the recasting of capital laws, none of the changes the colonists would make was distinctively Puritan. Instead, they owed this program to a long-standing tradition of complaints about the law that also prompted the Long Parliament and its successors of the 1650s to attempt—but never accomplish—a major reworking of the English legal system. Yet again, the colonists owed their success to the social consequences of immigration, which reduced or eliminated the interest groups that blocked reform in England.

The General Court took the first steps in this direction in response to agitation about magisterial authority, appointing a two-person committee in 1635 (Winthrop and Richard Bellingham) to review "all orders already made" and advise the government on what should be "repealed, corrected, inlarged, or explained." Fourteen months later, with Henry Vane now installed as governor, the court appointed three ministers and five laymen to a committee to "make a draught of lawes agreeable to the word of God, which may be the Fundamentalls of this commonwealth." Out of this process came a document that, for the first time, revealed the far-reaching aspirations of the colonists, John Cotton's *Abstract of the Lawes of New-England,* an inaccurate title invented by the London bookseller who printed the text in 1641. By the close of the 1630s, others in the colony, especially Ward, a minister noted for his knowledge of the law, had drafted the Body of Liberties, which the General Court approved in 1641 for a provisional period of three years. In the mid-1640s, another group began the work of compiling the statutes in force and writing others that seemed necessary. Thus came into being *The Book of the General Lawes and Liberties Concerning the Inhabitants of the Massachusets,* printed locally in 1648. Other colonies rapidly followed suit, often by borrowing heavily from the *Lawes and Liberties.*[50]

Hailed by legal historians as the first printed code of laws in the Western world,[51] the *Lawes and Liberties* was the fruit of prolonged agitation in England about the excessive costs of doing legal business, the length of time it took to resolve civil disputes, the remoteness of most courts from where people actually lived, the obscurity of the law, the greediness of lawyers, the corruption of justice, the harsh treatment of thieves and debtors, and the privileges granted the aristocratic class. Conservative though he was in most respects, Thomas More shared some of this discontent, arguing in *Utopia* that theft should not be a capital crime. Another political conservative, Francis Bacon, was proposing in the early seventeenth century that the law should be simplified in order to curtail the uncertainties built into the English system. These, he warned, were the reason why so much litigation, with its "endless delays and evasions," had arisen. In the 1620s, many in the House of Commons complained about the courts most closely associated with the king's prerogative, like the Star Chamber, and few had good things to say of the Court of Chancery or the ecclesiastical courts administered through the Church of England. Early in its tenure, the Long Parliament abolished the Star Chamber and curtailed the ecclesiastical courts, the Rump Parliament called for all proceedings to be in English, and the Barebones Parliament of 1653 attempted to abolish the Court of Chancery. Little else changed during the decades of the English Revolution despite broadly felt hopes for reform.[52] Those hopes found their strongest advocates among the Levellers and Fifth Monarchists. For the Levellers, the principal fault of the English legal system was that it perpetuated the Norman Yoke, a system of privileges and procedures, like legal proceedings in the archaic language law French, imposed (so it was argued) on the English in the aftermath of the Conquest of 1066. For the Fifth Monarchists, the goal of reform was to align the law with Scripture, although they also wanted broader changes. To this end, William Aspinwall arranged for a new printing in 1655 of Cotton's *Abstract*.[53]

As Aspinwall realized, Cotton's *Abstract* and an associated text, "Moses Judicialls," which circulated only in manuscript, were forceful expressions of godly rule because they aligned capital law with biblical precedents, secularized other aspects of the law, and discarded certain privileges embedded in the English system. Cotton never alluded to the Norman Yoke, but he wanted to disengage inheritance from the feudal principle of primogeniture, which remained normative for some in England. In its place he proposed that eldest sons receive a double proportion of a parent's estate, with equal shares for their male siblings. Wanting something closer to economic justice in everyday affairs, Cotton included a provision (based on Deuteronomy 15) that debts be forgiven every seven years "because no brother should grow poore," and he warned against allowing towns to make extensive grants of land to "gentlemen," a statement possibly directed at the likes of Lord Saye and Sele.[54] Via the *Abstract*, which circulated in handwritten copies, and in reaction against the perceived corruptions of the English system, the Massachusetts General Court gradually filled out a system of courts and created a body of law that fulfilled long-deferred aspirations. No longer faced with the special interests—most significantly, the lawyers themselves—that thwarted meaningful change in England, the colonists jettisoned Chancery and ecclesiastical courts and never recreated any equivalent of the Star Chamber. All this happened without controversy.[55]

Four major strands of reform figured in the making of the Body of Liberties, the *Lawes and Liberties,* and the system of courts put in place by the middle of the 1640s.

The first of these concerned procedures and the geography of doing legal business. Out went law French, still in use in England in the 1630s, and in came a cluster of rights or privileges for plaintiffs and defendants with virtually no equivalent in English law: a rule that no one could be imprisoned "before the Law hath sentenced him," the possibility of bail in all but exceptional cases, the right of appeal to a higher court, and the privilege of plaintiffs and defendants to represent themselves.[56] Out went barristers, eliminated in order to prevent "unjust, frequent and endless sutes," together with any arguments or pleas based on legal technicalities.[57] In came the relocating of legal business to towns and counties, with local magistrates or committees of freemen empowered to "hear and determin . . . small causes," and "Quarter Courts" or county courts authorized to decide all cases save those "extending to life, member or banishment," which had to be decided by the General Court or the magistrates collectively. In came procedures for reimbursing witnesses and a resolution to avoid delay, with cases to be taken up "at the next Court" once someone had been charged. In came careful record-keeping of evidence and decisions, "so such as shall have just cause to have their causes reviewed" could put it to "good use."[58] In came what was expected to be a much more impartial method of selecting juries than was the norm in England, a requirement that jurymen be chosen by the "freemen" of the "towne where they dwell," a rule in keeping with the attempt to relocate the workings of justice more closely to towns. Out went the sale of offices and the possibility of judges' enriching themselves through fees. Out went torture.[59]

A second strand concerned crimes and penalties. In came a dramatic simplifying of felonies for which the death penalty was mandated—no reiteration, for example, of the English rule that theft of property valued at more than one shilling was a capital offense. As many as a third of all criminal cases for theft and other crimes in early-seventeenth-century England concluded with judges' imposing the death sentence, a percentage that would have been much higher had juries and magistrates not colluded to avoid some aspects of the law. In place of the death penalty for theft, the colonists introduced restitution, the "most frequent punishment assigned" for such crimes. The colonists added a procedural rule, based on Scripture, that no one could be convicted of a capital crime for any offense "without the testimonie of two or three witnesses."[60] The colonists also curtailed the possibility of imprisonment for debt and recast the legal consequences of suicide, mitigating the "revolting barbarities of the English law" that mandated the confiscation of a person's property.[61]

A third strand of reform concerned economic or social privileges and, less explicitly, the imbalance between men and women in their control of property. Monopolies were easily dispensed with; with rare exceptions (for example, the ironworks in Saugus, Massachusetts), there would be no New England equivalent of the Stuarts' practice of granting them to certain kinds of business as a means of gaining extra revenue. So were any and all "fines and licences" that the English government applied to "lands and heritages" as property was dispersed after someone's death.[62] Nor would there be any

Court of Wards, another much-abused aspect of the English system that successive kings used to enhance their revenue. A cluster of laws spelled out certain rights or privileges involving wills and the distribution of estates: empowering any male twenty-one and over to make a will even if "excommunicate or condemned"; allowing a widow or an underage child to convey property with the consent of a court;[63] and, of most significance, the introduction of partible inheritance in contrast to a system of inheritance built around primogeniture, which favored the male line and, in particular, the eldest son. Though not followed to the letter in every will, partibility, which the Levellers would advocate for England in the late 1640s, laid the ax to the root of primogeniture and encouraged the practice of providing something to every female child. Less resolutely than the Levellers but far more effectively, the colonists eliminated all but a few traces of the social privileges that pervaded the English system and remade justice into a matter of equal treatment before the law.[64]

A fourth strand concerned the law as an instrument of righteousness. As the ministers tirelessly explained, the righteousness God expected of a people in covenant was embodied in the "judicial laws of Moses." Long before the colonists set sail for New England, this reasoning had become a commonplace of English and Reformed reflections on the law, although never a formal principle in England itself. Now, with hopes running high that the colonists could restore divine law to its proper place, the Body of Liberties introduced twelve "Capitall Laws" drawn from Exodus, Leviticus, Deuteronomy, and Numbers, a shorter version of the list Cotton had specified in his *Abstract.* Two more were added in the mid-1640s, one for rape, the other for disobedience of parents by any son sixteen years or older.[65] Righteousness coincided with intriguing elements of flexibility and improvisation. One of these has already been noted in Chapter Two, the near-complete absence of executions in any of the colonies for the crimes deemed "capital," with witchcraft the notable exception. A second was the "evidence of substantial non-Scriptural influences" in the actual language of these statutes. Seemingly an example of Puritan literalism and moral ferocity, the capital laws were never of one piece or kind. The statute on adultery grew out of dissatisfaction with ecclesiastical courts in England, which from a Puritan point of view had been far too lax, and the statutes on disobeying parents, not added until 1646, coincided with the colonists' uneasiness about the collapse of authority in England. An alternative means of being righteous appears in the provisions for restitution in cases of theft, a biblical principle with a considerably different flavor. Meanwhile, the colonists were detaching some aspects of social and moral life from the reach of religious law, notably by making marriage entirely secular (a step also taken by the Barebones Parliament) and by allowing for divorce.[66]

Apart from righteousness, equity, and fairness, what values guided this reworking of the law? The foremost value was a commonplace of English social thought—to many observers of Stuart rule in the 1620s and 1630s, an endangered commonplace—that every person in a commonwealth possessed immutable "liberties Immunities and priveledges" that must be protected. No less important to the colonists was a second value, a version of the equality that figured in other aspects of their social ethics: justice itself must be rendered equally to all, or, as was stipulated in Liberty No. 2 in 1641, "every person . . . whether Inhabitant or other shall enjoy the same justice and law, that is generall for this Plantation." Here the context was the colonists' animus against hierarchies of privilege and their effects on the system of justice.[67] The Body of Liberties incorporated another commonplace of English social thought, the principle that no person could be deprived of life or property "unlesse it be by virtue or equitie of some expresse law of the Country," with two provisos attached, that such laws must be "established by a generall Court" (not, that is, by mere prerogative) and must be "sufficiently published"—that is, made known.[68] In general, the colonists wanted a legal system that was transparent and accessible. Hence the singularity of having a printed code with an alphabetical index to facilitate locating statutes, a book with no counterpart in seventeenth-century England. A printed code, a cluster of rules protecting the procedural rights of defendants and allowing appeals should anyone believe that "injustice" had been "done him" in any court—these and other provisions, including partible inheritance, brought to a conclusion a movement for reform that, on the other side of the Atlantic, was stymied throughout the seventeenth century.[69]

The tears that flowed when people reconciled with their congregations, the expressions of love that prompted legacies to the poor or a man asking to be buried next to John Cotton—alongside these moments of high emotion, law reform and the guiding principle of equity can seem bloodless. To propose that a rule or normative value "does" something is always questionable and is especially so with equity, given its ubiquity. Based on that very fact, however, it seems plausible that equity was something people could presume as the way governments, churches, and civil courts would function. In this regard it played the role that two English historians attribute to the "rule of law" in seventeenth-century England, calling it a "shibboleth" that "bound all members of the polity."[70] Equity was not unique in this regard, for the colonists also trusted the "rule of law." But the more thoughtful of the colonists knew that "all members of the polity" were *not* united around a particular form of religious experience (the new birth), an apocalyptic reading of Scripture, a mentality of persecution in their English years, or the Congregational Way, and, knowing this, supported other principles and practices that encompassed everyone. Inclusive, not exclusive—the realism of such a strategy lay behind the Mayflower Compact, signed in late 1620 by a mixture of "pilgrims" and others, Davenport's hedging the privileges of the saints in his *Discourse,* and the decision in Connecticut and Plymouth to loosen the connections between voting and church membership. Hence, too, the significance of equity as a moral rule that anyone and everyone could use in calling others to account. Social peace in any early-modern society was precarious—and in New England, where so much was provisional and so many risks were being taken with authority, especially so. That the colonists enjoyed as much peace as they did suggests the importance and effectiveness of an inclusive ethics and its consequences for the law.

IV

"AUTHORITY" WAS another master word in the moral vocabulary of the colonists and, in courtrooms, congregations, and General Courts, a master word with real bite, for anyone who slurred the men who held office as magistrates and ministers was quickly called to account. It was good to believe in authority, good because, as Thomas Shepard pointed out in a treatise he wrote on obedience, God had made submission to His will the threshold to being a true Christian. The benefits of divine grace and providence would flow only to those who willingly obeyed the moral law out of sincere love for God. Mere rote or show was inadequate. Authority was a living thing, a vital presence in the world. So was obedience. "Such is the wildness, boldness, and carelessness of men's hearts," Shepard declared in this treatise, "that they do not only need laws, but watchmen over them, to see they be kept; and hence the Lord appointed some chief, some judges in every city, and also some in every village. . . . Now, this was the blessed wisdom of God to put all into sweet subordination one to another for himself."[71]

Authority was a concept that prompted a great deal of rhetorical excess, most of it devoted to describing what went wrong when people ignored this principle. The dangers were many, all of them held at bay only by resolute rulers. Writers resorted to sensationalism in evoking the horrors of lawlessness, using extreme language and assembling lengthy catalogues of words and actions to bring home those horrors. Thomas Weld's preface to *A Short Story of the Rise, reign, and ruine of the Antinomians, Familists and Libertines* (London, 1644) was a classic of this kind, a New England version of the genre known as heresiography that reached something of a climax in the English Presbyterian Thomas Edwards' *Gangraena: Or A Catalogue and Discovery of . . . Errours, Heresies, Blasphemies and pernicious Practices of the Sectaries* (London, 1646). Both men resorted to the trope of "monster," both lingered on the damage being done to community peace, and both were appalled by the outbursts of uneducated people who claimed the authority of the Holy Spirit. "Now, oh their boldness, pride, insolency, alienations from their old and dearest friends, the disturbances, divisions, contentions they raised among us," Weld wrote at the beginning of a catalogue that ran for several pages, part of it recapitulating the anti-clericalism of the antinomians: "Now the faithfull Ministers of Christ must have dung cast on their faces, and be no better then Legall Preachers, Baals Priests, Popish Factors, Scribes, Pharisees, and Opposers of Christ himselfe." Like so many others confounded in the 1640s by such behavior, Weld resorted to the influence of Satan. Who else was Anne Hutchinson but "an instrument of Satan so fitted and trained to his service for interrupting the passage [of his] Kingdome in this part of the world"—an argument reinforced by another catalogue of her actions and ideas.[72]

Satan (and his agent the Antichrist) versus Christ and the saints: from these extremes descended others, like "anarchy" versus government, and Winthrop's distinction between "civil" and "natural" liberty. Presbyterians angered by the Congregational Way pulled out the rhetorical stops, arguing that it would divide husbands from wives (because of how church membership was construed) and introduce "anarchy" into the churches in place of clerical office. Winthrop was excessive in responding to critics of "arbitrary" rule, and Cotton in painting the "tyranny" of Roman Catholicism. The specter of disobedient children informed the capital law inserted into the *Lawes and Liberties* of 1648, and a recurrent theme in these years was the horrors that would follow from allowing a true liberty of conscience.[73]

This frenzied language colored the workings of everyday politics and congregational governance, but it cannot be regarded as a perfect transcript of Puritan authoritarianism, for two reasons: the limited ways in which the rhetoric of authority at risk shaped social practice, and, of equal importance, the checks and balances built into the very notion of authority. The second of these points has been demonstrated repeatedly in this and previous chapters—the compromises that figure so prominently in the judicial system, and the remarkable safeguards against abusive power built into every code of law; the empowering of laymen in church governance, and, despite some tweaks and second thoughts, the preserving of that power throughout the 1640s; the persistence of private meetings in the wake of Anne Hutchinson's; the attempts to distribute land fairly; the openness to popular participation in political and religious affairs, especially the vigorous uses of petitioning; and the insistence on the rule of law that lay behind the movement to create a Body of Liberties. The social history of authority in early New England is at odds, therefore, with the rhetoric; most of the time, bark was not really bite.

Nor was authority so authoritarian in the fullness of theological and social speculation among the colonists. God was unmistakably sovereign and all-powerful, a figure to whom obedience was due. But the God of the colonists had willingly decided to curtail the reaches of His power by working through the secondary "means" of church, ministry, and magistrates. The same point was made using scholastic language, that, because humans were "reasonable" beings, God had to respect the faculties of reason (understanding) and will by using persuasion instead of force.[74] A self-limiting God was also a God who imposed limits on everyone who held office as magistrates (kings) and ministers. As Cotton insisted in the Revelation sermons and others said elsewhere, the authority of these officers was "ministerial" or delegated, the point being that, instead of receiving a blank check to do as they wished, their rule was strictly bounded by obligations and regulations spelled out in Scripture and reiterated within a history of interpretation as recent as the latest sermon. Properly understood, authority was always and everywhere a matter of obligations, some descending from above, others emerging within the sphere of social life. The naked affirmation of hierarchy in the opening sentence of Winthrop's "Charitie" discourse—some are born to rule, others to obey—was overtaken in the larger discourse by the theme of obligation rooted in a mutual covenant among the saints as well as between them and God. God's covenant was more testament than contract, more proclamation than the work of a committee. But in the covenanted towns and congregations of New England, the crucial feature of all covenants was a people's willing consent: covenant as instrument and expression of popular decision-making.

Thus did authority and liberty become intertwined. To treat them as opposites, either in the thinking or the practice of the colonists, is probably the most serious mistake we can make, for it fosters a "liberal" misreading of the men who struggled to sustain authority as if they were an oligarchy. Obligation and limits are the crucial middle terms that inflect these categories and, as the case history that follows will demonstrate anew, shaped practice on the ground.

CHAPTER FIVE

"Already in Heaven"?
Church and Community in Cambridge, Massachusetts

Something about the land bordering the Charles River upstream from Boston, a place named Newtown by the first people to settle there, was bothersome. Within a year of arriving in Newtown in 1633, Thomas Hooker and the "company" that had followed him from England were looking elsewhere, having decided that the "plowable plaines were too dry and sandy" and the supply of meadow insufficient.[1] By 1636, Hooker and his friends had departed for the Connecticut River Valley, where they founded the town of Hartford. Fortunately for them, several groups that arrived in 1635, most of them connected with the minister Thomas Shepard, agreed to buy the houses and fields that were being abandoned.[2] Soon, these newcomers were complaining about shortages of land to anyone who would listen. What gave urgency to their complaints was the possibility that Shepard would join Hooker, his father-in-law, in Connecticut. When the political leaders of the colony heard that such a move was in the offing, they offered Shepard and the church an eight-thousand-acre tract bordering the Shawsheen River, some twenty miles to the northwest. To lose a trusted confidant of John Winthrop, a pillar of orthodoxy during the Antinomian Controversy, and a minister already the subject of near-hagiographical praise would be too great a blow, especially since the court knew that he was sure to be followed by others in the town. A bargain was struck: the court would confirm the grant on the condition that "the church and present elders" remain in Cambridge.[3]

The townspeople of Cambridge had already begun to distribute common lands and regulate the town's other resource, its supply of timber. Here as elsewhere, handing out land, agreeing on the location of roads, and curbing the damage done by wandering animals dominated the business of town meetings and the work of local magistrates and selectmen. But by the late 1640s, the question of most interest to the people of Cambridge was how the Shawsheen grant would be shared. What made this process problematic and potentially disruptive was the nature of the grant that the General Court had assigned to Shepard and his congregation. It was no secret that some people in the town were not church members. Would they participate in the distribution of the Shawsheen grant, or would the church favor its own? Did godly rule in Cambridge benefit some and not others? What consequences would the distinction between saints and others, a distinction embedded in the granting of freemanship and celebrated in Shepard's many evocations of the special fellowship that prevailed within the church, have for local politics? Or were church and town not really separated or distinct? When Shepard spoke of the people within the church as "already in heaven," could he have reasoned that, church members or not, the townspeople as a whole shared the same values? To answer these questions, all of which must be explored if we are to achieve a critical understanding of the much-invoked concept of Puritan "communalism," the thesis of authoritarian or oligarchic control, and the workings of godly rule, we must turn to the broader history of congregation and town, gathering up the threads of ministry, ethics, economy, and politics as fully as the records permit.[4]

I

CAUGHT UP in the expectations of restoration and kingdom that animated so many of the colonists, Shepard had high hopes for the congregation he and a handful of others founded in Cambridge in February 1636. (All but a few members of Hooker's congregation had departed with him.) At the beginning of the ceremony that brought the church into being, the prospective ruling elder, probably Edmund Frost, prayed. "After this, Mr. Shepard prayed with deep confession of sin, &c., and exercised out of Eph[esians 5:27] that he might present it to himself a glorious church, not having spot, or wrinkle, or any such thing, but that it should be holy and without blemish," a verse that comes near the end of an exhortation to "walk in love . . . as becometh saints" (5:2–3). Accepting the counsel of the other ministers on hand that seven persons were needed to "make a church," Shepard and six or seven men "declare[d] what work of grace the Lord had wrought in them" and "gave a solemn assent" to the church covenant. The ceremony concluded with Shepard's ordination to office and a brief sermon in which he exhorted the "rest of his body [the congregation], about the nature of their covenant, and to stand firm in it."[5]

By the close of this remarkable day, it was apparent to everyone in the town that the church would be selective or gathered in its membership. Thereafter, no one could join unless she or he testified convincingly about the "work of grace" and accepted the obligations of covenant. For one new member, Henry Dunster, an experienced minister who became the first president of Harvard College in 1640, covenanting created an all-important boundary between the pure and the unclean, the true followers of Christ and those who could not bring themselves to obey his rule. In Dunster's words, it was a two-step process that began with a renunciation of the world and concluded with a commitment to submit and obey: "You that have been baptized and have made a covenant . . . to forsake [the] devil, away then with pride, world and lusts of flesh . . . give up yourselves to Christ so for obedience." Even more pointedly, Dunster insisted on "difference" as the founding principle of congregational churches: "There should be a difference between [the] precious and the vile," with the latter excluded from participating.[6]

Shepard agreed. That he chose a passage from Ephesians is indicative of how fervently he wanted the new congregation to be "a glorious church . . . holy and without blemish," as Paul had counseled those early Christians. Shepard's first act on the day the church was organized, the prayer he made "with deep confession of sin," was one element in a process of self-cleansing. As the "great assembly" of people on hand to watch and learn would have recognized, the ceremony underscored the rupture between a corrupt Church of England and the purity of the Congregational Way: reordination for Shepard, a selective membership, no liturgy taken from the Book of Common Prayer. Always a moderate nonconformist in his English ministry, Shepard had begun to change his mind in the aftermath of being "silenced" by William Laud, the major architect of Charles I's reshaping of English Protestantism. Now he was willing to denounce "the evil of the English ceremonies, cross, surplice, and kneeling" and, in a treatise defending the Congregational Way written in the 1640s, explained to its English critics that he and his fellow immigrants could no longer "study some distinctions to salve our Consciences in complying with so manifold corruptions in Gods Worship" or abide the unlawful "power of . . . tyrannicall Prelates." For him, New England in general and New World Cambridge in particular were sites of much-needed reformation.[7]

What gave this day in February 1636 its particular significance for him was its consequences for his wife, Margaret. Mortally ill, she was visited late that afternoon by the men who brought the congregation into being. They "ask[ed] her if she was desirous to be a member with us," and when she said she was, they "took her by the hand and received her as one with us, having had full trial and experiences of her faith and life before." For Margaret, this was no ordinary moment. The brief description that someone, probably Thomas, wrote of the event concludes with what those present took to be a sign of God's "presence" and a "seal of his accepting of us," the response of the dying Margaret to this simple rite of incorporation: "The Lord hereby filled her heart [with] such unspeakable joy and assurance of God's love, that she said to us she had enough now"—meaning, enough to satisfy her yearnings for union with Christ.[8]

One by one, other women and men in Cambridge became members. For them, too, this New World congregation had a special significance as a place free from the prejudices, conflicts, and corruption that had tainted their lives in England. A unique set of documents conserves sixty-seven of their "relations" in which many looked back on the experience of being a Puritan in England and recalled their passage from sin to grace—a halting, troubled passage, but a transition universally accepted as authentic by the congregation. Shepard's church was no respecter of persons: young servant women came forward alongside the learned Dunster. Those with firsthand knowledge of the "scoffs and scorns" directed at the godly in England may have been especially pleased with "the privileges of saints" they were gaining. Chief among these was, as someone said, the "sweetness" of fellowship, but others also mattered, like the "purity" of a religious service cleansed of human inventions, the "love" among those in covenant, and the membership accorded children who, thanks to a parent's situation, were brought "under covenant." All these possibilities and expectations lay behind one Cambridge man's declaration, "I loved Sabbaths and saints," and resonated in a newcomer's prayer, "Make me fit for church fellowship." Goodwife Champney summed up these expectations in a sentence: "I saw the Lord's people were the most happy in the world."9

Shepard shared these same hopes and expectations. A sermon series on the Parable of the Ten Virgins (Matthew 25:1–13) he began to preach in June 1636 is suffused with an idealization of the church as community or, as he remarked, the true "kingdom of heaven" on earth. In New England, he told the congregation, they had set up "pure, chaste, virgin churches, not polluted with the mixture of men's inventions, not defiled with the company of evil men." Wanting this purity sustained, he urged the church to keep careful watch on who was admitted; never should it open the "doors to all comers" now that it had the satisfaction of celebrating the Lord's Supper with the "saints alone." How different this was from their English experience, during which, in his words, godly people had grieved "when . . . profane persons" were admitted to the sacrament. With purity ensured, the saints would enjoy a fellowship akin to that of the saints in heaven. So he assured them in the *Parable* sermons, telling the congregation that they would know what it was like to "walk as men come down from heaven, and returning thither again; and that as it were already in heaven." A community this heavenlike was a community committed to the rules of mutuality, peace, and love (charity) Paul had prescribed and John Winthrop had reiterated in his "Charitie" discourse of 1630. All within the bonds of the covenant, Shepard told the congregation in the mid-1640s, should perform "the mutuall offices of love." By love he meant the imperative to "seek the good of the whole kinde . . . the welfare of the whole."[10]

In doing so, the congregation relied on practices akin to those that other congregations were adopting. The economic turbulence of the late 1630s and early 1640s gave new significance to one such practice, the assistance provided to those in need. Shepard was emphatic that the congregation do something. Remarking in the privacy of his journal that he was "much troubled about the poverty of the churches," he asked that every member "look over the congregation, and consider such a brother's or sister's estate; one is poor and low, another falling, another very much altered."[11] In December 1638, urged on in this manner, the congregation initiated a special voluntary offering for "the supply of the wants of the Church of Christ," stipulating that any funds collected for this purpose could also be used for "the needy people of Cambridge." Some gifts were contributed during church services, but the first major gift was made by a "dear friend" of Shepard's, the wealthy Roger Harlakenden, who, on his deathbed in 1638, provided legacies of forty pounds for Shepard and twenty more "to the pore brethren of our congregation"; he also canceled his claims to "that which is in the . . . hands" of the church elders. Herbert Pelham, another high-status resident, gave a cow to the church fund in 1640, the same year Thomas Bittlestone left five pounds to Shepard and, provisional on the death of his wife and only child, a third of his estate to the church. When Robert Skinner, unmarried and childless, died in 1641, he left the church half of the value of his "lands and hose" and willed the indenture of his servant to Elder Frost. Matthew Day, a printer who died in 1649, had no children to worry about and distributed his estate widely: gifts to Shepard and his wife, Elder Frost, Harvard College, his mother, and various friends. Shepard himself provided a legacy of five pounds "unto the Elders to be equally divided" in his will of 1649. Among the entries in a notebook listing disbursements from this fund are: "Given my brother Towne toward his expenses in a sicknesse," one pound; "given to our brother Hall toward the rearing of his house that was blown down," one pound; "given our sister Francis More (to suply them in there need)," five shillings; and "Payd our brother Briggam for something for clothinge for his sone," seven shillings sixpence.[12]

Once the economic crisis eased, church members who became disabled or slipped into poverty may have relied on the town for support, as happened elsewhere. But the congregation persisted in other practices associated with the ethics of mutuality and love. Among themselves, they used "brother" and "sister" as terms of address. In continuity with the culture of Puritanism in England, some withdrew into private meetings to discuss the Bible and revisit the sermons they were hearing, using for this purpose the notes people took as Shepard was preaching. From time to time, the members held "private fasts." At moments of illness or life crises, people prayed for one another, confident that doing so in the proper manner would benefit the sick and the troubled. Shepard may have received requests for special prayer, for a journal entry records him praying "for our brother Collins at sea," a gesture in keeping with the rule he established for himself that, as town minister, he was "to pour out the affections, thoughts, and desires of all the people to God in prayer." When a young woman experienced a "distemper" her family blamed on the malice of a neighbor, "many prayers [were] made for her," and an "elder" came to pray by her bedside. Some in the congregation supported Elizabeth Holman, the woman named as a witch, vouching for her piety even though she was not a member of the congregation. Two deacons and twenty-one lay members, twelve of them women, deposed to the Middlesex County Court that Holman "hath always been a diligent hearer of and attender to the word of God."[13] In situations such as this, as well as in the practical workings of charity, an ethics of mutuality and fairness extended beyond the boundaries of a covenanted congregation.

The men who held lay office in the congregation as deacons and elders were at the center of another aspect of congregational life, requests that they serve as executors of a will and guardians of young children. It may have been expected that one of the elders would help distribute the estate of his brother John Champney, who died in 1650, but either John's widow or he himself as he was dying had also asked John Bridge, a deacon (and former elder), to participate as well. After Simon Crosby died in 1645, leaving a widow and three sons, the "elders and deacons" of the church, together with Shepard, helped her work through the disposition of the estate. A deacon helped appraise the estate of John French, who also died in 1645, and Bridge reappeared in 1651 as one of two witnesses to a will. Henry Dunster, described by a man who died in late 1651 or early 1652 as "my trusty and loving friend," was coexecutor with his widow, and, after the death of George Cooke in Ireland in 1652, became the guardian of his daughter and, along with another Cooke, the person responsible for disposing of his property in New England; several years later, although alienated from the church because of the stand he took against infant baptism, Dunster left a legacy of twenty shillings "to the holy servant of the Lord Elder Frost." Participating in the distribution of an estate was a significant responsibility and, as Dunster would learn to his dismay when he was sued for mismanaging the property of someone else, never without risk of conflict. Yet those who did the task well were among the peacemakers of Cambridge, trusted to act fairly in situations where trust was sometimes betrayed.[14]

For many in the congregation, the most important benefit of membership was access to the sacrament of baptism. Near the end of his life, Shepard defended infant baptism at a moment when English Baptists were beginning to publicize their opposition to the practice. In the 1650s, a few in the congregation turned against infant baptism, including Henry Dunster. But most continued to regard the ritual action of including their children within the covenant as powerfully significant. Making their relations of the work of grace before the church, several people emphasized the connections between church membership and the welfare of their children. Mary (Angier) Sparhawk remembered feeling anxious when her husband decided to immigrate and how she reconciled herself to his decision by "thinking that [if] her children might get good it would be worth my journey." Here the implied context was the difference between the sacraments as administered in their primitive purity in New England and how they were performed in England. Mrs. Crackbone (we do not know her first name) remembered the sadness she felt when one of her children died and how she worried about the others, thinking they would go "to hell . . . because I had not prayed for them," a statement of self-blame followed in her relation by the sentence "And so came to New England." There she received the comforting message that she "was under [the] wings of Christ," as (theologically) were her children once she became a church member. The same feeling of responsibility for one's children, combined with a high opinion of the sacraments, was voiced by Ann Errington when she told the church that she knew of children who "would curse parents for not getting them to means" (i.e., the means of grace).[15]

Words were matched by behavior. That people credited baptism with a distinctive significance is apparent in the promptness with which they brought their newborn children to the church to be baptized. Two examples must suffice. Within the family of the printer and land speculator Samuel Green, the intervals between the birth and baptism of three of his children were two days, six days, and one day respectively. Shepard's successor in the Cambridge pulpit, Jonathan Mitchell, had not been able to baptize a newborn son before the baby died, though he baptized another of his children seven days after it was born. Distressed that he had failed his infant son, Mitchell wrote in his journal that "to be deprived of [the sacrament] is a great frown, and a sad intimation of the Lord's anger."

The feelings of Shepard and his wife, Margaret, were just as strong as those of Mitchell and the laypeople in the church. Shortly before husband and wife set sail for New England in 1635, Margaret had given birth to a son they named Thomas. Not until the congregation was organized in February 1636 was this Thomas baptized— in time, it seems, for Margaret to know before she died. During the the long delay, she had "made . . . many a prayer and shed many a tear in secret" for her unbaptized infant. Why she felt this way is indicated in a passage in Shepard's autobiography that may contain language from the ritual itself. Addressing his son several years after the event, Shepard reminded him that through "the ordinance of baptism . . . God is become thy God and is beforehand with thee that whenever thou shalt return to God, he will undoubtedly receive thee—and this is a most high and happy privilege, and therefore bless God for it." As he remarked elsewhere, children may have been "of wrath by nature" but, once baptized, became "sons of God by promise." The difference was not that sin had been swept away but that God had become the child's benefactor and—in the context of recurrent illnesses of the kind little Thomas was suffering—a source of protection. Baptism was a privilege that Shepard as parent and pastor wanted for his children.[16]

So he argued openly in his short treatise on baptism and in other writings. In the treatise he appealed directly to parents concerned about the spiritual well-being of their children, assuring them that through the sacrament "God gives parents some comfortable hope of their children's salvation, because they be within the pale of the visible church; for as out of the visible church (where the ordinary means of grace be) there is ordinarily no salvation," a situation he characterized as "very hard, and horrible to imagine." He reiterated this point in another text, this time underscoring the long-term consequences of having—or not having—a child baptized. To withhold a child from being baptized, he declared, was to "undermine all hopes of posterity for all time to come." The time frame of posterity was extensive, stretching for "generations without limitation in the Lyne of Beleevers," an argument warranted by the covenant God made with Abraham (Genesis 17:7).[17]

He knew his audience. Within the popular religiosity of the colonists, it was second nature to worry about the generations to come. Dying men and women crafted wills that provided something for all of their children or, if there were none, for sisters, brothers, nieces, nephews, cousins, and sometimes close friends. Baptism itself was a legacy, explicitly likened to legacies of land by another first-generation minister and, as Shepard was promising his parishioners, a gift that would keep on giving through succeeding generations.[18] Baptism thus joined church and family in ways that had long-term consequences. One of them was unexpected, the reluctance of some Cambridge children to come forward and make a "relation" once they became adults. That reluctance was acutely visible in the family of Elder Edmund Frost, the exemplary Christian to whom people made gift after gift in their wills, referring to him sometimes as a "holy servant of the Lord." But by 1668, none of his eight children had made a relation of the work of grace.[19]

Church and town were never synonymous. Was there something in Shepard's preaching or his understanding of the church that prevented people from affiliating? In his English years, he had taught a strenuous version of the "practical divinity" that spelled out the steps or stages leading to the "new birth" and its aftermath, the recurrent self-examination that marked the Christian's pilgrimage through this world. There, in the context of a parish system that lacked effective means of excluding the ungodly, he could set the bar as high as he liked without affecting who actually belonged to the church. Telling people that "very few are saved" out of all who professed to be Christians, a ratio he placed at one to a hundred, had little or no bearing on who brought their children to be baptized or turned up for the Eucharist.[20] But in New World Cambridge, his was the only show in town, his sermons, prayers, catechism, and pastoral counseling the principal doorway to church membership and the sequence of experiences that, within the framework of the practical divinity, constituted the work of grace.

Committed to that framework and the high standards it implied, Shepard took advantage of its built-in ambiguities to preach in several keys to his congregation.[21] One major theme emerged at the time of the Antinomian Controversy. Doctrinally a tiger in the contest between John Cotton and the rest of the Massachusetts clergy, Shepard participated in drafting a list of sixteen questions he and his colleagues gave to Cotton. At the center of these questions was the figure of the "weak" Christian who could not gain assurance of salvation. How should the clergy counsel such people and give them "comfort"? For Cotton, the right answer was to press on them the emptiness of "duties" and, as means of assurance, the "immediate witness of the Spirit." For Shepard, it was just as plausible—and, in the absence of any "clear" signal from the Holy Spirit, more effective—to rely on "sanctification" or the "saving Worke[s] of Christ" as manifested in someone's behavior.22

The *Parable* sermons he began to preach in 1636 defend the recourse to sanctification as helping "all those doubting, drooping, yet sincere hearts that much question the love of Christ to them." The voice of Shepard the caring pastor resonates in passages in which he urged townspeople and congregation not to fall into despair because Christ "hides his face, and departs sometimes from you," assuring them of the "tender-heartedness" of Christ even though he seemed absent. This was no easy out, for Shepard continued to excoriate the figure of the hypocrite and insist on rigorous self-examination. But his pastoral sympathies set Shepard's church-manship on a different course from what was implied by John Wheelwright's fast-day sermon of January 1637, with its apocalyptic scenario of the few against the many. Shepard was on the side of the many, be they persons of weak faith or strong. In the *Parable* sermons he argued that the story of the ten virgins referred to the visible church at the time of Christ's return to earth; if some in the church were ready for his return and others not (those without oil in their lamps), both groups would coexist until that moment came; "there is and will be a mixture of close hypocrites with the wise-hearted virgins in the purest churches." Shepard wanted those he deemed hypocrites to awaken to their situation, but nowhere did he commend a church of the few who were assured of their state of grace. Treasuring the separation of church and world, he also distanced himself from a central premise of godly rule, that the visible church must practice greater stringency as it approached the New Jerusalem.23

Like his father-in-law Hooker in Connecticut, someone well-known for the breadth of his churchmanship, Shepard tilted toward the judgment of charity even as he urged "the watchmen of the churches" to be wary of the hypocrites among them. When a woman began to make her relation to his congregation but faltered and fell silent soon after she began, Shepard intervened and told the congregation that "testimonies" in her favor "carried it." Of the sixty-seven people for whom relations survive, all but one became church members at once, and a man who was turned away entered several years later.[24] No list of members survives from Shepard's ministry, and any attempt at estimating how many joined the congregation is hampered by the rate at which people moved in and out of the town. Nonetheless, some families stayed put, and the history of their membership—parents, children, and, by the late 1660s, grandchildren—was recorded in a "catalogue" kept by Jonathan Mitchell. Starting from the sixty-seven relations that survive, adding in the number of adult men who became freemen (a status open only to church members), and counting the first-generation families listed in the Mitchell catalogue yields a membership that encompassed, at a minimum, 60 percent of households in the town, and possibly as many as 80 percent.

The people who remained outside the church should not be understood as hostile to its values. So the testimony on behalf of Elizabeth Holman reminds us. In the judgment of many of her neighbors, she was as good a Christian as they were, someone who attended services regularly and was manifestly pious. Other nuances emerged within Cambridge families, with wives generally joining the church (sometimes by reaffirming their baptismal covenant) earlier than their husbands. The gradual gendering of church membership made for tensions of the kind revealed in the speech of a man who ridiculed his wife for becoming a member, telling her that the congregation "saw nothing in her wherefore they received her in but that she made two or three fine kerchies." In this case as in others, church membership in Cambridge was not an all-or-nothing thing; affiliation happened at different times for different people, and in most families one parent was a member, be it "full" or in the lesser category of the baptized.[25]

Churchmanship and preaching were thus slightly askew, as they also were for many of Shepard's colleagues. Thanks to his churchmanship, the congregation gradually became more diverse in its spiritual and social temperatures. It is certain he sympathized with Richard Mather, the minister in Dorchester, when he proposed that congregations allow all who were baptized as children to include their own children in the sacrament. Rejected by the synod that drafted *A Platforme of Church Discipline* (1649), this step was approved some fourteen years later by a great majority of the ministers, including Shepard's son Thomas Jr.[26] Set apart though the Cambridge congregation was from the wider town, its commitment to infant baptism brought the two closer together. Family continuity was powerfully significant, so much so that no one writing a will and making legacies ever singled out children or kinfolk who were church members from those who lagged behind. Nor is there any evidence of the religiously engaged turning away from spouses who may not have been so caught up in affairs of the Spirit. With baptism on its way to becoming symbol and instrument of continuity within families, the social and the religious would slowly converge.[27]

Another bridge between the two was a program of moral order for which both church and civil state were responsible. Shepard was firm in his support of righteousness as an aspect of godly rule. In the absence of church records, when and how his congregation exercised church discipline cannot be recovered, though from other sources we learn that in 1639 it excommunicated Nathaniel Eaton, the first "schoolmaster" of Harvard. What is not a mystery, however, is Shepard's thinking about the connections between true religion, manners, and civil society. In the autobiography he wrote for his son, he included a telling anecdote from his English years, when, after leaving East Anglia, he became a house pastor to a wealthy family in Yorkshire. Realizing as soon as he arrived that he was living in a "profane house, not any sincerely good," he turned the powers of his tongue on the crowd that gathered to celebrate a wedding. No doubt expecting to dance, drink, and make merry, the people listening to him began to experience "great terrors for sin" and, as Shepard remarked guilelessly, to "look about them." The groom, a "most profane young gentleman," "fell to fasting and prayer and great reformation," as did others who were present, including Shepard's future wife, a servant in the household.[28]

Nothing this dramatic happened in New World Cambridge, which was certainly not a "vile wicked town" of the kind he encountered in Yorkshire. The deputies from Cambridge assented to the capital laws of 1641, and, a year later, the printing office in Harvard

Yard issued them as a broadside. Shepard believed in the alliance of church and godly magistrate that was official policy in Massachusetts. When he learned that some Congregationalists in England were calling for liberty of conscience, he wrote to Hugh Peter, a former colleague who had returned to England, to express his dismay that anyone would turn away from magisterial Protestantism.[29] How frequently local people flouted the Sabbath or overindulged in alcohol cannot be determined, for the Middlesex County Court records do not begin until 1649. Certainly, those records indicate that the people of Cambridge were as human as their neighbors. A man who punished a servant so severely that he died, lawsuits between high-status residents over stray animals and fences, conflict among siblings about the meaning of a will—behaviors of this kind that came before the County Court in the 1650s bear out Shepard's observation that "the wildness, boldness, and carelessness of men's hearts" demonstrate how much they "not only need laws, but watchmen over them."[30]

For someone as alert as Shepard was to the spiritual temperature of his congregation and the moral temperature of the wider community, there was always a difference between the high hopes he had for peace and what he saw around him. How could it have been otherwise? Inheriting a rhetoric of complaint that dominated English preaching from the late Middle Ages onward, he fretted about prosperity and the distractions of the world. Hearing of anti-clericalism in England and possibly responding to local discontent with ministerial authority, he wrote a treatise on the proper meaning of liberty—not the liberty of nineteenth-century liberalism but the liberty achieved by wholehearted submission to Christ, its fruit a "peace" experienced by everyone who accepted Christ in their hearts and "bound themselves" to be his in a covenant. As though he were holding up a mirror to the social world of the colonists, Shepard noted the contraries that were the stuff of everyday life in Cambridge: a reluctance to undergo the "church trial" required of candidates for membership, the indifference of church members to the process of discipline and its "admonitions for sin," the rowdiness of militia companies, the cry of "injustice" when town meeting disagreed on measures for "keeping pigs out of corn," and the poison of a "rigid, censorious, unloving spirit." These were the perverse underside of liberty, the very opposite of a scriptural injunction he cited, St. Paul's counsel to the Ephesians to exercise the "power of communication of good one to another, in way of edification" (Ephesians 4:16).[31]

Shepard's social ethics began with Paul and the promise of recovering the near-perfect love and fellowship of the early church. But where did the distribution of land fit into this set of values as the moment approached when the Shawsheen grant would be divided?

II

HUNDREDS OF people passed through Cambridge between 1636 and 1650. Some arrived as families, to stay and put down roots. Others, also arriving as families, left within a few years. As children grew up and married, some found partners outside the town and moved elsewhere, or left for economic reasons. Because of Harvard College, which acquired its first cohort of students in 1638, the town contained a group of teenage boys together with their slightly older tutors and a college president, the post Henry Dunster held between 1640 and 1654. All told, the town may have contained six hundred people in the mid-1640s.[32]

Some Cambridge families had been persons of status and means in England and remained so in their new community.[33] The "gentry" of the town included Roger Harlakenden, whose father, Richard, had been instrumental in securing Shepard a post as lecturer in the town of Earle's Colne, Essex. In that ministry his preaching "mightily" transformed the eldest of Richard's sons, Roger, who traveled on the same ship as Shepard in 1635. Another brother, who remained in England, invested in the town. Aged all of twenty-six, Roger was named lieutenant colonel of militia in Massachusetts, and in 1637 became an overseer of newly founded Harvard; he died in November 1638. Second to him in status was Herbert Pelham, whose maternal grandfather and great-uncle were, successively, Barons de la Warr, and whose uncle was a prominent merchant in London.

Named treasurer of Harvard in 1643, five years after arriving in the colony, and elected a magistrate of Massachusetts in 1645, the year he became a freeman, he married Harlakenden's widow, Elizabeth; in 1647, he returned to England, having been of little consequence in town affairs. George and Joseph Cooke, sons of a well-to-do "country gentleman," had been part of Shepard's circle of friends in England and came with him in 1635. The two brothers quickly became "active and energetic citizens," holding office as selectmen, deputy, town clerk, local officer of the law, and captain of the militia; both were also prominent as entrepreneurs and landowners. They, too, returned to England, George in 1645 and Joseph in 1658, George becoming a lieutenant colonel under Oliver Cromwell.

Others of middling or high social status included Edmund Angier, whose wife was the daughter of William Ames, the Puritan theologian and polemicist who in 1610 had moved to the Netherlands; intending to immigrate, Ames died before he could do so. Nicholas Danforth, an English friend of Shepard's, was a substantial yeoman who immediately entered the service of town and commonwealth before he died in 1638. His son Thomas would ascend the political and economic scale in town and colony, first serving as a constable and, in 1647, becoming a selectman, a post to which he would be reelected for twenty-seven years; in 1659, he became a magistrate in the colony government. Edward Oakes, of the same generation as Nicholas Danforth, would emerge as the most trusted official in the town, elected selectman for twenty-nine years and deputy for seventeen. Edward Collins, cited in Shepard's autobiography as among his special friends, became a church deacon, selectman, and deputy in his new home. Edward Goffe, who arrived with Shepard in 1635, was "surveyor general" of Massachusetts in the 1640s and selectman for sixteen years, and Edward Mitchelson, another of the newcomers in 1635, was appointed marshal general of the colony in 1637. Having such men was advantageous to the town and, as Shepard's warm words about them in his autobiography indicate, to his personal status. Sons of theirs went to Harvard in large numbers, several of them becoming ministers: two Collinses, an Oakes, an Angier, and two of Shepard's own sons. Of more importance, these men provided the capital to create bridges and mills and make loans to people in need.[34] None of them wavered at the time of the Anti-nomian Controversy, and none seems to have questioned Shepard's leadership of the congregation.

Most of the families in Cambridge were of middling social status. Some earned a living as artisans (carpenters, blacksmiths, and house wrights), a few were merchants with shares in boats that carried goods up and down the coast, and a few others, including a deacon of the church, ran a tavern or a wine shop. Harvard College employed a steward and several women, and a printer labored in the sole printing office in New England. But the dominant activity was farming, centered for virtually everyone on animal husbandry (pigs, sheep, milk cows, cattle, and oxen), with surpluses sold to markets outside of the town. As the economy strengthened in the mid-1640s, the people in Cambridge could begin to share in the prosperity that Edward Johnson celebrated in *The Wonder-Working Providence of Sions Saviour*.[35] That the situation was changing for the better is indicated by the inventory of Shepard's estate after his death in 1649. At the end of the 1630s, he was encumbered by debts, but in 1649, the inventory of household goods, silver, cattle, and land he owned was valued by his executors at some seven hundred pounds, together with another hundred pounds' worth of books. Yet a rising tide did not lift all boats. The men in a few Cambridge families worked as day laborers, owned very little land or cattle, and had more run-ins with the law than their better-off neighbors. Meanwhile, Edward Goffe was on his way to becoming the largest landholder in the town.[36]

The formation of a town government happened easily. In November 1636, the townspeople named seven "townsmen to order the towne Affayres," two others to serve as constables, and still others to serve as surveyor and hog reeve. Two years later, they agreed to reduce the number of townsmen to five. Frequent in the mid-1630s, town meetings were eventually fixed for November and March, though special meetings were always a possibility. To this body of townsmen fell the all-important business of arranging the distribution of land or instructing the selectmen how to do so; supervising the construction of roads and fences; ordering surveyors to lay out boundaries; conserving the town's scant resources of timber; encouraging someone to build a mill; and pestering householders to control their wayward pigs and cattle. In town meeting, the townspeople also wrestled with the workings of the market in land and houses. As was true elsewhere, the founding families wanted a say in who came to live there. On the eve of the departure of Hooker and his friends, the town established a list of "those men whoe have houses in the Towne at this present as onely are to be acconted as houses of the Towne," a measure implying a determination to bring order to the flow of people in and out of the community. In February 1636, the same month the new congregation was organized, the townspeople agreed to deny anyone the "preveledge[s]" of residency unless such newcomers had been given the "liberty" to build a house. Absentee ownership (exacerbated, perhaps, by the departure of so many people for Connecticut) was addressed by a rule that prospective renters of house and land had to be approved by "the townsmen," with an interesting exception: "unlesse it be to a memb[er] of the congregation." Clearly, some were more welcome than others, with the congregation front and center in determining who was legitimate. Realizing that these restrictions threatened the workings of the market, the townsmen added a proviso that, if no one turned up to rent or purchase, the owner "shall then be free to sell or lett" his property "unto anie oth[er] provided the townsmen think them fitt to be received in." An order of 1638 reiterated that renters and purchasers must be persons the townsmen "shall like," again with an exception for church members. When the town repeated most of these restrictions in 1644, no reference was made to the church.[37]

The great majority of Cambridge households received their land as freehold; a few rented from one of the major landowners, usually someone associated with the Massachusetts Bay Company. Because of its allocations, Cambridge had little or no control over some of the land within its boundaries. Out in what would eventually become East Cambridge, Atherton Haugh, another person of wealth, owned scores of acres and a house; he also had a house and other property in Boston, where he was occasionally elected to political office. Other residents had economic interests in nearby Watertown and, of course, Boston, where the merchant Hezekiah Usher moved after living for a few years in Cambridge; the town was never a self-contained economic entity. By the 1650s, some families had left the place of initial settlement, crossing the Charles to the south or heading north-northwest to the area known as Menotomy, where the edge of a glacial moraine enabled the Cookes to set up a gristmill. Here trees grew more abundantly than along the flood plain of the Charles. By the early 1650s, the southsiders were beginning to agitate for a church of their own, a privilege they finally gained in 1661.

One way of describing the interplay of economic, social, and political power in 1640s Cambridge is to assume that the sixteen men who recurrently served as selectmen, constables, commissioners for small causes (the equivalent of justices of the peace), and deputies to the General Court constituted a kind of oligarchy. If oligarchy implies having better access to privileges than does the rest of the community, then there is something to this interpretation, for the town leaders secured much larger grants of land than other householders did. Some of these grants were in keeping with the rule of proportionality that, like most of its neighbors, Cambridge used to distribute the land it owned. Others were a means of rewarding people for their "worke, and place," as was said of Dunster and Deacon Edward Collins in 1648, when they were voted special allotments.[38]

But if oligarchy implies a self-perpetuating group of leaders, as was the case in some English towns, or the abuse of office for personal benefit via fees and inequitable taxation, as also happened in England, the alignment of office-holding, elections, and privilege worked in different ways in Cambridge. In the two most important spaces where a much larger group of townspeople shared certain privileges, the congregation and town meeting, these local leaders seem less imposing. No evidence suggests that they or their families had easier access to church membership, and although townspeople elected and re-elected some of them to office, none of the core group of leaders was invulnerable. Most elections in the 1640s saw some turnover, and occasionally a clean sweep: in 1648, all of the sitting selectmen were turned out of office, and in 1652 something similar occurred.[39] Of more importance, the men who administered town affairs and represented Cambridge in the General Court were constrained by a local version of the culture of participation sketched in Chapter Two and the social ethics described in Chapter Four. Leaders had to respect the "public good," and, as Shepard was emphasizing in the early 1640s, they were accountable to town meeting in the specific sense of sharing their decisions with everyone. The "due and prudent publication, that all may know of town orders, with records of them," was his way of stating this rule of town governance.[40] The authority of the few was contingent or mediated, resting on trust and expectations of reciprocity as much as it did on social rank or wealth.

Town meeting was where the largest number of townspeople gathered to discuss, argue, and decide matters of policy. The town records do not clearly indicate whether those known as "admitted inhabitants" (this phrase does not appear in the records) could attend and vote, but the language of several entries, including one from 1651, an agreement "to call the inhabitants to gether . . . to consider of Shawshine," suggests that this happened some of the time. Each November the town meeting filled a substantial list of offices—deputies, selectmen, constables (in Cambridge, a high-status position), and surveyors of highways (ditto); some months later, others were appointed as hog reeves, fence viewers, and field drivers (who looked after the town herds as they moved out to pasture). Separately, the local militia company chose some of its officers. Annually, the freemen also elected three (or, by the 1640s, two) deputies and voted for magistrates, governor, and deputy governor. Somewhere around 55 percent of adult men were freemen in the mid-1640s. The town may not have supervised the process of voting very closely, for in 1652 George Bowers was charged by the county court for voting out of turn (he was not a freeman); in his defense, Bowers said he had done so "every yeere since he came into these parts."[41] The two ruling elders during the years of Shepard's ministry, Frost and Richard Champney, excused themselves from holding office as deputies or selectmen. So did two of the deacons, Nathaniel Sparhawk and Gregory Stone, and, until the mid-1650s, a third, Edward Collins. In the course of time, responsibilities large and small fell to half of the men in the town, a process abetted by the departures of leading citizens like the Cookes and the indifference of some residents, including persons of means, to the duties of office.

If we turn away from elections and, for the moment, how land was distributed, the people of Cambridge seem remarkably alike in alternately enforcing and ignoring the principles of community peace and mutuality. Rich, poor, or middling, every householder in Cambridge lost control at some point of his pigs and cattle, which promptly did their best to destroy other families' gardens and fields. Nor could people keep their fences in order. The amount of fencing to be built and maintained was enormous—in a single instance, a half mile's worth was assigned to one of the Cookes. Together with the incessant demand for firewood and lumber for constructing buildings, bridges, and occasional boats, fences strained the town supply of timber. Regulating pigs and cattle, limiting access to timber, and policing the system of fences were perennial topics on the agenda of town and selectmen's meetings, and the fallout from ineffective regulation kept local courts busy with suits between neighbors. The General Court having given up its attempts to resolve the problem of runaway pigs and, as a consequence, "muche Damage done by swine in this towne," a town meeting in early 1639 ordered that, "with a generall Consente of the greastest number of the Inhabitants the[n] present," every pig must be "suffitientelye yoaked and Ringed after the judgement" of the two hog reeves, with any violation subject to a fine of two shillings. The same town meeting addressed the looming shortage of timber by ordering that no more trees be felled in a nearby area "without a warrant under all the townsmens hands granted at a Generall meeting monthly," and nothing cut in a more distant area without "warrant from the major part of the Townesmen." Many more such orders followed in the 1640s.[42]

A well-known saying has it that all politics is local. So it was in the town in 1639, as evidenced by the complicated wording of the order about pigs. Every householder may have resented having pigs do their damage, but some may have rightly blamed those who owned a larger number of the animals. The resentment that accumulated around this situation was probably the source of a town order specifying that no one could "keep" more than two pigs "Abroad on the Common," an interpretation made more likely by an accompanying statement that the rule applied to both "riche" and "pore." The lobbying of the "pore"—who surely outnumbered the rich in the town meeting—is also apparent in how the system of fines was to function. Those who broke the law could use the excuse of an "unexpected providence" to have the fine mitigated; "otherwise" these were to be levied "without all excuses."

Clearly, the townspeople were not of one mind about who was to blame for runaway animals and the damage they caused. So the General Court had discovered when protests forced it to give up any attempt at regulation. Clearly, too, some of the Cambridge elite were flouting the rules, for in 1646 Edward Goffe was singled out for being "delinquent in the Breach of the hog order," having "severall times" pastured ten animals. By this time, the town had adopted a policy of letting pigs that were ringed run free. The bad effects of this policy had been felt more by the people "least" able to recoup what they lost when their crops were "in great part destroyed," a situation the townspeople tried to remedy by ordering that, until the corn was harvested, everyone keep his pigs "at home in a close yarde." That Goffe was called to account a few months later suggests that he had become a convenient target for the resentments of those "least" able to deal with the pig problem. Indeed, he was not re-elected a selectman in 1648.⁴³

The most striking pages in the town records are those listing the people fined for letting pigs and cattle wander. In the late fall of 1646, thirty-three men and one woman were censured in this manner. Fourteen of the men have the designation of "brother" and the one woman "sister," possibly a sign of their church membership. Had a spasm of discontent come over the town meeting? Cambridge was no respecter of persons: Shepard was not on the list, but Elder

Frost was, along with Angier and Pelham. Beyond the time frame of this chapter, a list of 1657 included forty-six men, a veritable who's-who of the town, all of them fined for cutting down trees in violation of town statutes. In 1666, Lieutenant Edward Winship, sometime selectman and, for the two preceding years, deputy to the General Court, acknowledged "selling wood out of the Towne," a no-no.[44]

That everyone was accountable to the town meeting, and that, when leading citizens flouted the basic rules of community well-being, they were punished call into question the argument for oligarchy. At the very least, the influence of the town's elite was constrained by the social ethics Shepard persistently impressed upon everyone. The foundational premise of this ethics was charity or love, the obligation to care for the welfare of the whole. The men who may have been especially responsive to this ethics were the lay officers of the congregation. It is a social fact of some importance that the elders and deacons refrained from holding town or colony office. Doing so underscored the status they owed to a different hierarchy. Meanwhile, a few men of high status and considerable wealth, such as Edmund Angier and Herbert Pelham, were consistently passed over by the town meeting.

As in the colony as a whole, so in Cambridge, social peace and effective governance depended on the willingness of the selectmen to acknowledge the superior authority of the town meeting and, in particular, the authority of the town to name others to manage the crucial business of distributing land. Thus, in 1645, five men joined the selectmen in carrying out the apportioning of "lotts on the other side of Menotime," most of it as "small farmes," and (to look ahead once again) in 1660, seven were appointed to arrange the location of an exceptionally lengthy fence. It helped, too, that selectmen and townspeople agreed with the colony-imposed mandate to keep careful records of land sales and transfers. When it was "found that there is many blotts, upon many figures . . . that it can hardly be discerned, what is every mans Right and intrest" in the records, five men, one of them Dunster, another a ruling elder, were assigned the task of preparing a fresh copy of the original. And it helped that people could request abatements on their rates, resort to arbitration, or seek other kinds of assistance.[45] Governance in Cambridge was constructed around obligation, accountability, transparency, and trust. And, although the reasons may be difficult to discern, governance was certainly affected by the willingness of the deacons and elders to remain outside any contests for office.

Shawsheen brought home the complexities of this politics. From the mid-1630s onward, the town had necessarily grasped that nettle of local politics, the distribution of town lands. As elsewhere, the townspeople in Cambridge made such distributions in keeping with three principles or traditions. The first of these was proportionality or "proportion," that resources should be distributed in relation to wealth, status, and service. The second was equity or "equal," words the townspeople explicitly associated with the levying of taxes, meaning that all were treated alike in how these were levied. Like their neighbors in nearby towns, the townspeople also attempted a third principle, the responsibility of giving every adult man (and a few widows) a share of town lands, however modest this might be, and of helping those in need.[46]

That the distribution of the Shawsheen grant took four years to complete, and that, in its immediate aftermath, many of the townspeople were aggrieved, indicates the difficulty of navigating among these rules. One hurdle was removed at the start when the congregation agreed to transmit control of Shawsheen to the town. It did so subject to certain conditions. Although the records do not say this directly, one was probably a town-meeting decision in April 1648 to lay out "a farme . . . of a thousand acres, to be for a publick stocke and improved for the Good of the Church." Simultaneously, the town gave substantial allocations of land to Henry Dunster, "Brother Edward Oakes," Deacon Edward Collins, and two other important laymen, these latter on the condition of continuing to reside in the town. In keeping with the principle of equity, town and church also gave land to persons who had not yet been fully admitted to the privilege of participating in divisions, and took other steps to help the people who "resign[ed] there small farmes for the good of the town" or who lacked acreage of the right kinds and quality.[47]

A town meeting in May 1651 to discuss "Shawshine" was followed by another in November 1652, when 115 shares were assigned, but only after Mitchell, newly installed as town minister (Shepard died in 1649), was awarded a "Ministeriall Grant" of five hundred acres, no doubt to make up for the fact that he had no rights to future distributions, and Edward Oakes and his brother Thomas received three hundred and one hundred acres, respectively. Thereafter, the process unfolded according to the rule of proportionality. Twenty-two of the 115 allocations, five of them to widows, were in the range of one to forty-nine acres; another fifty-five ranged from fifty to ninety-nine; ten people received from a hundred to 149 acres each; twelve a grant of 150 to 249, and ten (not counting Dunster, who had received four hundred acres in 1649) received more than 250. The largest single allocation was to Edward Collins, possibly the same allocation voted him in 1648 and now confirmed. The other elders and deacons all got at least two hundred acres apiece. Taken as a whole, half of the householders received reasonably sizable grants, and another thirty-five did much better.[48]

The thirty-five persons who received a hundred acres or more were church members, and most had served the town in one office or another. The men with grants of ten to forty acres look very different. One was listed in Mitchell's church register as a full member, and one or two were sons of members, but the rest may not have belonged to the church at the moment Shawsheen was divided up, although several had wives who were or would become full members. None of these men had held any kind of political office before 1652; several had yet to marry. The town had previously allocated small plots of land to two of them, almost surely as a form of welfare. William Clements, son of a father by the same name who was also at the bottom of the list, had a childless, troubled marriage and in 1656 sued unsuccessfully for divorce.[49]

Something troubled the townspeople about this decision-making, for at the next town meeting, in November, the three sitting constables and two of the sitting selectmen were not re-elected. This was not an uprising of the poor against the rich but an attempt to reaffirm certain values and to align them with the workings of town government. At the request of the town meeting, a special five-man committee that included a deacon and a ruling elder and three men with intermittent service as selectmen (but not in 1652) brought in a set of "instructions to be given the Townsmen." Ratified at another "General meeting" in December, the first of these instructions called for all "worke or buissines" enacted by the townsmen to "conduce to a publique good." The second, a request that the selectmen "give publique notice to the inhabitants to meet together" and that orders made "by a publique vote of the Towne" be "execute[d] . . . without respect of any mans person," drew on the moral tradition of equity or fairness and the principle of transparency. Equal in the sense of impartial was underscored in an instruction calling for an "equall rate" to meet town expenses. Five more instructions followed, one of them requiring a yearly report on disbursements from the town's "publique stocke," to be rendered "before the yearly election of the Townsmen," a means of putting teeth into accountability. It was also mandated that all such disbursements should be "kept . . . in a booke fairely written." The final instruction had to do with the taking of land for highways, the townspeople requesting that "no man . . . be wronged . . . more than his due proportion," a phrasing that converted proportionality into something much closer to fairness.[50]

The disposing of Shawsheen was conventional in one respect, the resort to proportionality. Hierarchies arranged around office (civil and ecclesiastical), wealth, service, age, family, and length of time in the town came into play. Just as striking, however, was the willingness of the church to relinquish most of its claims to the grant. Congregations may not have been so willing to cede their status or privileges in every community, yet it is worth recalling John Davenport's insistence that every householder in New Haven, church member or no, have the same rights or privileges when it came to land. The measures taken at the Cambridge town meeting in 1652 to revitalize certain rules of governance were in keeping with the spirit of Davenport's counsel and Shepard's preaching about outreach. The mutuality among the "saints" was immensely significant, but so was a broader mutuality sustained by specific social values and practices.[51]

In the event, only a few of the people who received land at Shawsheen moved there, for a group from nearby towns bought out most of their shares and established the town of Billerica. In its next major distribution of land, this time on the south side of the Charles, the town meeting put on record a set of rules that, once again, combined aspects of proportionality with "just right" (or equity) and the possibility of making "free gift . . . unto other inhabitants . . . that have no interest."[52]

III

WAS SHEPARD'S Cambridge an example of Puritan communalism, with social and economic power conserved in the hands of minister, church members, and their allies, all of them bent on muting disagreement and implementing a program of moral discipline? Or was it divided, some in the town relying on the moral authority of the congregation, others asserting their economic and social rank, and still others employing the possibilities for popular participation to complain and, at moments such as in 1652, to contest the authority of the local hierarchy?

None of the above, we may be tempted to exclaim, for each of these possibilities seems too stark or incomplete. The least adequate interpretation is a "theocratic," top-down, religion-centered reading of social and political history. To understand why warrants returning to Shepard and the policies he pursued. The theocratic interpretation is useful in one important respect, for it recognizes that he wanted unity and peace and, as the means to these ends, called on everyone in the town to commit themselves to obeying divine law. It is also true that Shepard upheld the root principle of the Congregational Way, a gathered church from which the unworthy were excluded. But he was neither a Wheelwright calling for the "few" to withdraw from a corrupt multitude nor an aggressive enforcer of uniformity as, in his own experience, Archbishop Laud had been. To the contrary, Shepard insisted that the promise of divine grace and forgiveness of sin was available to everyone through the "means" of his ministry, and he welcomed into the congregation the many people of "weak faith" who never quite transformed their repentance and dutifulness into full assurance of salvation. He asked for more, but reluctantly accepted less, a reluctance voiced in an aside in *The Clear Sun-shine of the Gospel Breaking Forth upon the Indians in New-England* (London, 1648), where, after noting the "several gracious impressions of God" he observed among the Indians touched by the missionary John Eliot's preaching, he remarked that "it might make many Christians ashamed, who may easily see how far they are exceeded by these naked men."[53]

Perhaps it is a paradox that, in his everyday churchmanship, he refused to regard the church on earth as comprised of a spiritual elite. The high significance he gave to incorporating newborn children into the bonds of the covenant bespoke a generosity that overrode abstract principles of doctrine, especially the doctrine of election. He wanted to persuade every adult in the town to apply for church membership and every parent in the church to have his or her children baptized. His success in doing so is measured in the large number of people who became church members; his failure in the people who spurned his pleas or, as he complained from time to time, relaxed the temper of their piety and became less compelling as Christians than the Indians he cited. But he never told the lukewarm to leave the church or enlisted the machinery of church discipline against them.

Nor did Shepard seek authority in civil affairs. Except as a recipient of two grants of land, his name does not appear in the town meeting records, and he had little to do with measures as important as land distribution or the implementing of legal reforms that gave local people easy access to magistrates and juries well known to them. Although John Winthrop consulted Shepard from time to time, as magistrates, deputies, and town officers must also have done, he complied with the rule that ministers should never hold political office. He believed in ministry as a divinely ordained office and lamented the traces of anti-ministerial sentiment he detected in the 1640s. Yet he defended a crucial aspect of the Congregational Way—the empowering of the laity. Describing congregational governance, he resorted to the language of "mixed" government: the foundation was "democratical and popular" in giving lay church members a large place in decision-making and "aristocratic" in entrusting the clergy with a cluster of privileges, with both of these tiers subordinate to Christ as king. This was language aimed at placating conservative critics of the Congregational Way, not a transcript of how church government actually worked, which was much more likely to be consensual and collective.[54]

In their social life together, he and the townspeople relied on practices such as record keeping to preserve the peace. Certain compromises also helped. Even though one plank in the program of righteousness called for strong controls on the sale and consumption of alcohol, how better to promote "the weal publick" than by giving a Cambridge woman a license to brew beer, a step defended by no less than Henry Dunster when he asked the local court to overlook "the wholesome orders and prudential laws of the country" and permit a fellow church member, "Sister Bradish," to do her brewing. Insisting that, contrary to rumor, Bradish had never catered to "students unseasonably spending their time and parents' estate," Dunster argued that a license would help her business of baking bread and benefit "all that send unto her" for beer, because she charged less than her competitors. Thus did local circumstances stretch the meaning of "public weal" or complicate the meaning of freeman, as when townspeople looked the other way whenever George Bowers voted.[55] Few classifications were hard and fast, not even church membership, as the sympathy for Elizabeth Holman indicated. Coalitions formed and reformed, and, when disagreements threatened social peace, the most trusted and effective remedy was a fresh election or calling on the lay leadership of the church, men who otherwise played little part in town politics.

Shepard sanctioned these compromises and fashioned other bridges between church and town, leaders and people. He implored the church members to take seriously the plight of everyone in need, and encouraged the town leaders to practice transparency and accountability, a principle that looms large in the list of rules adopted by the town meeting in 1652. Winthrop was reluctant to kowtow to English grandees, and a version of his resentment flavors Shepard's recollections of his English years. Liberated from the

unjust authority of bishops in the Church of England and spared
the role of household chaplain to people who were his social superiors, he surely welcomed the disappearance of aristocratic or gentry
ownership of church livings and, in New World Cambridge, the
shortening of the social scale that accompanied the process of colonization. If it was irritating that townspeople were obsessed with
rampaging pigs, unbuilt fences, and the parceling out of land, this
was not too high a price to pay for the liberties associated with a
purified church and reformed community.

In the end, he pressed one value on the townspeople: deferring
self-interest in order to enhance the general good. The worm in the
apple of social peace was the all too visible ways in which the general
good was violated by men of high rank and low. Ever alert to ethical lapses in town and congregation, Shepard sympathized with
Hooker's response to the economic crisis of 1640. "The churches
of the commonwealth," Hooker declared in a letter that year,
". . . must make a privy search what have been the courses and sin-
ful carriages which have brought in and increased this epidemical
evil; pride and idleness, excess in apparel, building, diet, unsuitable
to our beginnings or abilities; what toleration and connivance at
extortion and oppression; the tradesman willing the workman may
take what he will for his work, that he may ask what he will for his
commodities." In Shepard's sermons of the 1640s he voiced a similarly troubled reading of community among the colonists. But to
regard his discontent as indicating the decay of ethical commit-
ments—of self-interest triumphing over religion, a scenario that
informs most modern descriptions of "declension"—is to ignore the
capacity of congregation and town to practice such contraries without allowing one to overtake the other, a capacity exactly parallel to
Shepard's churchmanship.[56]

Taking these readings into account, the "heaven" that Cambridge seemed to resemble becomes a place where ever-present greed
and self-interest were mediated and sometimes held in check by
ethical values and social practices. As well, it was a place where the
figure of the saint became blurred and several versions of status, participation, and community met and coexisted: saints and strangers,

"full" church members and those who entered via baptism, the core group that came with Shepard but also those who arrived without this affiliation, outliers and those with house lots in the historic center, the better-off and the people who needed economic assistance, freemen and nonfreemen, women and men, town and gown, officers of the church and officers of the town, all of them wanting fairness and equity, though not always able to live up to these rules. Would that the workings of capitalism and the diminished form of democracy in twenty-first-century America gave us as much.

CONCLUSION

Aт а тense moment in New England politics, the arrival of four commissioners dispatched by the government of Charles II to terminate the colonists' de facto independence from England, ninety-one men in the town of Hadley, Massachusetts, petitioned the General Court in 1665 about the rights or privileges they wanted to preserve. The first of these was "the right from God and man to chuse our own governors, make and live under our own laws." Drawing on a commonplace of continental humanism, the distinction between slavery and freedom, they justified this right by evoking the "liberties and privileges" that made them "freemen and not slaves." To this assertion they added another: "Our privileges herein as Christians in regard of the kingdom, name, glory of our God is far more precious than our lives." For the many in New England who agreed with the men of Hadley, these statements pointed back to the key decisions of the 1630s about religion and civil government—first and foremost, the decision to install popular participation, consent, and "Fundamental" law at the heart of civil governance, and, second, the decision to create a purified church, the Congregational Way.[1]

Both were in jeopardy in the 1660s, disliked by some colonists and vigorously challenged by the four commissioners, one of whom had been calling for major changes in church and civil governance since 1646, when he joined with Dr. Robert Child in a "remonstrance and petition." Samuel Maverick viewed the Massachusetts government as arbitrary and oppressive, specifying a franchise limited to church members in colony elections, and suggesting that laypeople were intimidated by the ministers and would welcome other opportunities for being religious. In the late 1670s, another English official who investigated the situation in Massachusetts, Edward Randolph, was certain that Anglicanism would attract large numbers of disaffected colonists and that any opposition to royal policies was the doing of, as he put it, a "faction" unrepresentative of the people as a whole.[2]

Yet again, two versions of New England history collide, the opinion that people in the colonies were "freemen and not slaves" and its obverse, the assumption that arbitrary, top-down governance prevailed. Were we to rely on numbers to settle this difference of opinion, the men of Hadley would come out ahead, for the great majority of the colonists accepted the first of these interpretations and acted accordingly. When Anglican churches were founded after 1680 and toleration was gradually extended to Baptists and Quakers, only a tiny fraction of people quit the Congregational Way for any of these alternatives.[3] Active supporters of direct royal rule and an appointed council, the scheme Randolph favored, were few— a small circle of such people in Charlestown, an irascible Gershom Bulkeley in Connecticut, some of the merchants in Boston. Apparently, the men of Hadley got the story right.

But in the nineteenth and again in the twentieth century, the Mavericks and the Randolphs gained a fresh hearing, not in person but for what they represented, outsiders who claimed to unveil the workings of a closed society. Any nineteenth-century liberal who assumed that Calvinism was a benighted form of religion, with a terrifyingly authoritarian God and an overbearing ethics of righteousness, would have favored this interpretation. So would anyone anxious then or now about the risks to civil society of empowering the religiously committed. Hence the ease with which some historians resorted to words such as "despotism," "oligarchy," and "rigid orthodoxy" to describe the political and religious culture of early New England.[4]

Would that all of us could resist the appeal of this language when we seek to understand the workings of public life among the colonists. Opinions about good religion and sound theology will continue to vary, and the search for people in the past who resemble us is unending. But anyone of a liberal persuasion who claims to find fellow liberals in the seventeenth century is going to be anachronistic, for none of the likely candidates fit the bill, not even Roger Williams. (As I write this, there comes to mind a script I once reviewed for a projected TV drama about Anne Hutchinson that included a scene in which she conversed, presumably in Algonquian, with Squaw Sachem of Menotomy about herbal remedies: Hutchinson as feminist and earth mother who bonded with Native Americans.)

Nor is it easy to find authoritarians and authoritarianism (as we understand these words) among the colonists. Consider, to begin with, the ambition to restore the kind of church government that, according to the colonists, the apostles had sanctioned and the earliest Christian communities had practiced. The Congregational Way struck many contemporaries in England as a risky experiment in "democratical" governance, as indeed it was in contrast to the Church of England and Presbyterianism. Consider the manner in which civil governments were fashioned, with local representatives taking their place alongside magistrates and governors, all of them elected annually, and with many arguing that those in office received their authority by delegation from the people. Consider the possibilities for participation and, in particular, the practice of petitioning. Consider the transformation of the law, the workings of the courts, and the limited but real support for liberty of conscience. Consider especially the animus against "tyranny" and "arbitrary" power that pervaded virtually every sermon and political statement. Faced with deciding whom to trust with freemanship, two of the colonies severed their connections with wealth or property and opted for church membership. But it is impossible to translate this fact into an inflexible authoritarianism that enclosed the rest of the colonists in a severe disciplinary regime, if only because civil courts acted otherwise and because a healthy share of adult men became freemen in Massachusetts and New Haven. Instead of agreeing on any sort of authoritarian policies, these freemen fought tenaciously among themselves (at least in Massachusetts) over matters of governance. Instead of practicing rule by a self-selected minority—whether an aristocracy of status and wealth or an aristocracy of saints—all five colonies instituted the rule of law in continuity with English culture, a rule greatly enhanced by their strong feelings about the dangers of unlimited power, the theme of John Cotton's Revelation sermons. Just as tellingly, local and colony governments never turned the saints into an autocratic, self-sustaining elite that monopolized resources such as land. So we learn from Thomas Shepard's Cambridge, where the category of "saint" became increasingly elastic and comprehensive. Eager to reform civil society and the church, the colonists also learned that social peace depended on compromise and mediation. Compromises of one kind or another had marked the Puritan movement from its inception in mid-sixteenth-century England, and although some of the colonists hoped to start afresh, their daring coexisted with attitudes and practices of the kind that prevailed in Shepard's Cambridge.

Always, Puritanism wore two faces. From the mid-sixteenth century onward, it was a movement aimed at taking over a national church and improving it in certain ways. Simultaneously, it was a movement driven by deep feelings about obeying "conscience" and divine law even when doing so made for tensions with civil rulers and the state church. If the art of being a Puritan in early Stuart England lay in holding these two possibilities together, the art of being a Puritan in New England lay in placing divine law and the workings of grace and the Holy Spirit at the heart of civil and religious society while clinging to elements of corporate, comprehensive Protestantism. What worked in New England during the 1630s and 1640s did not work in Civil War England. There, the social and religious situation saw a rupturing of a precarious synthesis; there, the hopes for creating a "free commonwealth" came to naught, as Milton would lament as the Restoration dawned. Only in the colonies was it possible to sustain a civil state with so limited a version of executive authority and a Puritanism that combined a vigorous role for ministry with the empowering of laymen (and in more limited ways, laywomen) over against the customary hierarchies of state church and civil society. Should it surprise us, therefore, that out of these divergent pressures and possibilities there should emerge the high appreciation for "consent" and "liberty" voiced in 1665 by the men of Hadley?[5]

That there were moments of strain within the political culture of the colonists as they sorted through the choices they had to make is, I hope, fully acknowledged in these pages. That hierarchies of several kinds persisted, that the Indians were kept at arm's length and their self-governance seriously abused, that there were moments when the culture of godly rule *threatened* to create acute divisions, all this is also part of the broader story. But in comparison with governance in any other British colonies in North America before 1650 and short-lived Providence Island, and in comparison with governance and social practice in England itself, the colonists may rightly be regarded as unusual for their times.

The tenor of *A Reforming People* may suggest that I find the New Testament ethics embraced by the colonists and their heartfelt craving for peace and mutuality appealing, perhaps enchanting. True. But, like everyone who delves into the sources, I know that sermons and court records bespeak a different mood, an awareness of possibilities not fully accomplished, of goals unmet. Many people experienced the tension between self-interest and the general good, a tension palpable in Shepard's Cambridge. By the 1640s and increasingly thereafter, the colonists were beginning to contrast a founding moment of near-perfect community with the conflicts they were experiencing, divisions well documented in town and colony records as fights broke out over who had access to land and other key resources.[6] "Loving and Christian Freinds," Henry Vane wrote from England in early 1654 to the people of Providence, "How is it, that there are such divisiens amongst you, such headinesses tumults disorders Injustice? . . . Is not the love of christ in you to fill you with [y]earning bowells one towards anothr and Constraine you not to live to your selves but unto him that Died for you yea and is risen againe? Are there noe Wise men amongst you, noe publike self denying Spirits that att least upon grounds of Common Safety Equity and Prudence can finde out some Way or Meanes of Union and reconceluetion . . . amongst your selves"? In such statements lay the making of a literary tradition that already had shaped William Bradford's *Of Plimoth Plantation* and would shape much that was written in New England after 1660.[7]

This is a literary tradition we may want to revisit in our own time. A historian reminds us that, "with varying degrees of self-consciousness, deliberation, and explicitness, the New Englanders were . . . attempting to carry out most of the expressed goals of a revolutionary challenge to the status quo in English society, economy, politics, and law as well, no matter how traditionalistic local life, family, and farming may have been."[8] To read these words in 2010, at a moment in American political history when every attempt at salutary reform is being thwarted by self-interest of the most egregious kind, and when any appeal to "compassion" is deflected in order to protect a corrupt status quo, is to experience a disenchantment as troubling as any the colonists may have undergone. They, too, were stigmatized by their opponents as divisive and unpatriotic even as they worked to introduce justice and equity into the fabric of social, religious, and economic life. Where is equity today? And can we take heart from the capacities of the colonists to break through abuses of power and language in early-seventeenth-century England?

Notes

ABBREVIATIONS

Cambridge Records
  The Records of the Town of Cambridge (Formerly Newtowne), Massachusetts, 1630–1703 (Cambridge, Mass.: City Council, 1901)

Coll. MHS
  Collections of the Massachusetts Historical Society

CW Williams
  The Complete Writings of Roger Williams, 7 vols. (New York: Russell & Russell, 1963)

Gardiner, *Constitutional Documents*
  Samuel Rawson Gardiner, *The Constitutional Documents of the Puritan Revolution, 1625–1660,* 3rd ed. (Oxford: Clarendon, 1906)

Hall, *AC*
  David D. Hall, *The Antinomian Controversy, 1636–1638: A Documentary History* (Middletown, Conn.: Wesleyan University Press, 1968)

Hall, *Faithful Shepherd*
  David D. Hall, *The Faithful Shepherd: A History of the New England Ministry in the Seventeenth Century* (Chapel Hill: University of North Carolina Press, 1972)

Kenyon, *Stuart Constitution*
  J. P. Kenyon, *The Stuart Constitution: Documents and Commentary,* 2nd ed. (Cambridge: Cambridge University Press, 1986)

Lawes and Liberties
  The Laws and Liberties of Massachusetts Reprinted from a Copy of the 1648 Edition in the Henry B. Huntington Library, ed. Max Farrand (Cambridge, Mass.: Harvard University Press, 1929)

NEHGR
  New England Historic Genealogical Register

Proc. MHS
    Proceedings of the Massachusetts Historical Society
Pub. CSM
    Publications and Transactions of the Colonial Society of Massachusetts
Recs. Conn.
    The Public Records of the Colony of Connecticut, 1636 to 1665, ed. J. Hammond
    Trumbull (Hartford, 1850)
Recs. Mass.
    Records of the Governor and Company of the Massachusetts Bay in New-England,
    ed. N. B. Shurtleff, 5 vols. (Boston, 1853–54)
Recs. New Haven
    Records of the Colony and Plantation of New Haven, ed. Charles J. Hoadly,
    2 vols. (Hartford, 1857–58)
Recs. Plymouth
    Records of the Colony of New Plymouth in New England, ed. Nathaniel B.
    Shurtleff and David Pulsifer, 11 vols. (Boston, 1855–61)
Recs. Southampton
    The First Book of Records of the Town of Southampton with Other Ancient Documents of Historic Value (Sag Harbor, N.Y., 1874)
Shepard, *Works*
    The Works of Thomas Shepard, ed. John A. Albro, 3 vols. (Boston, 1853)
Walker, *Creeds and Platforms*
    Williston Walker, *The Creeds and Platforms of Congregationalism* (New York,
    1893)
Whitmore, *Colonial Laws*
    William H. Whitmore, *The Colonial Laws of Massachusetts* (Boston, 1887)
Winthrop, *Journal*
    The Journal of John Winthrop, ed. Richard S. Dunn, James Savage, and Laetitia Yeandle (Cambridge, Mass.: Harvard University Press, 1996)
Winthrop Papers
    Winthrop Papers, 6 vols. (Boston: Massachusetts Historical Society, 1929–)
WMQ
    William and Mary Quarterly

INTRODUCTION

1. George Yerby, *People and Parliament: Representative Rights and the English Revolution* (Basinstoke: Palgrave Macmillan, 2008), p. 140; Winthrop, *Journal,* p. 66; Thomas Hutchinson, *The History of the Colony and Province of Massachusetts-Bay,* ed. Thomas Shaw Mayo, 3 vols. (Cambridge, Mass.: Harvard University Press, 1936), 1:54n; Brian Manning, *The English People and*

the English Revolution, 1640–1649 (London: Heinemann, 1976), pp. 11–13. For Charles I's criticism of the Petition of Right, see Kenyon, *Stuart Constitution,* p. 72. What John Wilson actually said from his perch in the tree is not indicated, but he was certainly urging the election of Winthrop, his ally in a Boston congregation divided between supporters and opponents of "Antinomians."

2. Larzer Ziff, *John Cotton on the Churches of New England* (Cambridge, Mass.: Harvard University Press, 1968), pp. 71, 101; John Cotton, *An Exposition upon the Thirteenth Chapter of the Revelation* (London, 1655).

3. John Morrill, *The Revolt of the Provinces: Conservatives and Radicals in the English Civil War, 1630–1650* (London: Longman, 1980), p. 47 and passim.

4. Winthrop, *Journal,* p. 107.

5. "A Remonstrance and Petition of Robert Child, and Others," in *Hutchinson Papers,* 2 vols. (Albany: Prince Society, 1865), 1:216, 217.

6. Gardiner, *Constitutional Documents,* pp. 100–101.

7. *Winthrop Papers,* 4:162, 266–67.

8. Tocqueville owed this theme to the Boston minister-antiquarian Jared Sparks, as George Wilson Pierson showed in *Tocqueville and Beaumont in America* (New York: Oxford University Press, 1938), pp. 397–416.

9. Nineteenth-century Unitarian stigmatizing of "Calvinism" as cruel, arbitrary, and superstitious is sketched in David D. Hall, "Calvin and Calvinism Within Congregational and Unitarian Discourse in Nineteenth-Century America," in *John Calvin's American Legacy,* ed. Thomas J. Davis (New York: Oxford University Press, 2010), pp. 147–64. As part of revisionist scholarship (American-style) of the 1960s, I attempted to demonstrate the severe limitations of the "theocratic" interpretation in Hall, *Faithful Shepherd,* chap. 6.

10. Brooks Adams, *The Emancipation of Massachusetts* (Boston, 1887).

11. Vernon Louis Parrington, *Main Currents in American Thought,* 3 vols., vol. 1: *The Colonial Mind* (New York: Harcourt, Brace, 1927), 23–46.

12. Perry Miller, *Orthodoxy in Massachusetts, 1630–1650* (Cambridge, Mass.: Harvard University Press, 1933), pp. 150, 175–76. A much less informed historian, Thomas J. Wertenbaker, put "oligarchy" in the title of his study of early New England, *The Puritan Oligarchy* (New York: Scribner, 1947).

13. George Bancroft, *An Oration Delivered Before the Democracy of Springfield and Neighboring Towns, July 4, 1836* (Springfield, Mass., 1836). The colonists affirmed other "rights" than these, of course; see below, Chapters One and Four. That the Reformed (Calvinist) tradition was a source of rights language adopted by the colonists is argued (with varying degrees of accuracy) in John Witte, Jr., *The Reformation of Rights: Law, Religion, and Human Rights in Early Modern Calvinism* (Cambridge: Cambridge University Press, 2007), a reference I owe to David Little.

14. Gilbert Sheldon's repressive policies as archbishop of Canterbury and the death toll they caused (possibly higher than the toll under Mary Tudor) are described in J. R. Jones, *Country and Court: England, 1658–1714* (Cambridge, Mass.: Harvard University Press, 1978), pp. 145–50.

15. Robert Bolton, quoted in William M. Lamont, *Godly Rule: Politics and Religion, 1603–1660* (London: Macmillan, 1969), p. 49; Winthrop, *Journal*, p. 587. Just how conventional Winthrop was is indicated by the parallels between the "little speech" and Ephraim Huit's comments on liberty run amuck (Huit, *The whole Prophecie of Daniel Explained* [London, 1643], p. 116).

16. Their claims on electoral office are emphasized in Mark A. Kishlansky, *Parliamentary Selection: Social and Political Choice in Early Modern England* (Cambridge: Cambridge University Press, 1986).

17. Cotton Mather, *Memorable Providences, Relating to Witchcrafts and Possessions* (Boston, 1689), p. 45.

18. Robert O. Paxton, *The Anatomy of Fascism* (New York: Alfred A. Knopf, 2004). In Hitler's Germany, on the other hand, the mediating elements of traditional society were suppressed.

19. Anthony Fletcher, *Reform in the Provinces: The Government of Stuart England* (New Haven: Yale University Press, 1986), pp. 62, 57, 52–53; Clive Holmes, *Seventeenth-Century Lincolnshire*, vol. 7 of *History of Lincolnshire*, ed. Maurice Barley (Lincoln, U.K.: History of Lincolnshire Committee, 1980), chaps. 5, "The Brokers: The Professions," and 6, "The Brokers: The Gentry"; Ann Hughes, *Politics, Society and Civil War in Warwickshire, 1620–1660* (Cambridge: Cambridge University Press, 1987), p. 61. Everyday compromises in civil and criminal justice are described in Cynthia B. Herrup, *The Common Peace: Participation and the Criminal Law in Seventeenth-Century England* (Cambridge: Cambridge University Press, 1987); see also Herrup, "The Counties and the Country: Some Thoughts on Seventeenth-Century Historiography," in *Reviving the English Revolution: Reflections & Elaborations on the Work of Christopher Hill*, ed. Geoff Eley and William Hunt (London: Verso, 1988), pp. 289–304. As another historian has pointed out, "By late 1641 . . . [Archbishop] Laud had ranged against him a powerful opposition of common lawyers, civil lawyers . . . and many of the gentry and nobility, who had been humiliated by clergy bent on advertising their new professional confidence" (Julian Davies, *The Caroline Captivity of the Church: Charles I and the Remoulding of Anglicanism, 1625–1641* [Oxford: Clarendon, 1992], p. 86).

20. Stephen Brachlow, *The Communion of Saints: Radical Puritan and Separatist Ecclesiology, 1570–1625* (Oxford: Oxford University Press, 1988); Murray Tolmie, *The Triumph of the Saints: The Separate Churches of London, 1616–1649* (Cambridge: Cambridge University Press, 1977); David R. Como,

Blown by the Spirit: Puritanism and the Emergence of an Antinomian Under-ground in Pre–Civil War England (Stanford: Stanford University Press, 2004).

21. Herrup, *Common Peace,* chap. 2.

22. Valerie Pearl, *London and the Outbreak of the Puritan Revolution: City Government and National Politics, 1625–43* (Oxford: Oxford University Press, 1961).

23. Anthony Milton, "Licensing, Censorship, and Religious Orthodoxy in Early Stuart England," *The Historical Journal* 41 (1998): 625–51.

24. Harold Love, *Scribal Publication in Seventeenth-Century England* (Oxford: Clarendon, 1993), pp. 13–22; Adam Fox, *Oral and Literate Culture in England, 1500–1700* (Oxford: Clarendon, 2000), chap. 7.

25. J. G. A. Pocock, *The Ancient Constitution and the Feudal Law: A Study of English Historical Thought in the Seventeenth Century* (Cambridge: Cambridge University Press, 1957); Glenn Burgess, *The Politics of the Ancient Constitution: An Introduction to English Political Thought, 1603–1643* (University Park: Pennsylvania State University Press, 1992). My few sentences cannot encompass the complexities of what was meant by the common law, as described by Burgess.

26. Kenyon, *Stuart Constitution,* pp. 31, 70.

27. J. H. Gleason, *The Justices of the Peace in England, 1558–1640* (Oxford: Clarendon, 1969), p. 13; Herrup, *Common Peace,* pp. 54–55.

28. A point central to theories of patriarchy, as demonstrated in Gordon J. Schochet, *Patriarchalism in Political Thought: The Authoritarian Family and Political Speculation and Attitudes, Especially in Seventeenth-Century England* (New York: Basic Books, 1975).

29. Quentin Skinner, *The Foundations of Modern Political Thought,* 2 vols. (Cambridge: Cambridge University Press, 1998); J. H. M. Salmon, *The French Religious Wars in English Political Thought* (Oxford: Clarendon, 1959), esp. chaps. 2, 4, and 5; Conrad Russell, *Unrevolutionary England, 1603–1642* (London: Hambledon, 1990), p. xiii, which covers a point Russell demonstrated at greater length in *Parliaments and English Politics, 1621–1629* (Oxford: Clarendon, 1979). The "revisionist" perspective I briefly summarize in this paragraph is described more fully in Richard Cust and Ann Hughes, "Introduction: After Revisionism," in *Conflict in Early Stuart England: Studies in Religion and Politics, 1603–1642,* ed. Cust and Hughes (London: Longman, 1989). The contrary case, that "fundamental disagreements" on political questions arose in this period, is argued by (among others) J. P. Sommerville, *Politics and Ideology in England, 1603–1640* (London: Longman, 1986), and Yerby, *People and Parliament.*

30. Michael Mendle, *Henry Parker and the English Civil War: The Political Thought of the Public's "Privado"* (Cambridge: Cambridge University Press,

1995), p. 32. Before this date, scribal publication was the preferred mode for "political reflection" (ibid.).

31. Kenyon, *Stuart Constitution,* p. 9.

32. Richard Tuck, *Philosophy and Government, 1572–1651* (Cambridge: Cambridge University Press, 1993), p. 223; Mendle, *Henry Parker,* p. 43; Pauline Gregg, *Free-Born John: A Biography of John Lilburne* (London: J. M. Dent, 1961), p. 207. English Puritan clergyman John White assigned the phrase a moral significance (see *Winthrop Papers,* 3:322).

33. These meanings may be found, respectively, in John Cotton, *The Keyes of the Kingdom of Heaven* (London, 1644), p. 36; in documents associated with the founding of Rhode Island (see below, Chapter One); in Winthrop, *Journal,* p. 453; in John Cotton's letter to Lord Saye and Sele in *The Correspondence of John Cotton,* ed. Sargent Bush, Jr. (Chapel Hill: University of North Carolina Press, 2001), p. 245; and in a letter from an unknown New England writer printed in Thomas Edwards, *The Second Part of Gangraena* (London, 1646), p. 166.

34. Joel Hurstfield, *Freedom, Corruption and Government in Elizabethan England* (Cambridge, Mass.: Harvard University Press, 1973), pp. 13–14, 23–49.

35. Conal Condren, *The Language of Politics in Seventeenth-Century England* (New York: St. Martin's, 1994), p. 45; Martin Dzelzainis, "Republicanism," in *A Companion to Milton,* ed. Thomas N. Corns (Oxford: Blackwell, 2001), pp. 294–308. The earliest explicit statements of "republican" theory in England date from the end of the period of New England history I am describing. Humanist reflections on republicanism were available to the colonists, as Tuck remarks in *Philosophy and Government* (p. 222), noting also that in much scholarship there remains "an unclarity about what republicanism meant in a mid-seventeenth-century context." The tendency to discern republican elements in pre-1640 political reflection is questioned in Glenn Burgess, *British Political Thought, 1550–1660* (New York: Palgrave Macmillan, 2009), pp. 324–26, and in Blair Worden, "Republicanism, Regicide and Republic: The English Experience," in *Republicanism: A Shared European Heritage,* ed. Martin van Gelderen and Quentin Skinner, 2 vols. (Cambridge: Cambridge University Press, 2002), 1:307–27. In an essay that overlaps in some respects with my argument, Michael P. Winship applies the term to the colonists, although conflating it with a category (the godly) I prefer to keep separate (Winship, "Godly Republicanism and the Origins of the Massachusetts Polity," *WMQ,* 3rd ser., 54 [2006]: 427–62).

36. Leo Damrosch, *The Sorrows of the Quaker Jesus: James Naylor and the Puritan Crackdown on the Free Spirit* (Cambridge, Mass.: Harvard University Press, 1996). The meaning of "liberty" as framed in A. S. P. Woodhouse's introduction to *Puritanism and Liberty* (Chicago: University of Chicago Press, 1951)

has been widely criticized—e.g., in Hurstfield, *Freedom, Corruption and Government,* pp. 56–58; William Lamont, "Puritanism, Liberty and the Putney Debates," in *The Putney Debates of 1647: The Army, the Levellers and the English State,* ed. Michael Mendle (Cambridge: Cambridge University Press, 2001), pp. 241–55; and J. S. Davis, "Religion and the Struggle for Freedom in the English Revolution," *The Historical Journal* 35 (1992): 507–30. Conal Condren's wide-reaching critique of language and category confusion among modern historians has influenced these observations. That millenarianism was too widely shared to be attached to any specific political program is demonstrated in Lamont, *Godly Rule,* and B. S. Capp, *The Fifth Monarchy Men: A Study in Seventeenth-Century English Millenarianism* (London: Faber and Faber, 1972), chap. 1.

37. Kenyon, *Stuart Constitution,* pp. 207–17. This is perhaps the place to look back at the thesis that Puritanism created a "new kind of person, the citizen, the activist, the ideologically committed radical," as Michael Walzer argued in *The Revolution of the Saints: A Study in the Origins of Radical Politics* (Cambridge, Mass.: Harvard University Press, 1965). For critical responses, see David Little, "Max Weber Revisited: The 'Protestant Ethic' and the Puritan Experience of Order," *Harvard Theological Review* 59 (1966): 416–28, and Patrick Collinson, "Magistracy and Ministry: A Suffolk Miniature," in Collinson, *Godly People: Essays on English Protestantism and Puritanism* (London: Hambledon, 1983), pp. 445–66. But see Stephen Baskerville, *Not Peace but a Sword: The Political Theology of the English Revolution* (London: Routledge, 1993), introduction (quotation, p. 8).

38. These questions are raised directly and indirectly in Patrick Collinson, "The Cohabitation of the Faithful with the Unfaithful," in *From Persecution to Toleration: The Glorious Revolution and Religion in England,* ed. Ole Peter Grell et al. (Oxford: Oxford University Press, 1991), pp. 51–76. The ways in which Collinson uses Thomas Shepard in this essay differ from my own; see below, Chapter Five.

39. In the introduction to *Fear and Polemic in Seventeenth-Century England: Richard Baxter and Antinomianism* (Aldershot: Ashgate, 2001), Tim Cooper summarizes the recent scholarship that establishes the rhetorical qualities of political discourse. As Condren and others have noted, the category of "radical" was a nineteenth-century invention. I have avoided it as much as possible in these pages.

40. This point is forcefully made about the Levellers by David Wootton in "Leveller Democracy and the Puritan Revolution," in *The Cambridge History of Political Thought, 1450–1700,* ed. J. H. Burns (Cambridge: Cambridge University Press, 1991), pp. 412–42. For Parliamentarians and their spokesmen, the writer Henry Parker is a case in point. As Mendle remarks, he "was a par-

liamentarian and an absolutist, a spokesman for the self-proclaimed defenders of liberty and property and a brutally dismissive critic of the ancient constitution" (Mendle, *Henry Parker,* p. xv). For Milton, see Dzelzainis, "Republicanism." Specifying a Leveller position on any single issue is greatly complicated by the fact that this was not a consolidated, coherent movement.

41. *Recs. Mass.,* 1:115, 117, 139.

42. [John White], *The Planters Plea: Or, The grounds of plantations examined and usuall objections answered* (London, 1630), reprinted in *The Founding of Massachusetts: A Selection from the Sources* (Boston: Massachusetts Historical Society, 1930), pp. 168, 197–98; Winthrop, "Modell of Christian Charitie," in *Winthrop Papers,* 2:282; ibid., 3:335. Earlier, after visiting Plymouth, the Puritan minister Richard Cushman had noted the importance of putting community ahead of self in *A Sermon Preached at Plimmoth in New-England* (London, 1621).

43. *Winthrop Papers,* 3:486; Gardiner, *Constitutional Documents,* pp. 124–34 (quotations on p. 124).

44. Bush, ed., *Correspondence of John Cotton,* p. 184; Isabel M. Calder, ed., *Letters of John Davenport* (New Haven: Yale University Press, 1937), p. 39; John Ball, *A Tryall of the New-Church Way in New-England and in Old* (London, 1644), sig. [a4r]; Hall, *Faithful Shepherd,* chap. 4. The accelerating radicalism of the immigrants, especially the laity, is a major theme of Stephen Foster, *The Long Argument: English Puritanism and the Shaping of New England Culture, 1570–1700* (Chapel Hill: University of North Carolina Press, 1991), chap. 4.

45. Ronald G. Walters, "New England Society and the *Laws and Liberties of Massachusetts,* 1648," *Essex Institute Historical Collections* 106 (1970): 145–68.

46. Donald Veall, *The Popular Movement for Law Reform, 1640–1660* (Oxford: Clarendon, 1970).

47. See below, Chapter One.

48. A process traced below, in Chapter Three.

49. The indecision of the Long Parliament, and, longer-term, its conservatism, had no equivalent in New England. The situation of the colonists is illuminated by Ann Hughes' observation that if "a majority [in England] preferred peace . . . a minority [of gentry] were prepared to take up arms for what they believed in; and that several, albeit a smaller minority, were, in a hierarchical, deferential society, prepared to fight the supreme authority in the land" (Hughes, *Politics, Society, and Civil War,* p. 167). This argument should not be taken as implying that the "English Revolution" was destined for grander things. The phrase is an artifact of periodization and cannot be equated with a necessary teleology of "revolution" that somehow was thwarted. Nonetheless, the peculiar conditions of this period made it possible for different groups to advocate a thorough remodeling of political and religious structures.

50. The colonists were sympathetic to the reforms undertaken by the Long Parliament, sided with Parliament during the period of civil war (one of John Winthrop's sons became an officer in the New Model Army, as did others who returned to England), and thought well of Oliver Cromwell. See James O'Toole, "New England Reactions to the English Civil Wars," *NEHGR* 129 (1975): 238–49; Timothy J. Sehr, *Colony and Commonwealth: Massachusetts Bay, 1649–1660* (New York: Garland, 1989), chap. 1.

CHAPTER ONE. "ARBITRARY" OR "DEMOCRATICAL"?

1. Winthrop, *Journal*, p. 38; John Noble and John F. Cronin, eds., *Records of the Court of Assistants of the Colony of the Massachusetts Bay, 1630–1692*, 3 vols. (Boston: Suffolk County, 1901–28), 2:1–2.
2. Gardiner, *Constitutional Documents*, pp. 6, 4; Francis Oakley, "Jacobean Political Theology: The Absolute and Ordinary Powers of the King," *Journal of the History of Ideas* 29 (1968): 323–46; Roger Mainwaring, *Religion and Allegiance: In Two Sermons Preached Before the Kings Majestie* (London, 1627).
3. Kenyon, *Stuart Constitution*, pp. 68, 72.
4. Gardiner, *Constitutional Documents*, p. 60.
5. Winthrop, *Journal*, p. 381. Another disquieting rhetoric was the apocalypticism that people sometimes turned against the government or, in the case of the religious radical Samuel Gorton, any government. See, e.g., ibid., p. 362.
6. Sargent Bush, Jr., ed., *The Correspondence of John Cotton* (Chapel Hill: University of North Carolina Press, 2001), p. 245. My account is indebted to T. H. Breen, *The Character of the Good Ruler: A Study of Puritan Political Ideas in New England, 1630–1730* (New Haven: Yale University Press, 1970), where the focus is on "discretionary" and constrained forms of authority.
7. Winthrop, *Journal*, p. 63.
8. Ibid., pp. 68, 74, 77.
9. Ibid., pp. 77, 113–14.
10. Ibid., p. 116.
11. Ibid., p. 127. A familiar phrase in English politics by this time, the "negative voice" (or negative vote) had crossed over into debates about church government dating from the early decades of the century (Hall, *Faithful Shepherd*, p. 40).
12. Everett Emerson, ed., *Letters from New England: The Massachusetts Bay Colony, 1629–1638* (Amherst: University of Massachusetts Press, 1976), pp. 149, 145, 148; Winthrop, *Journal*, p. 142. The contents of Stoughton's "treatise," which does not survive, may be discerned from the letter he wrote his brother John Stoughton, and from Winthrop's account of the episode. In *The Colonial American Origins of Modern Democratic Theory* (Cambridge:

Cambridge University Press, 2008), J. S. Maloy points out (p. 35) that the understanding of "magistrate" as merely a "steward" of a sovereignty possessed by the political community as a whole can be traced back to John of Paris and the Sorbonnists, who differentiated "ministerium" from "dominium." This genealogy may be enlarged to include attempts within the Reformed tradition to describe ministerial or delegated authority as what ministers possessed, in distinction from magisterial authority; see, e.g., W. J. Torrance Kirby, *The Zurich Connection and Tudor Political Theology,* Studies in the History of Christian Traditions vol. 131 (Leiden and Boston: Brill, 2007). For the distinction as used by the ministers, see John Cotton, *The Keyes of the Kingdome* (London, 1644), reprinted in Larzer Ziff, *John Cotton on the Churches of New England* (Cambridge, Mass.: Harvard University Press, 1968), p. 88. Maloy (chap. 4) also cites Separatist minister John Robinson's reasoning about church governance as a source of "ministerial" understandings of office. Thomas Shepard characterized "magisterial power" as able "to do what they will" and implied that it was an "anti-Christian illimited power" (Shepard, *Works,* 3:333). That the language of governance employed by the Separatists and Puritan exiles in the Netherlands overlapped in several ways with the language of civil politics in Massachusetts is certain, though how explicitly influential the first was upon the second is debatable.

13. Winthrop, *Journal,* p. 146.

14. [John Cotton], *An Abstract of the Lawes of New-England, as They Are Now Established* (London, 1641), pp. 3–4, 2. At almost the same time, Cotton was declaring that in churches, ministers could "transact no publique act, but in their [congregation's] presence, and with their consents" ([Cotton], *A Coppy of a Letter of Mr. Cotton . . . Sent in Answer to Certaine Objections* [London, 1641], pp. 3–4). See also Winthrop's report of a mediating sermon Cotton preached, in Winthrop, *Journal,* p. 128.

15. Kenyon, *Stuart Constitution,* pp. 12, 11; *Winthrop Papers,* 4:476 (referencing judges); John Calvin, *The Institutes of the Christian Religion,* trans. Ford Lewis Battles, 2 vols. (Philadelphia: Westminster, 1960), 2:1489.

16. *Recs. Mass.,* 1:196. Vane's place in the campaign for godly rule is noted below, in Chapter Three.

17. Henry Vane, "A briefe Answer to a certaine declaration, made of the intent and equitye of the order of court, that none should be received to inhabite within this jurisdiction but such as should be allowed by some of the magistrates," in [Thomas Hutchinson], *A Collection of Original Papers Relative to the History of Massachusetts-Bay* (Boston, 1769), pp. 84, 86 (emphasis added).

18. *Hutchinson Papers,* 2 vols. (Albany: Prince Society, 1865), 1:100, 111.

19. *Recs. Mass.,* 1:174; *The Book of the General Laws of the Inhabitants of the Juris-*

diction of New-Plimouth (Cambridge, Mass., 1672), p. 3; Kenyon, *Stuart Constitution,* p. 100.

20. Whitmore, *Colonial Laws,* p. 33.

21. *CW Williams,* 3:254; Whitmore, *Colonial Laws,* p. 35.

22. Winthrop, *Journal,* pp. 390–91, 395; *Winthrop Papers,* 4:359–61. In October 1643, "all the elders" prepared a response that, as summarized by Winthrop, rejected the concept of a council "with a kind of transcendent authority" but, on the grounds of necessity, warranted having such a body (*Journal,* pp. 418–20).

23. Winthrop, *Journal,* pp. 395, 398.

24. *Winthrop Papers,* 4:382–83; Kenyon, *Stuart Constitution,* pp. 18–20.

25. [John Norton?], "The Negative Vote, 1643," *Proc. MHS* 46 (1913): 276–85.

26. *Recs. Mass.,* 2:90–96; Winthrop, *Journal,* p. 561.

27. *Lawes and Liberties,* pp. 21, 24.

28. *Winthrop Papers,* 4:468.

29. Winthrop, *Journal,* p. 589, a passage that also suggests the opposition to Winthrop had turned to *salus populi suprema lex.* The drift to local authority is perceptively argued (in the service of a dismissal of "Puritanism") by Darrett B. Rutman, "The Mirror of Puritan Authority," in *Law and Authority in Colonial America: Selected Essays,* ed. George A. Billias (Barre, Mass.: Barre Publishing Company, 1965), pp. 149–67.

30. Emerging regionalism is a principal theme of Robert E. Wall, *Massachusetts Bay: The Crucial Decade, 1640–1650* (New Haven: Yale University Press, 1972).

31. *Winthrop Papers,* 4:468–72.

32. Ibid., 4:469; Ziff, *Cotton on the Churches of New England,* p. 130; like his fellow ministers, Cotton was also employing the language of "mixt" government (ibid., p. 134).

33. *Winthrop Papers,* 2:114, 3:162; Winthrop, *Journal,* 280. The Latin tag may be translated as a plea to protect the power of the magistrates from their inferiors. Winthrop's preference for something close to secrecy is described in David D. Hall, *Ways of Writing: The Practice and Politics of Text-Making in Seventeenth-Century New England* (Philadelphia: University of Pennsylvania Press, 2008), chap. 5.

34. Bush, ed., *Correspondence of John Cotton,* p. 245; Winthrop, *Journal,* p. 324.

35. Who was responsible for drafting the Fundamental Orders has never been determined. I date it as of 1638; the formal document was ratified in January 1639.

36. Winthrop, *Journal,* pp. 145–46.

37. Charles M. Andrews, *The Colonial Period of American History,* 4 vols. (New Haven: Yale University Press, 1934–38), 2:94.

38. *Recs. Conn.,* pp. 20–25.

39. *Winthrop Papers,* 4:81–82; the month is conjectural. Maloy, *Colonial American Origins,* points out (p. 100) that the Separatist minister John Robinson had used the same phrase.

40. *Collections of the Connecticut Historical Society* 1 (1860): 20.

41. Antithetical interpretations of Thomas Hooker may be found in Vernon L. Parrington, *Main Currents in American Thought,* vol. 1, *The Colonial Mind* (New York: Harcourt, 1927), pp. 53–62 (representing him as a founder of American democracy), and Perry Miller, "Thomas Hooker and the Democracy of Connecticut," *New England Quarterly* 4 (1931): 663–712. More recently, Maloy has interpreted Hooker as taking an important step toward democracy in making rulers accountable (Maloy, *Colonial American Origins,* pp. 148–60).

42. Thomas Hooker, *A Survey of the Summe of Church-Discipline* (London, 1648), pt. 1, pp. 188–203. Because he explicitly differentiated civil government from ecclesiastical (Christ being the source of all authority in the latter), we should not hastily turn him into a theorist of secular democracy.

43. *Laws 1623–1686,* vol. 11 of *Recs. Plymouth,* pp. 6, 7, 3 (brackets eliminated).

44. Ibid., pp. 7, 31, 34–35; John D. Cushing, ed., *The Laws of the Pilgrims* (Wilmington, Del.: Michael Glazier, 1977), p. 21.

45. William Brigham, *The Compact with the Charter of the Colony of New Plymouth* (Boston, 1836), p. 61.

46. A fifth community, Warwick, did not participate in this meeting.

47. Glenn W. LaFantasie, ed., *The Correspondence of Roger Williams,* 2 vols. (Hanover, N.H.: University Press of New England, 1988), 1:53.

48. Howard M. Chapin, *Documentary History of Rhode Island,* vol. 2, *Being the History of the Towns of Portsmouth and Newport to 1647* (Providence: Preston and Rounds, 1919), p. 108; William R. Staples, *Annals of the Town of Providence* (Providence, 1843), p. 39. The theocratic aspects of governance on Newport Island are described below, in Chapter Three. This brief summary scants the disarray within these towns, foregrounded in Sydney V. James, *The Colonial Metamorphoses in Rhode Island: A Study of Institutions in Change* (Hanover, N.H.: University Press of New England, 2000), chap. 1.

49. John D. Cushing, ed., *The Earliest Acts and Laws of the Colony of Rhode Island and Providence Plantations, 1647–1719* (Wilmington, Del.: Michael Glazier, 1977), p. 12.

50. Ibid.; G. B. Warden, "The Rhode Island Civil Code of 1647," in *Saints and Revolutionaries: Essays on Early American History,* ed. David Hall et al. (New York: W. W. Norton, 1984), p. 146.

51. *CW Williams,* 3:249–50, 4:28–29; see also 3:214, where he insisted that "the Soveraigne power of all Civill Authority is founded in the consent of the People, that every Common-weale hath radically and fundamentally in it a power of true discerning the true feare of God, which they transfer to their Magistrates and Officers."

52. [Henry Parker], *Observations upon Some of His Majesties Late Answers and Expresses* (London, 1642), pp. 1, 2.

53. *Recs. New Haven,* 2:24, 52–57.

54. The methods of distributing land did not always coincide with this principle; see below, Chapter Two.

55. Quoting the Massachusetts delegates to the New England Confederation; see *Acts of the Commissioners of the United Colonies of New England,* vols. 9–10 of *Recs. Plymouth,* 10:76.

56. *Recs. Conn.,* p. 119; *New-Havens Settling in New-England, and some Lawes for Government* (London, 1656), reprinted in *Recs. New Haven,* 2:570.

57. Karen Ordahl Kupperman, *Providence Island, 1630–1641: The Other Puritan Colony* (New York: Cambridge University Press, 1993), pp. 51–52.

58. Kenyon, *Stuart Constitution,* p. 180. This all-too-brief sketch of the politics of 1640–42 omits the fractures within Parliament that dogged attempts at anything more thoroughgoing. As John Morrill has pointed out, a coalition fashioned around fears of "popery" and a distaste for some of Charles's policies was not a coalition champing at the bit to make major changes. Indeed, the word "radical" is questionable even for Pym and his allies. (Morrill, *The Revolt of the Provinces: Conservatives and Radicals in the English Civil War, 1630–1650* [London: Longman, 1980], p. 47.) Pym's efforts to fashion and hold together a majority in the House of Commons in behalf of reform are detailed in J. H. Hexter, *The Reign of King Pym* (Cambridge, Mass.: Harvard University Press, 1941).

59. Kenyon, *Stuart Constitution,* p. 184.

60. Or, better, agreed on a single definition of sovereignty. Competing theories are described in Corinne Comstock Weston and Janelle R. Greenberg, *Subjects and Sovereignty: The Grand Controversy over Legal Sovereignty in Stuart England* (Cambridge: Cambridge University Press, 1981).

61. See esp. Edmund S. Morgan, *Inventing the People: The Rise of Popular Sovereignty in England and America* (New York: W. W. Norton, 1988), chap. 3.

62. [Parker], *Observations,* p. 23; Kenyon, *Stuart Constitution,* p. 184.

63. William Haller and Godfrey Davies, eds., *The Leveller Tracts, 1647–1653* (New York: Columbia University Press, 1944), pp. 60, 78; A. S. P. Woodhouse, *Puritanism and Liberty* (Chicago: University of Chicago Press, 1951), p. 66; Glenn Burgess, *British Political Thought, 1550–1660* (New York: Palgrave Macmillan, 2009), pp. 248–52. See also Ian Gentles, "The *Agreements of the*

People and Their Political Contexts, 1647–1649," in *The Putney Debates of 1647: The Army, the Levellers and the English State,* ed. Michael Mendle (Cambridge: Cambridge University Press, 2001), pp. 148–74; David Wootton, "Leveller Democracy and the Puritan Revolution," in *The Cambridge History of Political Thought, 1450–1700,* ed. J. H. Burns (Cambridge: Cambridge University Press, 1991), pp. 412–42.

64. *Winthrop Papers,* 5:44, 37.

CHAPTER TWO. LAND, TAXES, AND PARTICIPATION

1. Bernard C. Steiner, *A History of the Plantation of Menunkatuck and . . . of Guilford, Connecticut* (Baltimore, 1897), p. 168; Don Gleason Hill, ed., *The Early Records of the Town of Dedham, Massachusetts, 1636–1659* (Dedham, Mass., 1892), p. 54. On the tug of war involving pigs, fences, and fence viewers, see Sumner Chilton Powell, *Puritan Village: The Formation of a New England Town* (Middletown, Conn.: Wesleyan University Press, 1963), pp. 109–10. For litigation in relation to land, see David Thomas Konig, *Law and Society in Puritan Massachusetts: Essex County, 1629–1692* (Chapel Hill: University of North Carolina Press, 1989), pp. 40–63. Throughout this chapter, I use a deceptively inclusive term, "townspeople," because the appropriately gendered alternative, "townsmen," was used by the colonists to designate the small number of men elected each year to manage a town's affairs. In the pages that follow, "townspeople" refers solely to the adult men of a town, unless otherwise noted.

2. Grants of land made by the Massachusetts Bay Company or government to shareholders in the Company or others deemed important are not included in the description of land issues that follows. John Frederick Martin's study of the founding of towns and the distribution of land amplifies and, in one major respect, differs from what I argue in this chapter. Demonstrating that some town foundings were the doing of entrepreneurially minded proprietors, an interpretation less suited to towns of the 1630s than those that came into being after 1640, he emphasizes the privileges of the shareholders in a land corporation (or town), chief among them access to future allocations. Accordingly, the original shareholders fared much better than the people who subsequently settled in a town. Martin interprets the word "equal" to mean equal rights for shareholders, and takes less seriously than I do the ethics that (in my reading of town records) prompted these communities to ensure the welfare, however limited, of a broader group of residents. We agree, however, on questioning the emphasis in some town studies on "communalism," and he makes an important point in demonstrating that no land corporation required church membership of its shareholders, a point sup-

ported by other kinds of evidence I cite in this chapter. See Martin, *Profits in the Wilderness: Entrepreneurship and the Founding of New England Towns* (Chapel Hill: University of North Carolina Press, 1991).

3. *Hartford Town Votes 1: 1635–1716, Collections of the Connecticut Historical Society* 6 (1897): 5, 9.

4. Hill, ed., *Dedham Records,* p. 25; Henry M. Burt, *The First Century of the History of Springfield,* 2 vols. (Springfield, Mass., 1899), 1:162 (by 1636); Joseph B. Felt, *History of Ipswich, Essex, and Hamilton* (Cambridge, Mass., 1834), p. 57; Frances Manwaring Caulkins, *History of New London, Connecticut* (New London, 1895), p. 79; Robert J. Dunkle and Ann S. Lainhart, eds., *The Town Records of Roxbury, Massachusetts, 1647 to 1730* (Boston: New England Historic Genealogical Society, 1997), p. 4; George Wingate Chase, *The History of Haverhill, from Its First Settlement, in 1640, to . . . 1860* (Haverhill, Mass., 1861), p. 56.

5. Expectations of war with the Narragansetts in 1645 led the New England Confederation to call for the mobilizing of three hundred men, forty of them at once in Massachusetts, an order that startled some of the deputies (William Bradford, *Of Plymouth Plantation, 1620–1647,* ed. Samuel Eliot Morison [New York: Alfred A. Knopf, 1952], pp. 330–34).

6. Powell, *Puritan Village,* p. 93; Frank Thistlethwaite, *Dorset Pilgrims: The Story of West Country Pilgrims Who Went to New England in the 17th Century* (London: Barrie & Jenkins, 1989), p. 84; Steiner, *History of Guilford,* p. 35.

7. Samuel Greene Arnold, *History of the State of Rhode Island and Providence Plantations, 1636–1700* (Providence, 1894), pp. 125–30; Glenn W. LaFantasie, ed., *The Correspondence of Roger Williams,* 2 vols. (Hanover, N.H.: University Press of New England, 1988), 1:53; C. S. Brigham, ed., *The Early Records of the Town of Portsmouth* (Providence, 1901), p. 35.

8. *Hartford Town Votes,* pp. 2–3, 12, 58; Burt, *First Century of Springfield,* 1:235; Samuel Sewall, *The History of Woburn, Middlesex County, Mass.* (Boston, 1868), p. 25; Arnold, *History of Rhode Island,* p. 131. For similar practices, see the case study of Cambridge below, in Chapter Five.

9. *Town Records of Roxbury,* p. 1; Amos E. Jewett and Emily Jewett, *Rowley, Massachusetts, "Mr Ezechi Rogers Plantation," 1639–1850* (Rowley, 1946), p. 119; *Hartford Town Votes,* p. 14.

10. Steiner, *History of Guilford,* p. 36; Burt, *First Century of Springfield,* 1:187.

11. For efforts to quantify a rate that may have reached half of a town's population in a dozen years, see Gloria L. Main, *Peoples of a Spacious Land: Families and Cultures in Colonial New England* (Cambridge, Mass.: Harvard University Press, 2001), pp. 43–48; Linda Auwers Bissell, "From One Generation to Another: Mobility in Seventeenth-Century Windsor, Connecticut," *WMQ,* 3rd ser., 31 (1974): 79–110; W. R. Prest, "Stability and Change in Old and

New England: Clayworth and Dedham," *Journal of Interdisciplinary History* 6 (1976): 359–74; T. H. Breen and Stephen Foster, "Moving to the New World: The Character of Early Massachusetts Immigration," *WMQ,* 3rd ser., 30 (1973): 189–222. Modern town studies that gave the impression of persistence and stability in the population were, as Prest demonstrates for Dedham, based on faulty calculations.

12. Thomas Weld to his former parishioners, 1632, in Everett Emerson, ed., *Letters from New England: The Massachusetts Bay Colony, 1629–1638* (Amherst: University of Massachusetts Press, 1976), p. 97. Studies of English towns and counties amply document the tensions between the "godly" and their antagonists; see esp. Patrick Collinson, "Cranbrook and the Fletchers: Popular and Unpopular Religion in the Kentish Weald," in Collinson, *Godly People: Essays on English Protestantism and Puritanism* (London: Hambledon, 1983), pp. 399–428.

13. *Winthrop Papers,* 3:216; Caulkins, *History of New London,* p. 57. Noting that a line is drawn through this order in the records, Caulkins speculates that it was never enforced.

14. Henry S. Nourse, ed., *The Early Records of Lancaster, Massachusetts, 1643–1725* (Lancaster, 1884), p. 28. For policies and practices relating to care of the poor, see Edward Warren Capen, *The Historical Development of the Poor Law of Connecticut* (New York: Columbia University Press, 1905), and below, Chapter Four.

15. *Second Report of the Record Commissioners of the City of Boston* (Boston, 1872), p. 5; Samuel A. Bates, ed., *Records of the Town of Braintree, 1640–1793* (Randolph, Mass., 1886), p. 2; Erastus Worthington, *The History of Dedham from the Beginning of Its Settlement* (Boston, 1827), p. 33; Henry R. Stiles, *The History of Ancient Wethersfield, Connecticut,* 2 vols. (New York, 1904), 1:78; Burt, *First Century of Springfield,* 1:164; *Hartford Town Votes,* p. 1.

16. Chase, *Haverhill,* p. 71.

17. Philip J. Greven, *Four Generations: Population, Land, and Family in Colonial Andover, Massachusetts* (Ithaca, N.Y.: Cornell University Press, 1970), chap. 3. That fifty-six households in Dorchester were able to sell their house lots in the course of moving to Connecticut in 1635 and 1636 bespeaks both a high level of activity and its benefits (Thistlethwaite, *Dorset Pilgrims,* p. 97).

18. *Recs. New Haven,* 2:567; [John Davenport], *A Discourse About Civil Government in a New Plantation Whose Design Is Religion* (Cambridge, Mass., 1663), p. 11.

19. Main provides a good brief overview in *Peoples of a Spacious Land,* pp. 53–61.

20. Arnold, *History of Rhode Island,* p. 121; LaFantasie, ed. *Correspondence of Roger Williams,* 1:53. In New Haven, the "planters" seem to have received the same kind of house lots others had, with family size taken into account for

future shares; they were also required to pay taxes (1646). The situation in Providence was immensely more complicated than my few words indicate; for a fuller account of the turmoil about land and rights, see Sydney V. James, *The Colonial Metamorphoses in Rhode Island: A Study of Institutions in Change* (Hanover, N.H.: University Press of New England, 2000), pp. 15–17.

21. Nourse, ed., *Early Records of Lancaster,* p. 41.

22. These regional differences as played out in Massachusetts are described in Powell, *Puritan Village;* John J. Waters, "Hingham, Massachusetts, 1631–1660: An East Anglian Oligarchy in the New World," *Journal of Social History* I (1967–68): 351–70; Richard P. Gildrie, *Salem, Massachusetts, 1626–1683; A Covenant Community* (Charlottesville: University Press of Virginia, 1975); and esp. David Grayson Allen, *In English Ways: Movements of Societies and Transferral of English Local Law and Custom to Massachusetts Bay, 1600–1650* (Chapel Hill: University of North Carolina Press, 1981). I have elected to generalize about practices, as contrasted with the much more particular analysis found in Allen.

23. Caulkins, *History of New London,* p. 48; Sewall, *History of Woburn,* p. 17n. See also Steiner, *History of Guilford,* p. 168; George D. Langdon, Jr., *Pilgrim Colony: A History of New Plymouth 1620–1691* (New Haven: Yale University Press, 1966), p. 35; Isabel M. Calder, ed., *The Letters of John Davenport, Puritan Divine* (New Haven: Yale University Press, 1937), p. 67.

24. Roger F. Thompson, *Divided We Stand: Watertown, Massachusetts, 1630–1680* (Amherst: University of Massachusetts Press, 2001), pp. 51–52; Hill, ed., *Dedham Records,* p. 92.

25. Greven, *Four Generations,* pp. 45–47; Jewett and Jewett, *Rowley, Massachusetts,* pp. 20, 23 (noting that church records before 1665 have been lost).

26. Kenneth Lockridge, *A New England Town: The First Hundred Years* (New York: W. W. Norton, 1970), pp. 9–10; Steiner, *History of Guilford,* p. 49; *Hartford Town Votes,* pp. 21–24; Chase, *Haverhill,* p. 56; Edward S. Perzel, "Landholding in Ipswich," *Essex Institute Historical Society Collections* 104 (1968): 303–28; James Russell Trumbull, *History of Northampton, Massachusetts, from Its Settlement in 1654,* 2 vols. (Northampton, 1898–1903), 1:7, 14; Gildrie, *Salem, Massachusetts,* pp. 56–57; Powell, *Puritan Village,* chap. 6; Thompson, *Divided We Stand,* chap. 5; Thistlethwaite, *Dorset Pilgrims,* pp. 139–40; William J. Davisson and Dennis J. Dugan, "Land Precedents in Essex County, Massachusetts," *Essex Institute Historical Collections* 106 (1970): 252–76. See also John Raymond Hall, "The Three Rank System of Land Distribution in Colonial Swansea, Massachusetts," *Rhode Island History* 43 (1984): 3–18, and the case study of Cambridge, below, in Chapter Five.

27. *Recs. New Haven,* 1:368. Another means of doing so was to license those in need to sell wine or strong drink from their homes.

28. Edward Johnson, *The Wonder-Working Providence of Sions Saviour in New England,* ed. J. Franklin Jameson (New York: Scribner, 1910), p. 213.

29. Hill, ed., *Dedham Records,* pp. 30, 47, 144–45; Burt, *First Century of Springfield,* 1:173–74; Steiner, *History of Guilford,* pp. 49, 50; for New Haven's response to complaints by the poor or less favored, see *Recs. New Haven,* 1:144, 164. Similar agitation and response occurred in Plymouth Colony in the 1630s; see *Laws, 1623–1682,* vol. 11 of *Recs. Plymouth,* pp. 14, 16.

30. *Hartford Town Votes,* p. 14.

31. LaFantasie, ed., *Correspondence of Roger Williams,* 2:400; see also 1:220; James, *Colonial Metamorphoses,* p. 16; Nourse, ed., *Early Records of Lancaster,* p. 29.

32. Powell, *Puritan Village,* p. 83; for similar language, see Lockridge, *New England Town,* p. 71.

33. Thompson, *Divided We Stand,* p. 60; Charles M. Andrews, *The River Towns of Connecticut* (Baltimore, 1889), p. 43 n. 1. It is easy to misread the consciousness of "class" among the colonists; a community as uneasy as Guilford was about discrepancies in social power also recognized, in the words of a group of residents creating a new village out of town lands, that they would be helped by having "some of better quality . . . to goe and set downe with them to be helpful in several wayes for their encouragement" (Steiner, *History of Guilford,* p. 168).

34. Winthrop, *Journal,* p. 138; Darrett Rutman, *Winthrop's Boston: Portrait of a Puritan Town, 1630–1649* (New York: W. W. Norton, 1972), pp. 72–89. For tensions in Watertown, see Thompson, *Divided We Stand,* pp. 60–61, 63, where a clean sweep of selectmen in 1647 is linked to these issues. Looking back on the 1630s, Joshua Scottow acknowledged the plight of the poor but recast the situation as one of self-sacrificing generosity among the "Mean Ones" in Boston, who, putting Christianity before prosperity, agreed that "he who had but an Acre of Land for his House Lot, parted with one half of it to a desireable Neighbour" ([Joshua Scottow], *A Narrative of the Planting of the Massachusets Colony Anno 1628* [Boston, 1694], reprinted in *Coll. MHS,* 4th ser., 4 [1858]: 307). Turning the other cheek does not seem to be the primary motive of the "generality" in 1630s Boston.

35. Powell, *Puritan Village,* p. 38. The inequities of the English system are described in Anthony Fletcher, *A County Community in Peace and War: Sussex, 1600–1660* (London: Longman, 1975), chap. 10.

36. "Salem Town Records," *Essex Institute Historical Collections* 5 (1863): 223. For other examples, see *Hartford Town Votes,* p. 14; *Recs. Plymouth,* 1:91; Steiner, *History of Guilford,* p. 50.

37. *Recs. New Haven,* 1:97; *New-Haven's Settling in New England, and Some Lawes for Government* (London, 1656), reprinted ibid., 2:581; *Recs. Plymouth* 11.

38. *Recs. Mass.*, 1:140, 240, 295; 3:87–88; *Recs. New Haven*, 1:60; 2:581–82; *Recs. Conn.*, p. 79.

39. Burt, *First Century of Springfield*, 1:307; Sewall, *History of Woburn*, p. 24.

40. Thistlethwaite, *Dorset Pilgrims*, p. 166; *Coll. MHS*, 2nd ser., 10 (1843): 187. In other towns, such as Cambridge, the position of constable was held by high-status men.

41. Johnson, *Wonder-Working Providence*, p. 259n.; *Recs. Mass.* 4, pt. 1:37–38; *Recs. New Haven*, 2:23–24, 47. See also Burt, *First Century of Springfield*, 1:282–83, 302. Every aspect of taxes and taxation deserves much fuller attention than I give them here.

42. Bissell, "From One Generation to the Next," p. 82; Allen, *In English Ways*, p. 210, adding (as I do as well) an emphasis on geographic mobility (p. 215); Steiner, *History of Guilford*, p. 50.

43. *A Relation, or Journal* (London, 1622), reprinted in Edward Arber, *The Story of the Pilgrim Fathers, 1606–1623 A.D.* (London, 1897), 409.

44. Kenyon, *Stuart Constitution*, p. 232. As Dietrich Rueschemeyer points out, participation in modern societies does not always abet democracy if a voluntary group—regarded by theorizers from Tocqueville onward as key to participation—is not organized democratically or favors a different political system. Although the specifics of his argument have little pertinence to the seventeenth century, this warning (like others about trying to read "democracy" back into the past) informs the rest of this chapter. (Rueschemeyer, "The Self-Organization of Society and Democratic Rule: Specifying the Relationship," in *Participation and Democracy, East and West: Comparisons and Interpretations*, ed. Dietrich Rueschemeyer et al. [Armonk, N.Y.: M. E. Sharpe, 1998], pp. 9–25.) Had I come on Phil Withington, *The Politics of Commonwealth: Citizens and Freemen in Early Modern England* (Cambridge: Cambridge University Press, 2005), before I completed this book, I would have aligned some of my description of participation with his of "popular political participation." For reasons I outline briefly in *Ways of Writing: The Practice and Politics of Text-Making in Seventeenth-Century New England* (Philadelphia: University of Pennsylvania Press, 2008), chap. 5, I am wary of the term "public sphere." But see Peter Lake and Steve Pincus, "Rethinking the Public Sphere in Early Modern England," *Journal of British Studies* 45 (2006): 270–92, a reference I owe to Rachel Schneppers.

45. *Hartford Town Votes*, pp. 11–12.

46. One example must suffice: after Joseph Parsons of Northampton died in 1684, his wife and children rewrote his will in a court-approved process (the will was out of date); four sons, four daughters, and his wife signed the agreement (Henry M. Burt, *Cornet Joseph Parsons* [Garden City, N.Y., 1898], pp. 68–71).

47. Stephen Innes, "Introduction," in *Work and Labor in Early America,* ed. Innes (Chapel Hill: University of North Carolina Press, 1988), p. 37.

48. "The Trial of Ezekiel Cheever Before the Church at New Haven," *Collections of the Connecticut Historical Society* 1 (1860): 24; "Scituate and Barnstable Church Records," *NEHGR* 10 (1856): 41; Mary McManus Ramsbottom, "Religious Society and the Family in Charlestown, Massachusetts, 1630 to 1740" (Ph.D. diss., Yale University, 1987), chap. 2; Hall, *AC,* p. 393. At the Massachusetts General Court session of October 1650, ten women submitted petitions (two of them jointly with their husbands), and eleven men (*Recs. Mass.* 4, pt. 1:30–34). The most substantial mobilizing against the civil state occurred in 1649, when "five groups of women ranging in size from twenty-one to 130—each claiming to represent 'a greate many more'—flooded the General Court with petitions" protesting the treatment of the midwife Alice Tilley (Mary Beth Norton, *Founding Mothers & Fathers: Gendered Power and the Forming of American Society* [New York: Alfred A. Knopf, 1996], pp. 204–5; other aspects of women's participation, including gossip, are usefully described in this book). The earliest studies of women in seventeenth-century New England framed their history in terms of "powerlessness" and "resistance"; see, e.g., Lyle Koehler, *A Search for Power: The "Weaker Sex" in Seventeenth-Century New England* (Urbana: University of Illinois Press, 1980). More recent work, and especially studies of women in seventeenth-century England, have greatly expanded both the evidence of women's participation and the interpretive possibilities. See Patricia Crawford, " 'The Poorest She': Women and Citizenship in Early Modern England," in *The Putney Debates of 1647: The Army, the Levellers and the English State,* ed. Michael Mendle (Cambridge: Cambridge University Press, 2001), pp. 197–218, citing, among other studies not yet replicated for New England, a body of work on women as petitioners. This paragraph is informed as well by Susan Amussen, "Gender, Family, and the Social Order, 1560–1725," in *Order and Disorder in Early Modern England,* ed. Anthony Fletcher and John Stevenson (Cambridge: Cambridge University Press, 1985), pp. 196–217; Roger F. Thompson, *Sex in Middlesex: Popular Mores in a Massachusetts County, 1649–1699* (Amherst: University of Massachusetts Press, 1986); Amanda Porterfield, *Female Piety in Puritan New England: The Emergence of Religious Humanism* (New York: Oxford University Press, 1992); Dagmar Freist, *Governed by Opinion: Politics, Religion and the Dynamics of Communication in Stuart London, 1637–1645* (London: I. B. Tauris, 1997), chaps. 5–6; and Laurel Ulrich, "Martha Ballard and Her Girls," in *Work and Labor in Early America,* ed. Innes, pp. 70–105.

49. Keith Thomas, "The Levellers and the Franchise," in *The Interregnum: The*

Quest for Settlement, 1646–1660, ed. G. E. Aylmer (London: Macmillan, 1972), pp. 60–61.

50. George Selement and Bruce C. Woolley, eds., *Thomas Shepard's Confessions,* in *Pub. CSM* 58 (1981): 106–9, 65–66; Francis J. Bremer, "The Heritage of John Winthrop: Religion Along the Stour Valley, 1548–1630," *New England Quarterly* 70 (1997): 515–47; Clifford K. Shipton, "The Autobiographical Memoranda of John Brock, 1636–1659," *Proceedings of the American Antiquarian Society* 53 (1943): 97.

51. Michael McGiffert, *God's Plot: The Paradoxes of Puritan Piety, Being the Autobiography & Journal of Thomas Shepard* (Amherst: University of Massachusetts Press, 1972), p. 47; John Cotton, *The Way . . . Cleared* (London, 1648), reprinted in Larzer Ziff, *John Cotton on the Churches of New England* (Cambridge, Mass.: Harvard University Press, 1968), p. 217; Emerson, ed., *Letters from New England,* p. 167; Hall, *Ways of Writing,* chap. 2.

52. The informal negotiations around candidates are largely lost to us for the 1630s and 1640s but highly visible after 1650; see Hall, *Faithful Shepherd,* chap. 8.

53. *Winthrop Papers,* 4:32; Nathaniel Morton, *New-Englands Memoriall* (Cambridge, Mass., 1669), pp. 80–81.

54. Winthrop, *Journal,* pp. 204, 210; *Recs. Mass.,* 1:189; *Winthrop Papers,* 3:324–26; Hall, *Ways of Writing,* pp. 54–60.

55. Winthrop, *Journal,* pp. 343–44; *Winthrop Papers,* 4:286–87; 6:113–29; *Recs. Conn.,* pp. 97, 98.

56. Winthrop, *Journal,* pp. 151, 346–47.

57. Don Gleason Hill, ed., *The Record of Baptisms, Marriages and Deaths, and Admissions to the Church . . . in the Town of Dedham, Massachusetts* (Dedham, Mass., 1888), pp. 9–10; Whitmore, *Colonial Laws,* p. 57; Joseph Felt, *The Ecclesiastical History of New England,* 2 vols. (Boston, 1862), 2:53–54, 60, 62, 69; *Recs. Mass.,* 3:294; Deloraine P. Corey, *The History of Malden Massachusetts, 1633–1785* (Malden, 1899), pp. 126–64. The women's petition is printed in *The Bi-Centennial Book of Malden* (Boston, 1850), p. 140.

58. *Recs. Mass.,* 3:293–94, 359–60; 4, pt. 1:177; Chandler Robbins, *A History of the Second Church, or Old South, in Boston* (Boston, 1853), pp. 210–11; Felt, *Ecclesiastical History,* 2:96; Corey, *History of Malden,* pp. 160–61; Chase, *History of Haverhill,* p. 80.

59. Thomas Hooker, *A Survey of the Summe of Church-Discipline* (London, 1648), pt. 3, p. 6.

60. Winthrop, *Journal,* p. 275. In other places there were protests against the "gathered" concept of church membership; a few of these are noted in Hall, *Faithful Shepherd,* p. 97.

61. Jeremy Dupertuis Bangs, ed., *The Seventeenth-Century Town Records of Scituate, Massachusetts,* 3 vols. (Boston: New England Historic Genealogical Society, 2001), 3:513–14. Some months later, the offending members were reconciled with their brethren.

62. Robert G. Pope, ed., *The Notebook of the Reverend John Fiske, 1644–1675,* in *Pub. CSM* 47 (1977): 59–67 (an exceptionally drawn-out dispute).

63. Ibid., pp. 10, 12, 90–91, 3. Other congregations were more specific in their criticism of the *Platforme;* see Hall, *Faithful Shepherd,* pp. 116–17.

64. Cotton Mather, *Magnalia Christi Americana,* 2 vols. (1702; reprinted, Hartford, 1853–54), 1:437. See also George Leon Walker, "The Quarrel in Stone's Day," in Walker, *History of the First Church in Hartford, 1633–1883* (Hartford, 1884), pp. 146–81. James F. Cooper, Jr., *Tenacious of Their Liberties: The Congregationalists in Colonial Massachusetts* (New York: Oxford University Press, 1999), is the fullest description of the laity's energetic insistence on their privileges.

65. Whitmore, *Colonial Laws,* pp. 49, 35 (emphasis added); Langdon, *Pilgrim Colony,* p. 85.

66. Philip H. Round, *By Nature and By Custom Cursed: Transatlantic Civil Discourse and New England Cultural Production, 1620–1660* (Hanover, N.H.: University Press of New England, 1999), pp. 76–77; David Zaret, *Origins of Democratic Culture: Printing, Petitions, and the Public Sphere in Early-Modern England* (Princeton: Princeton University Press, 2000), chap. 3 (quotation, from a statement of 1536, is on p. 53); David Colclough, *Freedom of Speech in Early Stuart England* (Cambridge: Cambridge University Press, 2005); Freist, *Governed by Opinion,* introduction.

67. F. J. Levy, "How Information Spread Among the Gentry, 1550–1640," *Journal of British Studies* 21 (1982): 11–34; Richard Cust, "News and Politics in Early Seventeenth-Century England," *Past and Present* 112 (1986): 60–90.

68. These aspects of English practice are described in Adam Fox, *Oral and Literate Culture in England, 1500–1700* (Oxford: Clarendon, 2000), chap. 6; Joad Raymond, *Pamphlets and Pamphleteering in Early Modern Britain* (Cambridge: Cambridge University Press, 2003); Hall, *Ways of Writing,* pp. 121–22.

69. Hall, *AC,* p. 207; Whitmore, *Colonial Laws,* p. 57; Stephen Foster, *The Long Argument: English Puritanism and the Shaping of New England Culture, 1570–1700* (Chapel Hill: University of North Carolina Press, 1991), pp. 95–96.

70. Winthrop, *Journal,* pp. 107, 109; *Winthrop Papers,* 3:146–49; Hall, *Ways of Writing,* chap. 2; David D. Hall, "Scribal Publication in Seventeenth-Century New England: A Second Checklist," *Proceedings of the American Antiquarian Society* 118 (2008): 267–96.

71. For one example, see *Winthrop Papers,* 3:76. A fuller history of rumor in (and about) New England is needed.

72. Hall, *Ways of Writing*, p. 30; Bangs, *Town Records of Scituate, Massachusetts*, 3:512; Hall, *AC*, pp. 212–13.

73. Hall, *AC*, pp. 251–52; Winthrop, *Journal*, pp. 483, 584.

74. *Recs. Conn.*, p. 39.

75. Winthrop, *Journal*, pp. 314–15.

76. William K. Holdsworth, "Law and Society in Colonial Connecticut, 1636–1672" (Ph.D. diss., Claremont University, 1974), p. 135. Prior to having printed codes, the colony governments were distributing handwritten copies, one for each town (William Brigham, *The Compact with the Charter of the Colony of New Plymouth* [Boston, 1836], p. ix; Holdsworth, "Law and Society," p. 125).

77. Winthrop, *Journal*, pp. 395–98, 453–54; *Winthrop Papers*, 4:349–52.

78. Winthrop, *Journal*, pp. 136–37, 195–98, 453–54; *Winthrop Papers*, 4:349–52; Arthur Prentice Rugg, "A Famous Colonial Litigation: The Case Between Richard Sherman and Capt. Robert Keayne, 1642," *Proceedings of the American Antiquarian Society* 30 (1920): 217–50.

79. Winthrop, *Journal*, pp. 443, 467–68; *Winthrop Papers*, 4:394; *Recs. New Haven*, 1:97; *Recs. Mass.*, 3:7, 18–19.

80. Felt, *Ecclesiastical History*, 2:57; *Recs. Conn.*, p. 97; *Records of the Particular Court of Connecticut 1639–1663* (Hartford: Connecticut Historical Society, 1928), p. 71.

81. Winthrop, *Journal*, p. 423; Thompson, *Divided We Stand*, p. 69.

82. David D. Hall, *Witch-Hunting in Seventeenth-Century New England: A Documentary History, 1638–1693* (Boston: Northeastern University Press, 1999), chap. 2.

83. Gail Sussman Marcus, " 'Due Execution of the Generall Rules of Righteousnesse': Criminal Procedure in New Haven Town and Colony, 1638–1658," in *Saints and Revolutionaries: Essays on Early American History*, ed. David Hall et al. (New York: W. W. Norton, 1984), pp. 99–137; three of the missing four suspects subsequently turned up.

84. Anthony Fletcher, "Honour, Reputation and Local Office-Holding in Elizabethan and Stuart England," in Fletcher and Stevenson, eds., *Order and Disorder*, pp. 92–115. Because some witch trials are so fully documented, they make singularly visible the flexibilities of the justice system: witnesses disputing the evidence, juries refusing to convict, magistrates overruling a jury or improvising a penalty.

85. Edgar J. McManus, *Law and Liberty in Early New England: Criminal Justice and Due Process, 1620–1692* (Amherst: University of Massachusetts Press, 1993), app. C.

86. G. B. Warden, "The Rhode Island Civil Code of 1647," in Hall et al., eds., *Saints and Revolutionaries*, p. 149.

87. Marcus, " 'Due Execution,' " passim (quotation on p. 121); *Records of Particular Court,* p. 32. Thus, most of the fines or other penalties levied on the men who signed a petition favoring John Wheelwright were eventually canceled. For the role of confession in this culture, see David D. Hall, *Worlds of Wonder, Days of Judgment: Popular Religious Belief in Early New England* (New York: Alfred A. Knopf, 1989), chap. 4, and also below, Chapter Four. A fuller study of reconciliation as idea and practice is needed.

88. McManus, *Law and Liberty,* pp. 70–71, 174; Jules Zanger, "Crime and Punishment in Early Massachusetts," *WMQ,* 3rd ser., 22 (1965): 471–77, noting no executions at all in Connecticut and, more generally, the prevalence of fines in place of corporal punishment.

89. Keith Thomas, "The Puritans and Adultery: the Act of 1650 Reconsidered," in *Puritans and Revolutionaries: Essays in Seventeenth-Century History Presented to Christopher Hill,* ed. Donald Pennington and Keith Thomas (Oxford: Clarendon, 1978), pp. 257–82 (quotation on p. 257); Holdsworth, "Law and Society," p. 191, noting the "scarcity of offences" for nonattendance or refusal to contribute to a minister's maintenance and the utter absence of executions for neglecting the Sabbath. Important light is shed on the differences between stated law and social practice by Philip Benedict's careful review of data on church discipline within Reformed communities in Europe and Britain, demonstrating similar discrepancies, often because full enforcement jeopardized social peace (Philip Benedict, *Christ's Churches Purely Reformed: A Social History of Calvinism* [New Haven: Yale University Press, 2002], chap. 11).

90. "The overwhelming evidence for . . . parental evenhandedness, combined as it was with parity in age of marriage among brothers, sorely undercuts darker images of paternal despotism in Puritan New England" (Main, *Peoples of a Spacious Land,* p. 79, correcting previous arguments about fathers' control over sons). The same point is made even more emphatically in Barry Levy, *Town Born: The Political Economy of New England from Its Founding to the Revolution* (Philadelphia: University of Pennsylvania Press, 2009), chap. 9.

91. McManus, *Law and Liberty,* app. C. These statements are based on the tables in this appendix and on Thompson, *Sex in Middlesex,* chap. 2, "Courtship and Patriarchial Authority"; chap. 3, "Pregnant Brides and Broken Promises"; and chap. 5, "Adolescent Culture"; as well as Holdsworth, "Law and Society," chap. 5, "Law and the Family," and pp. 355–56, where he notes the rarity of mutilations and pillorying of criminals. Women or servants who had young children to care for were unable to attend most church services, and children themselves never were present.

92. Margaret Spufford, "Puritanism and Social Control?," in Fletcher and Stevenson, eds., *Order and Disorder,* pp. 41–57. For a specific example, see John

Noble and John F. Cronin, eds., *Records of the Court of Assistants of the Colony of the Massachusetts Bay, 1630–1692*, 3 vols. (Boston: Suffolk County, 1901–28), 3:34–35.

93. Zaret, *Origins of Democratic Culture*, pp. 85, 82.

94. Winthrop, *Journal*, p. 453; *Recs. Mass.*, 2:20. My account ignores petitions from any of the colonial governments to Parliament or committees thereof. Whether to count the entries in the Massachusetts records that imply a petition but do not use the word itself is among the uncertainties that stand in the way of exactitude. For the figure that follows in the next paragraph, I have counted some of these. If petitions to towns, congregations, and courts were added to this figure, the total would easily double.

95. *NEHGR* 2 (1848): 44–45; Lemuel Shattuck, *A History of the Town of Concord, Middlesex County, Massachusetts* (Boston, 1835), 152n.; Bernard Bailyn, *The Apologia of Robert Keayne: The Self-Portrait of a Puritan Merchant* (New York: Harper Torchbooks, 1965), p. 48.

96. *Winthrop Papers*, 3:432–33. When the Massachusetts General Court wedged Rowley between already founded Ipswich and Newbury, the predictable outcome was a steady drizzle of petitions (Jewett and Jewett, *Rowley, Massachusetts,* passim).

97. *Recs. Mass.*, 2:51, 64; Winthrop, *Journal*, pp. 611, 629.

98. David Zaret, "Petitions and the 'Invention' of Public Opinion in the English Revolution," *American Journal of Sociology* 101 (1996): 1497–1555 (quotation, p. 1499). As Zaret has pointed out (p. 1513), the practice of petitioning was acceptable because it satisfied the criterion of deference and made no "claims about the supremacy of popular will over petitioned authority."

99. *Hutchinson Papers*, 2 vols. (Albany: Prince Society, 1865), 1:72–74.

100. Zaret, *Origins of Democratic Culture*, pp. 90–91.

101. *Winthrop Papers*, 4:8–9; *Recs. Mass.*, 3:17–26; Winthrop, *Journal*, pp. 575–95, 617. The editors of the *Winthrop Papers* propose January 1638 as the date of Winthrop's response to the petitioners of 1637, but the context suggests 1637.

102. George Lyman Kittridge, "Dr. Robert Child, Remonstrant," *Pub. CSM* 21 (1919): 1–146; Edward Winslow, *New-Englands Salamander, Discovered* (London, 1647), reprinted in *Coll. MHS*, ser. 3, 2 (1830): 120.

103. *Recs. Conn.*, pp. 86, 90, 97–99; *Winthrop Papers*, 4:9.

104. *Recs. Mass.*, 1:189, 207–9, 213. The possibilities for voicing political criticism are described more fully in Hall, *Ways of Writing*, chap. 5.

105. The best point of entry to this literature is B. Katherine Brown, "The Controversy over the Franchise in Puritan Massachusetts, 1954 to 1974," *WMQ*, 3rd ser., 33 (1976): 212–41, which cites the relevant scholarship; see also James A. Thorpe, "Colonial Suffrage in Massachusetts: A Review Essay," *Essex Insti-*

tute Historical Collections 106 (1970): 169–81. For Plymouth, see George D. Langdon, Jr., "The Franchise and Political Democracy in Plymouth Colony," *WMQ*, 3rd ser., 20 (1963): 513–26; for New Haven, Bruce C. Steiner, "Dissension at Quinnipiac: The Authorship and Setting of *A Discourse about Civil Religion in a New Plantation Whose Design Is Religion*," *New England Quarterly* 54 (1981): 31, 31 n. 59; for Connecticut, David H. Fowler, "Connecticut's Freemen: The First Forty Years," *WMQ*, 3rd ser., 15 (1958): 312–33; for Rhode Island, Sydney V. James, "Rhode Island: From Classical Democracy to British Province," *Rhode Island History* 43 (1984): 124. Samuel Eliot Morison calculated the percentage for Roxbury, Massachusetts, as 65 to 75 in 1640 (Morison, *Builders of the Bay Colony* [1936; revised, Boston: Houghton Mifflin, 1958], p. 381). For Cambridge, see below, Chapter Five. There is general agreement that the ratio of freemen to adult men began to widen after 1650 in Connecticut and Massachusetts.

106. John G. Palfrey, *History of New England During the Stuart Dynasty,* 3 vols. (Boston, 1865), 3:41 n. 3; the figure is repeated in James Truslow Adams, *The Founding of New England* (Boston: Little, Brown, 1921), p. 121, where it was simplified to one out of five, the same proportion adopted by Perry Miller in *The New England Mind: The Seventeenth Century* (Cambridge, Mass.: Harvard University Press, 1954), p. 440. In *Orthodoxy in Massachusetts, 1630–1650* (Cambridge, Mass.: Harvard University Press, 1933), Miller had characterized the connections between church membership and the franchise as establishing "a sort of religious soviet" (p. 243), an allusion possibly less compelling today than it was in 1933.

107. The dispute in Hingham turned in part on whether a local militia could elect its own lieutenant, a point picked up in the Child petition, which alleged that soldiers were denied this privilege. Responding, Edward Winslow insisted that the privilege was "common to the non-freemen [as] with such as are free" (Winslow, *New-Englands Salamander,* p. 121). Colony governments tended to require elections beyond the rank of sergeant to be approved by the government. The participatory aspects of militia companies are emphasized in T. H. Breen, "The Covenanted Militia of Massachusetts Bay: English Background and New World Development," in Breen, *Puritans and Adventurers: Change and Persistence in Early America* (New York: Oxford University Press, 1980), pp. 24–45.

108. *Mass. Recs.,* 2:197; *Recs. Conn.,* p. 23. Evidence for local voting cited in Brown, "Controversy," p. 229; in this same essay, she draws on two town studies in particular, Powell's *Puritan Village* and Lockridge's *New England Town.*

109. Steiner, *History of Guilford,* p. 36. So argued in Rutman, *Winthrop's Boston,* pp. 159–63n., although aspects of his evidence are questioned in T. H. Breen, "Who Governs: The Town Franchise in Seventeenth-Century Massachu-

setts," *WMQ,* 3rd ser., 27 (1970): 460–74. In a careful study of the role of admitted "inhabitants" and town voting, Martin argues that they were frequently involved (*Profits in the Wilderness,* pp. 167–75).

110. *Hartford Town Votes,* pp. 80–82; *Recs. Plymouth,* 11:6, 3:162.

111. *Recs. Mass.,* 2:38, 208; Winslow, *New-Englands Salamander,* p. 139 (admitting that "many that are not free" but describing them as unwilling to accept public service); Holdsworth, "Law and Society," p. 97; *NEHGR* 3 (1849): 41. During the Putney debates of 1647, Oliver Cromwell asked the men who pushed for popular sovereignty a leading question. Were "the people of this Nation . . . prepared" to exercise the privilege of voting? he wondered. For Cromwell and most of his contemporaries, voting was less a freestanding right than a practice framed in terms of reciprocity or obligation (Mendle, ed., *Putney Debates,* p. 116).

112. As with other aspects of participation, the English side of the story—in this case, elections to the House of Commons—is a necessary starting point. One historian of voting has observed that "few" people in early Stuart England "succeeded in thinking coherently on the matter." Among the certainties is that, as of 1620, a very small number of these elections were publicly contested, with candidates reaching out to voters for support, although rivals within the county aristocracy and upper gentry tried privately to outmaneuver one another when new elections were taking place. In general, elections were moments when "patronage and connection predominated." A second certainty concerns the property requirement for the franchise. It was up to each county to decide who owned or received the amounts that satisfied this requirement. They did so in inconsistent and confusing ways, in part because a long-term process of inflation was raising people's incomes in the early seventeenth century. Derek Hirst, *The Representative of the People? Voters and Voting in England Under the Early Stuarts* (Cambridge: Cambridge University Press, 1975), p. 13; Mark A. Kishlansky, *Parliamentary Selection: Social and Political Choice in Early Modern England* (Cambridge: Cambridge University Press, 1986), emphasizing the absence of contests.

113. Thistlethwaite, *Dorset Pilgrims,* pp. 158–60; Robert E. Wall, *Massachusetts Bay: The Crucial Decade, 1640 to 1650* (New Haven: Yale University Press, 1978), for the percentages of turnover; and see below, Chapter Five.

114. This interpretation is indebted to Kishlansky, *Parliamentary Selection,* esp. preface and chap. 1.

CHAPTER THREE. GODLY RULE

1. John Cotton, *An Exposition upon the Thirteenth Chapter* (London, 1655), pp. 20, 32.

2. John Cotton, *The Powring out of the Seven Vials: Or, An exposition of the 16. Chapter of the Revelation* (London, 1642), p. 84; Cotton, *Thirteenth Chapter*, pp. 4–7.

3. John Cotton, *The Churches Resurrection Or, The Opening of the Fifth and Sixth Verses of the 20th Chap. of the Revelation* (London, 1642), pp. 8, 16; *Winthrop Papers*, 4:36, 3:133. An early and still-pertinent description of the colonists' thinking is James F. Maclear, "New England and the Fifth Monarchy: The Quest for the Millennium in Early American Puritanism," *WMQ*, 3rd ser., 32 (1975): 223–60.

4. B. S. Capp, *The Fifth Monarchy Men: A Study in Seventeenth-Century English Millenarianism* (London: Faber and Faber, 1972), p. 108.

5. John C. Miller, ed., *The Works of Thomas Goodwin*, 12 vols. (Edinburgh, 1861–66), 3:15; *Winthrop Papers*, 3:56; Crawford Gribben, *The Puritan Millennium: Literature and Theology, 1550–1682* (Milton Keynes, U.K.: Paternoster, 2008), pp. 119–20; Gardiner, *Constitutional Documents*, p. 125.

6. A. S. P. Woodhouse, *Puritanism and Liberty* (Chicago: University of Chicago Press, 1951), p. 233. Published anonymously, *A Glimpse of Sions Glory* is usually attributed to Thomas Goodwin and may be based on a sermon he preached in the Netherlands while he was living there at the close of the 1630s. The Baptist William Kniffin may have been responsible for transmitting the text to the press. *A Glimpse* is reattributed to Jeremiah Burroughs in Paul Christianson, *Reformers and Babylon: English Apocalyptic Visions from the Reformation to the Eve of the Civil War* (Toronto: University of Toronto Press, 1978), pp. 251–52.

7. Peter Toon, *The Correspondence of John Owen* (Cambridge: James Clarke, 1970), pp. 29–30; John F. Wilson, *Pulpit in Parliament: Puritanism During the English Civil Wars, 1640–1648* (Princeton, N.J.: Princeton University Press, 1969), chap. 6; Capp, *Fifth Monarchy Men*, chap. 1; Christopher Hill, *The World Turned Upside Down: Radical Ideas During the English Revolution* (New York: Viking, 1972); *Reverend M. Brightmans Iudgment on Prophecies which shall befall Germany, Scotland, Holland, and the Churches adhering to them: With what shall befall England, and the Hierarchies therein . . . Declaring that the Reformation begun in Queene Elizabeth's dayes, is not sufficient for us under Greater light* (London, 1642). The dismay of moderate and Presbyterian-inclined reformers is registered in Thomas Edwards, *Gangraena* (London, 1646).

8. W[illiam] A[spinwall], *The Legislative Power Is Christ's Peculiar Prerogative* (London, 1656), p. 4.

9. Vane, "A briefe Answer to a certaine declaration, made of the intent and equitye of the order of court, that none should be received to inhabite within this jurisdiction but such as should be allowed by some of the magistrates,"

in [Thomas Hutchinson], *A Collection of Original Papers Relative to the History of the Colony of Massachusetts-Bay* (Boston, 1769), p. 75.

10. Sixteenth- and seventeenth-century English versions of the concept are described in William M. Lamont, *Godly Rule: Politics and Religion, 1603–1660* (London: Macmillan, 1969). Scholarship on biblical prophecy among the colonists has been dominated by arguments for their "millenarianism." See below, note 15.

11. Edward Johnson, *The Wonder-Working Providence of Sions Saviour in New England,* ed. J. Franklin Jameson (New York: Scribner, 1910), p. 25. The "Epistle Written by the Elders" was incorporated into John Ball, *A Tryall of the New-Church Way in New-England and in Old* (London, 1644).

12. Vane's thinking is described in David Parnham, *Sir Henry Vane, Theologian: A Study in Seventeenth-Century Religious and Political Discourse* (Madison, N.J.: Fairleigh Dickinson University Press, 1997), and in Parnham, "Politics Spun Out of Theology and Prophecy: Sir Henry Vane on the Spiritual Environment of Public Power," *History of Political Thought* 22 (2001): 53–83, a reference I owe to Monica Poole.

13. Winthrop, *Journal,* p. 132; Glenn W. LaFantasie, ed., *The Correspondence of Roger Williams,* 2 vols. (Hanover, N.H.: University Press of New England, 1988), 1:68; W. Clark Gilpin, *The Millenarian Piety of Roger Williams* (Chicago: University of Chicago Press, 1979). Godly rule was not for everyone, at least not in some of its details. A handful of Presbyterian clergy among the colonists, most notably James Noyes of Newbury, Massachusetts, contested the lay-centered governance of the Congregational Way. As noted below, Connecticut and Plymouth never tied voting rights to church membership. With very few exceptions, ministers and laypeople continued to sustain the "external" sacraments of baptism and the Lord's Supper, together with academic learning, in contrast to assertions by some Puritans that the Holy Spirit rendered these unnecessary.

14. *Recs. New Haven,* 1:12.

15. John Eliot, *The Christian Commonwealth: Or, The Civil Policy of the Rising Kingdom of Jesus Christ* (London, 1659), sig. [A4r]. My purpose in this chapter must be differentiated from two other inquiries that rely on some of the same texts I am using. First are efforts to describe the "errand" of the colonists as "millenarian" in the sense of expecting the imminent thousand-year reign of Christ, and New England as the place where the final "New Jerusalem" would be established. As Theodore Dwight Bozeman pointed out, the first argument relies on misreadings of the scriptural and theological language in John Winthrop's "Modell of Christian Charitie," among other texts, and on a failure to differentiate the millennium of Revelation from the phases of reform specified by Thomas Brightman. The second error is to

regard the colonists as expecting New England to play a unique role in the end times. The better scholarship includes Bozeman, *To Live Ancient Lives: The Primitivist Dimension in Puritanism* (Chapel Hill: University of North Carolina Press, 1988); Reiner Smolinski, "Apocalypticism in Colonial North America," in *The Encyclopedia of Apocalypticism,* ed. Bernard McGinn et al., 3 vols. (New York: Continuum, 1998), 3:36–71; and Jeffrey K. Jue, *Heaven upon Earth: Joseph Mede (1586–1638) and the Legacy of Millenarianism* (Dordrecht, Netherlands: Springer, 2006), chap. 9. Older studies that remain useful include Joy Gilsdorf, *The Puritan Apocalypse: New England Eschatology in the Seventeenth Century* (New York: Garland, 1999), and Michael Eugene Mooney, "Millennialism and Antichrist in New England, 1630–1760" (Ph.D. diss., Syracuse University, 1982).

16. Miller, ed., *Works of Goodwin,* 3:127; Michael Fixler, *Milton and the Kingdoms of God* (Evanston, Ill.: Northwestern University Press, 1964), chap. 3. The anonymous interlocutor in [John Davenport], *A Discourse About Civil Government in a New Plantation Whose Design Is Religion* (Cambridge, Mass., 1663), raised the question of "Tyranny" (p. 8), as would others in England during the 1640s.

17. Christopher Hill, *Antichrist in Seventeenth-Century England* (London: Verso, 1990), p. 4. Lutheran precedents are described in Irena Backus, *Reformation Readings of the Apocalypse: Geneva, Zurich, and Wittenburg* (Oxford: Oxford University Press, 2000). Subsequent editions of the Geneva Bible strengthened the identification of the beast (or beasts) with Rome and the Antichrist (Basil Hall, "The Genevan Version of the English Bible: Its Aims and Achievements," in *The Bible, the Reformation and the Church: Essays in Honour of James Atkinson,* ed. W. P. Stephens [Sheffield: Sheffield Academic Press, 1995], pp. 124–49).

18. This paragraph and those that follow draw on the following studies of apocalypticism in English culture: Richard Bauckham, *Tudor Apocalypse: Sixteenth-Century Apocalypticism, Millenarianism and the English Reformation, from John Bale to John Foxe and Thomas Brightman* (Appleford, U.K.: Sutton Courtenay Press, 1978); Christianson, *Reformers and Babylon;* Katherine Firth, *The Apocalyptic Tradition in Reformation Britain, 1530–1645* (Oxford: Oxford University Press, 1979); and Gribben, *Puritan Millennium.* Anti-popery also figures in this mix; see, e.g., Peter Lake, "Anti-Popery: The Structure of a Prejudice," in *Conflict in Early Stuart England: Studies in Religion and Politics, 1603–1642,* ed. Richard Cust and Ann Hughes (London: Longman, 1989), pp. 72–106.

19. Lamont, *Godly Rule,* p. 42.

20. Ibid., p. 31; Gribben, *Puritan Millennium,* pp. 106–7.

21. Lamont, *Godly Rule,* p. 34.

22. Mooney, "Millennialism and Antichrist," p. 36 (quotation in n. 53).

23. Ibid., quoting [Robert Browne], *A True and Short Declaration, Both of the Gathering and Ioyning together of Certaine Persons* [c. 1584].

24. William Bradford, *Of Plymouth Plantation, 1620–1647,* ed. Samuel Eliot Morison (New York: Alfred A. Knopf, 1952), pp. 6–7; William Bradford, *A Dialogue or Third Conference Between Some Young Men Born in New England, and Some Ancient Men Which Came Out of Holland and Old England,* ed. Charles Deane (Boston, 1870), p. 8 and passim. Separatist versions of apocalypticism are described more fully in Christianson, *Reformers and Babylon,* chap. 2.

25. Cotton, *Thirteenth Chapter,* p. 87. Brightman was also cited favorably by Thomas Goodwin, the possible author of *A Glimpse of Sions Glory.*

26. Not identical to the thousand-year reign, or to the return of Christ in person, but a restoration of the true church that will happen as the Antichrist is being defeated, and, in this respect, looking ahead to the end times. The distinction between pre and post millennial interpretations of the thousand years, much remarked upon in studies of prophecy and apocalypticism in the eighteenth and subsequent centuries, has little bearing on the writers considered in this chapter.

27. Lamont, *Godly Rule,* pp. 50–51, 95; Christianson, *Reformers and Babylon,* pp. 100–107; Gilsdorf, *Puritan Apocalypse,* pp. 27–31.

28. Christianson, *Reformers and Babylon,* pp. 98–99; Jue, *Heaven upon Earth.*

29. George H. Williams et al., eds., *Thomas Hooker: Writings in England and Holland, 1626–1633* (Cambridge, Mass.: Harvard University Press, 1975), pp. 195–96; *Winthrop Papers,* 2:138–39; [Richard Mather], *Church-Government and Church-Covenant Discussed* (London, 1643), pp. 26–27.

30. Geoffrey F. Nuttall, *The Holy Spirit in Puritan Faith and Experience* (Oxford: Blackwell, 1946); David R. Como, *Blown by the Spirit: Puritanism and the Emergence of an Antinomian Underground in Pre–Civil War England* (Stanford: Stanford University Press, 2004).

31. John Davenport, *A Sermon Preach'd at the Election . . . 1669* ([Cambridge], 1670), p. 15; Cotton, *Thirteenth Chapter,* p. 87. Acknowledging his indebtedness to Brightman, though differing in some respects from his glossing of the seals and trumpets, Goodwin speculated that the overthrow of the Antichrist would happen by 1666 (Miller, ed., *Works of Goodwin,* 3:157–58).

32. Cotton, *Thirteenth Chapter,* p. 77.

33. John Cotton, *A Sermon . . . Deliver'd at Salem, 1636,* in Larzer Ziff, *John Cotton on the Churches of New England* (Cambridge, Mass.: Harvard University Press, 1968), pp. 56, 58, 47.

34. Cotton, *Powring Out,* fifth pagination, pp. 8, 3–4, 11, 21. Cotton's role in the development of Congregationalism (or Independency) in England is de-

scribed in Geoffrey F. Nuttall, *Visible Saints: The Congregational Way, 1640–1660* (Oxford: Blackwell, 1957), pp. 15–16.

35. Don Gleason Hill, ed., *The Record of Baptisms, Marriages, and Deaths, and Admissions to the Church . . . in the Town of Dedham, Massachusetts* (Dedham, Mass., 1888) p. 3; Hall, *Faithful Shepherd,* pp. 104–10.

36. Cotton, *Thirteenth Chapter,* p. 72; Cotton, *The True Constitution of a Particular Visible Church* (London, 1642), p. 5; LaFantasie, ed., *Correspondence of Roger Williams,* 1:24; [Mather], *Church-Government and Church-Covenant,* pp. 41–42.

37. Thomas Hooker, *A Survey of the Summe of Church-Discipline* (London, 1648), pp. 7–8; pt. 1: 188, 190.

38. Cotton, *True Constitution,* pp. 5–7; [Mather], *Church-Government and Church-Covenant,* p. 77. The underlying premise was a confidence in the workings of the Holy Spirit. "Certaine it is, that God doth speake by his Spirit in private Meditation and Prayers, and conferences with Brethren" (Cotton, *True Constitution,* p. 8).

39. John Owen, quoted in Nuttall, *Visible Saints,* p. 53; [Thomas Goodwin], *A Glimpse of Sions Glory* (London, 1641), p. 22; [Mather], *Church-Government and Church-Covenant,* p. 19; Cotton, *True Constitution,* p. 4; Cotton, *Churches Resurrection* , pp. 9, 11.

40. Everett Emerson, ed., *Letters from New England: The Massachusetts Bay Colony, 1629–1638* (Amherst: University of Massachusetts Press, 1976), p. 94.

41. As the Continental Reformed theologian Heinrich Bullinger recognized once he read the *Admonition* (W. J. Torrance Kirby, *The Zurich Connection and Tudor Political Theology,* Studies in the History of Christian Traditions 13 [Leiden: Brill, 2007], pp. 30–37). A similar uneasiness is apparent in *A Glimpse of Sions Glory,* as Christianson points out in *Reformers and Babylon,* pp. 216–17.

42. Cotton, *Thirteenth Chapter,* pp. 86–87; *CW Williams,* 3:50–51.

43. The "Model" survives only because Roger Williams incorporated it into *The Bloudy Tenent of Persecution* (London, 1644).

44. *CW Williams,* 3:222, 248–49. The ban on ministers' holding office, although informal and not written into statute law, was a basic principle of Reformed thinking on church and state.

45. Whitmore, *Colonial Laws,* p. 57. The "liberty" of having private meetings was a remarkable affirmation of voluntary religion in the aftermath of the dismay about the one conducted by Anne Hutchinson.

46. Sargent Bush, Jr., ed., *The Correspondence of John Cotton* (Chapel Hill: University of North Carolina Press, 2001), p. 245; for the same point in the "Model," see *CW Williams,* 3:223–24. Cartwright's original statement dates from the *Admonition* controversy of the 1570s (see John Ayre, ed., *The Works*

of John Whitgift, D.D., 3 vols. [Cambridge, 1851–53], 3:189). Whether he or anyone else in New England sanctioned resistance to ungodly magistrates is unclear. Though Francis J. Bremer points to a passage in a treatise of 1646 that seems to do so (Bremer, "In Defense of Regicide: John Cotton and the Execution of Charles I," *WMQ,* 3rd ser., 37 [1986]: 103–24), Hooker specifically ruled it out (*Survey,* pt. 2, p. 80). While in England, Ephraim Huit argued against such a premise (Huit, *The whole Prophecie of Daniel Explained* [London, 1643], p. 46).

47. James Calvin Davis, *The Moral Theology of Roger Williams: Christian Conviction and Public Ethics* (Louisville: Westminster John Knox Press, 2004), pp. 76–77. In *The Sincere Convert,* Thomas Shepard spoke in passing of conscience as "God's register, or notary, which is in every man . . . which telleth them there is a God," mentioning as well the "terrors of conscience" that strike those who turn away from God (Shepard, *Works,* 1:11).

48. Hooker, *Survey,* pt. 1:120–30; *CW Williams,* 3:42, 163, 48.

49. In the sermons Cotton preached on Canticles during his English ministry, he was much more emphatic about the role of "good Kings" to uphold "the purity of Religion," noting that "it is no impeachment" of a people's "Christianity liberty" for them to do so (*A Briefe Exposition of the Whole Book of Canticles* [London, 1642], p. 44). Later in the same sermons, he described the civil magistrates as "the head of the Church under Christ" (p. 213).

50. John Cotton, "How Far Moses' Judicialls Bind Mass[achusetts]," *Proc. MHS,* 2nd ser., 16 (1902): 276–84; John Cotton, *Powring Out,* second pagination, pp. 16–17; William Perkins, *A Commentary on Galatians,* ed. Gerald T. Sheppard (New York: Pilgrim Press, 1989), pp. 201, 202; *CW Williams,* 3:179; [Richard Mather], *An Apologie of the Churches in New-England for Church-Covenant* (London, 1643), p. 30 (adding, however, that any use of force was unjustifiable). Debating Williams, Cotton was drawn into citing Constantine favorably.

51. Davis, *Moral Theology,* pp. 84–85; Cotton, *Powring Out,* 17–18; John Cotton, *The Bloudy Tenent, Washed, and Made White in the Bloud of the Lambe* (London, 1647), pp. 9, 125. Cotton also specified that the process of correction began within a congregation using the normal apparatus of church discipline; *CW Williams,* 3:44–45.

52. Hooker, *Survey,* pt. 1, p. 13; Walker, *Creeds and Platforms,* pp. 234–37. Richard Gildrie has suggested that the language of *A Platforme* represented a riposte by the ministers to perceived excesses by the civil government (Gildrie, *Richard Mather of Dorchester* [Lexington: University Press of Kentucky, 1976], pp. 112–20, though I question his references to "Erastianism").

53. Patrick Collinson, *The Elizabethan Puritan Movement* (London: Jonathan Cape, 1967), pp. 195–97.

54. Whitmore, *Colonial Laws*, p. 57; *CW Williams*, 3:227. Some of the tensions around this rule are described in Hall, *Faithful Shepherd*, p. 135. The issue had come up during the Antinomian Controversy (Hall, *AC*, p. 243).

55. Cotton, *Thirteenth Chapter*, pp. 24–42.

56. Woodhouse, *Puritanism and Liberty*, pp. 242, 246.

57. *CW Williams*, 3:412–13.

58. Bush, ed., *Correspondence of John Cotton*, p. 245; Huit, *The whole Prophecie of Daniel*, p. 67. See also Shepard, *Works*, 3:339.

59. *Recs. New Haven*, 1:11–14.

60. Attributed to John Cotton in 1663, but in recent twentieth-century scholarship the text was definitively credited to Davenport, e.g., in Bruce E. Steiner, "Dissension at Quinnipiac: The Authorship and Setting of *A Discourse About Civil Government in a New Plantation Whose Design is Religion*," *New England Quarterly* 54 (1981): 14–32.

61. J. A. W. Gunn, *Politics and the Public Interest in the Seventeenth Century* (London: Routledge, 1969).

62. [Davenport], *Discourse*, pp. 14–16.

63. *Recs. Conn.*, p. 22; Bernard Steiner, *A History of the Plantation of Menunkatuck and of Guilford, Connecticut* (Baltimore, 1897), p. 35.

64. *The Works of Thomas Carlyle*, 30 vols. (London, 1897), 8:62, 64, 54, 58–59.

65. Capp, *Fifth Monarchy Men*, chap. 9.

66. Samuel Greene Arnold, *History of the State of Rhode Island and Providence Plantations 1636–1700* (Providence, 1894), p. 124; Howard M. Chapin, *Documentary History of Rhode Island*, vol. 2, *Being the History of the Towns of Portsmouth and Newport to 1647* (Providence: Preston and Rounds, 1919), pp. 48–49.

67. Richard W. Cogley, *John Eliot's Mission to the Indians Before King Philip's War* (Cambridge, Mass.: Harvard University Press, 1999), pp. 76–82, 111–12.

68. *Winthrop Papers*, 5:126. By "Jewes come in" he was referring to the widely accepted premise that, as the seventh seal was being opened and the end times were at hand, the Jews would be converted.

69. Hall, *AC*, pp. 412, 48, 226, 227, 236; Ziff, *Cotton on the Churches of New England*, pp. 62, 63.

70. Hall, *AC*, pp. 159–60, 166, 163, 273.

71. Ibid., p. 209.

72. Winthrop, *Journal*, p. 635; the letter of 1645 is printed in *Winthrop Papers*, 5:23–25. For Thomas Shepard's reaction to this turn of events in England, see below, Chapter Five. An overview of the "rise of toleration" is provided in William Haller, ed., *Tracts on Liberty in the Puritan Revolution, 1638–1647*, 3 vols. (New York: Columbia University Press, 1934).

73. *Winthrop Papers*, 5:56; George D. Langdon, Jr., *Pilgrim Colony: A History of*

New Plymouth, 1620–1691 (New Haven: Yale University Press, 1966), p. 65. The petitioner may have been William Vassall of Scituate. A year later, he was among the signers of the "Remonstrance and Petition" organized by Robert Child. The troubled situation of ministers in Plymouth is ably described in J. M. Bumsted, "A Well-Bounded Toleration: Church and State in the Plymouth Colony," *Journal of Church and State* 10 (1968): 265–79.

74. "A Remonstrance and Petition," *Hutchinson Papers,* 1:214–23.

75. J. T. Cliffe, *Puritans in Conflict: The Puritan Gentry During and After the Civil Wars* (London: Routledge, 1988), pp. 112–20. Poem quoted is John Milton, "On the Forcers of Conscience Under the Long Parliament." See also W[illiam] R[athband], *A Briefe Narration of Some Church Courses Held in Opinion and Practise in the Churches Lately Erected in New England* (London, 1644), p. 26. The push back against church discipline was led by an "Erastian" bloc (state over church) in the Long Parliament; no such bloc existed in New England.

76. A succinct description of these processes may be found in Hall, *Faithful Shepherd,* chaps. 5, 9, and 11.

77. William K. Holdsworth, "Law and Society in Colonial Connecticut, 1636–1672" (Ph.D. diss., Claremont University, 1972), p. 124.

78. New England appropriations of the figure of the saint as always and everywhere a persecuted remnant are described in Adrian Chastain Weimer, *Martyrs' Mirror: Persecution and Holiness in Early New England* (New York: Oxford University Press, forthcoming). See also John Cotton's comments on diversity in New England as of 1650 (Bush, ed., *Correspondence of John Cotton,* pp. 500–503).

79. Alexandra Walsham, *Charitable Hatred: Tolerance and Intolerance in England, 1500–1700* (Manchester, U.K.: Manchester University Press, 2006).

CHAPTER FOUR. AN EQUITABLE SOCIETY

1. Helen C. White, *Social Criticism in Popular Religious Literature of the Sixteenth Century* (New York: Macmillan, 1944); Alexandra Walsham, *Providence in Early Modern England* (Oxford: Oxford University Press, 1999), chaps. 2, 3, 6; David D. Hall, *Worlds of Wonder, Days of Judgment: Popular Religious Belief in Early New England* (New York: Alfred A. Knopf, 1989), chap. 2; John Harvard Ellis, ed., *The Works of Anne Bradstreet in Prose and Verse* (Charlestown, Mass., 1867), pp. 40–42, 61.

2. *Winthrop Papers,* 2:284, 288, 289.

3. This emphasis on the Pauline context is informed by John S. Coolidge, *The Pauline Renaissance in England: Puritanism and the Bible* (Oxford: Clarendon, 1970), with its analysis of "edification."

4. *The First and Second Prayer Books of Edward VI* (London: J. M. Dent, 1910), pp. 33, 378, 381, 385; Ian Green, *The Christian's ABC: Catechisms and Catechizing in England, c. 1530–1740* (Oxford: Clarendon, 1996), pp. 455, 457.

5. Margo Todd, *Christian Humanism and the Puritan Social Order* (Cambridge: Cambridge University Press, 1987); Quentin Skinner, *The Foundations of Modern Political Thought,* vol. 1, *The Renaissance* (Cambridge: Cambridge University Press, 1978), chap. 9.

6. Mark Fortier, *The Culture of Equity in Early Modern England* (Aldershot: Ashgate, 2005), pp. 88–91; J. H. Gleason, *The Justices of the Peace in England, 1558–1640* (Oxford: Clarendon, 1969), p. 13; Clive Holmes, *Seventeenth-Century Lincolnshire,* vol. 7 of *History of Lincolnshire,* ed. Maurice Barley (Lincoln, U.K.: History of Lincolnshire Committee, 1980), chap. 2; Edward Lambert, *History of the Colony of New Haven* (New Haven, 1838), p. 94.

7. *Winthrop Papers,* 2:143, 144.

8. Everett Emerson, ed., *Letters from New England: The Massachusetts Bay Colony, 1629–1638* (Amherst: University of Massachusetts Press, 1976), p. 97.

9. In what follows, I omit the much-studied topics of wealth and "calling" that Max Weber posited as central to an understanding of Puritan social ethics. Separately, Bernard Bailyn has argued that Puritanism embodied a "traditional" ethics centered on the concept of a "just price." Both arguments are effectively questioned in Stephen Foster, *Their Solitary Way: The Puritan Social Ethic in the First Century of Settlement in New England* (New Haven: Yale University Press, 1972); see also Todd, *Christian Humanism and the Puritan Social Order,* contesting Christopher Hill's interpretation of the social values of Puritanism as a class-based instrument of social control. Other important aspects of ethics and ethical practice omitted from this chapter include "oppression," Sabbatarianism, virtue, the moral rules for husbands, wives, and families, and Protestant casuistry, to which an influential guide was William Ames, *Conscience with the Power and Cases Thereof* (in Latin, 1630; in English, 1643).

10. See below, Chapter Five.

11. William Bradford, *Of Plymouth Plantation, 1620–1647,* ed. Samuel Eliot Morison (New York: Alfred A. Knopf, 1952), pp. 324–28; "Narrative Concerning the Settlement of New England," *Proc. MHS,* 1st ser., 5 (1862): 129–31.

12. John Cotton, *The True Constitution of a Particular Visible Church* (London, 1642), p. 8.

13. Cotton, *True Constitution,* p. 5; Jonathan Mitchell, *A Discourse of the Glory To which God hath called Believers* (London, 1677), pp. 51, 53; *Winthrop Papers,* 2:284, 290.

14. Walker, *Creeds and Platforms,* p. 156; Lambert, *History New Haven,* p. 101; Samuel Sewall, *The History of Woburn, Middlesex County, Massachusetts*

(Boston, 1868), p. 21; Lemuel Shattuck, *A History of the Town of Concord, Middlesex County, Massachusetts* (Boston, 1835), p. 151; Walker, *Creeds and Platforms,* p. 131.

15. Richard D. Pierce, ed., *The Records of the First Church in Boston, 1630–1868,* in *Pub. CSM* 39 (1961): 52.

16. The broader context is sketched in Hall, *Worlds of Wonder,* chap. 4.

17. Pierce, *Records of First Church Boston,* p. 20; *Roxbury Land and Church Records,* 2nd ed., *Sixth Report of the Record Commissioners* (Boston, 1881), pp. 78, 79; Walker, *Creeds and Platforms,* p. 212.

18. James F. Cooper and Kenneth P. Minkema, eds., *The Colonial Church Records of the First Church of Reading (Wakefield) and the First Church of Rumney Marsh (Revere),* in *Pub. CSM* 72 (2006): 70, 71.

19. Pierce, *Records of First Church Boston,* p. 21; Hall, *AC,* 356, 364, 368. As Winthrop noted in reference to one group of ex-antinomians (*Journal,* p. 321), "The elders and most of the church would have cast them out, as refusing to hear the church; but, all being not agreed, it was deferred."

20. *NEHGR* 4 (1850): 124, a pledge that encompassed the "inhabitants"; David D. Hall, *Witch-Hunting in Seventeenth-Century New England: A Documentary History, 1638–1693* (Boston: Northeastern University Press, 1999), p. 257.

21. But see Henry S. Nourse, ed., *The Early Records of Lancaster, Massachusetts, 1643–1725* (Lancaster, 1884), p. 18.

22. Walker, *Creeds and Platforms,* p. 213.

23. Bernard Bailyn, *The Apologia of Robert Keayne: The Self-Portrait of a Puritan Merchant* (New York: Harper Torchbooks, 1965), p. 20; *Essex Antiquarian* 1 (1897): 160; *Recs. Conn.,* pp. 488, 468–72; Charles William Manwaring, comp., *A Digest of the Early Connecticut Probate Records,* vol. 1, *Hartford District, 1635–1700* (Hartford, 1904), pp. 30, 43, 4. Gifts to the Plymouth congregation are noted in *NEHGR* 4 (1850): 33, 35.

24. *Essex Antiquarian* 1 (1897): 13; *Roxbury Land and Church Records,* pp. 76, 81; Manwaring, comp., *Digest,* p. 35; *Recs. Conn.,* p. 471.

25. *Essex Antiquarian* 2 (1898): 161; *NEHGR* 2 (1848): 261; *NEHGR* 7 (1853): 337, 335; Bailyn, *Apologia of Robert Keayne,* pp. 41–42.

26. Don Gleason Hill, ed., *The Early Records of the Town of Dedham, Massachusetts, 1636–1659* (Dedham, Mass., 1892), p. 2; Nourse, ed., *Early Records of Lancaster,* pp. 28, 21; William R. Staples, *Annals of the Town of Providence* (Providence, 1843), pp. 41–42; *Recs. Conn.,* pp. 49, 53. This practice deserves a fuller account than I can provide in this chapter; civil courts and colony governments recurrently asked the parties in a dispute to use arbitration.

27. Nourse, ed., *Early Records of Lancaster,* p. 59.

28. The significance of legacies in wills is minimized in Kenneth A. Lockridge, "The Charitable Impulse in Old and New England: An Enquiry into the

Origins of the American Character," unpublished essay, cited in Foster, *Their Solitary Way,* p. 138 n. 31, and in Foster's own research, ibid., pp. 138–39.

29. Edward Johnson, *The Wonder-Working Providence of Sions Saviour in New England,* ed. J. Franklin Jameson (New York: Scribner, 1910), p. 27; Increase N. Tarbox, "Ruling Elders in the Early New-England Churches," *Congregational Quarterly* 14 (1872): 401–15; Bailyn, *Apologia of Robert Keayne,* p. 63. A similar preference for compromise and reconciliation is evident in the workings of ecclesiastical courts in England; in neither region should this preference be interpreted as evidence of "declension" or laxness, although Puritan critics of the ecclesiastical courts said just this (Martin Ingram, *Church Courts, Sex and Marriage in England, 1570–1640* [Cambridge: Cambridge University Press, 1987], chap. 11 and passim).

30. *Recs. Mass.,* 1:242, 271; 3:16; John Cotton, *An Exposition upon the Thirteenth Chapter of the Revelation* (London, 1655), pp. 17–18.

31. As demonstrated by a mid-1639 letter from the Salem congregation to the Dorchester church, listing fourteen persons censured in Salem who had left the town (Joseph B. Felt, *The Ecclesiastical History of New England,* 2 vols. [Boston, 1855], 1:379–80).

32. *Recs. Mass.,* 1:240; Winthrop, *Journal,* p. 288; Hall, *Faithful Shepherd,* pp. 146–47.

33. Winthrop, *Journal,* pp. 430–31, 572; Hall, *Faithful Shepherd,* chap. 10. A fuller description of the politics of declension may be found in Stephen Foster, *The Long Argument: English Puritanism and the Shaping of New England Culture, 1570–1700* (Chapel Hill: University of North Carolina Press, 1991), chap. 5.

34. *Records of the Town of Plymouth,* 3 vols. (Plymouth, 1889), 1:3, 12, 30, 35; Edward Warren Capen, *The Historical Development of the Poor Law of Connecticut* (New York: Columbia University Press, 1905); see above, Chapter Two.

35. *Recs. Southampton,* 1:3, 44; *Recs. Conn.,* pp. 37–38; John D. Cushing, ed., *The Earliest Acts and Laws of Rhode Island and Providence Plantations, 1647–1719* (Wilmington, Del.: Michael Glazier, 1977), pp. 33, 34.

36. This argument owes a great deal to David Thomas Konig, *Law and Society in Puritan Massachusetts: Essex County, 1629–1692* (Chapel Hill: University of North Carolina Press, 1979); see, in particular, chap. 2, "Real Property Litigation."

37. *Winthrop Papers,* 4:75–77.

38. Intercolonial fractures around territorial claims are described in Francis Jennings, *The Invasion of America: Indians, Colonialism, and the Cant of Conquest* (Chapel Hill: University of North Carolina Press, 1975); local struggles are described in a number of regional and community studies, including

Richard P. Gildrie, *Salem, Massachusetts, 1626–1683: A Covenant Community* (Charlottesville: University Press of Virginia, 1975).

39. Roger F. Thompson, *Sex in Middlesex: Popular Mores in a Massachusetts County, 1649–1699* (Amherst: University of Massachusetts Press, 1986), chap. 3, provides a comparative perspective on premarital pregnancies.

40. Frances Manwaring Caulkins, *History of New London, Connecticut* (New London, 1895), p. 153; D. Williams Patterson, *A Genealogical Study of the Grant Family Descended from Matthew Grant* (Hartford, 1892), p. 3. I add Eaton to this list on the basis of a now lost biography of him: *Coll. MHS*, 4th ser., 8 (1868): 282. See also *Plymouth Church Records, 1620–1859, Pub. CSM* 22 (1920): 110 (a passage extolling Bradford as "of an unbiased Justice in all his actings").

41. As it does in the Geneva Bible translation of Psalm 72:2: "Then shall he judge thy people in righteousness, and thy poore with equitie." The psalm as a whole celebrates the responsibility of kings to "the poor and nedie" (verse 13) and to peace, justice, and righteousness.

42. Fortier, *Culture of Equity,* chap. 1 (quotation on p. 43); Perkins's treatise is included in Ian Breward, ed., *The Work of William Perkins* (Appleford, U.K.: Sutton Courtenay Press, 1970), pp. 481–510; see also John Eliot, *The Christian Commonwealth* (London, 1659), sig. C3v.

43. Fortier, *Culture of Equity,* pp. 101–4.

44. *Suffolk Deeds,* 14 vols. (Boston: Suffolk County, 1880–1901), 1:iii–iv; Winthrop, *Journal,* p. 338; *Records of the Particular Court of Connecticut, 1639–1663* (Hartford: Connecticut Historical Society, 1928), p. 9.

45. *NEHGR* 3 (1849): 41; *Hutchinson Papers,* 2 vols. (Albany: Prince Society, 1965), 2:12; Erastus Worthington, *The History of Dedham from the Beginning of its Settlement* (Boston, 1827), p. 18.

46. *Winthrop Papers,* 4:80–81; Fortier, *Culture of Equity,* pp. 172–73.

47. Whitmore, *Colonial Laws,* p. 33; *Winthrop Papers,* 3:64; John Davenport, *A Sermon Preach'd at the Election of the Governour* ([Cambridge], 1669), p. 8; *Recs. Conn.,* pp. 206, 36; Nathaniel Ward, quoted in James O'Toole, "New England Reactions to the English Civil Wars," *NEHGR* 129 (1975): 7.

48. W[illiam] A[spinwall], *The Legislative Power Is Christ's Peculiar Prerogative* (London, 1656), p. 32.

49. Fortier, *Culture of Equity,* p. 159.

50. *Recs. Mass.,* 1:137, 174–75.

51. George Lee Haskins, *Law and Authority in Early Massachusetts* (New York: Macmillan, 1960), p. 120.

52. Donald Veall, *The Popular Movement for Law Reform, 1640–1660* (Oxford: Clarendon, 1970), p. 69 and passim; Ivan Roots, "Cromwell's Ordinances: The Early Legislation of the Protectorate," in *The Interregnum: The Quest*

for Settlement, 1646–1660, ed. G. E. Aylmer (London: Macmillan, 1972), pp. 143–64; Patrick Little and David L. Smith, *Parliaments and Politics During the Cromwellian Protectorate* (Cambridge: Cambridge University Press, 2007), chap. 8. The dates in Veall's title are misleading, for he covers in some detail the nature of the law before 1640. Accusations of corruption surrounded officials who bought their offices and repaid themselves by charging large fees or receiving undercover bribes. Francis Bacon became notorious for doing so and was charged with corruption by a parliamentary committee (ibid., p. 43).

53. H. N. Brailsford, *The Levellers and the English Revolution* (Nottingham, U.K.: Spokesman University Paperbacks, 1983), pp. 129–30; Brian Manning, *The English People and the English Revolution, 1640–1649* (London: Heinemann, 1976), chap. 10; B. S. Capp, *The Fifth Monarchy Men: A Study in Seventeenth-Century English Millenarianism* (London: Faber and Faber, 1972), chap. 7 (without noticing the New England connections). Hugh Peter sketched a program of legal reform in *Good Work for a Good Magistrate* (London, 1651), as did Aspinwall in *Legislative Power.*

54. [John Cotton], *An Abstract of the Lawes of New England, as They Are Now Established* (London, 1641), pp. 4–7; Cotton, "How Far Moses' Judicialls Bind Mass[aschusetts]," *Proc. MHS,* 2nd ser., 16 (1902): 281–82.

55. The "Judicialls" was copied into the town records of Southampton, Long Island, carried there by the group from Lynn, Massachusetts, that founded the town (*Recs. Southampton,* 1:18–22). See also Theodore Dwight Bozeman, *To Live Ancient Lives: The Primitivist Dimension in Puritanism* (Chapel Hill: University of North Carolina Press, 1988), chap. 5.

56. *Lawes and Liberties,* p. 28; Whitmore, *Colonial Laws,* pp. 41, 39, 45. For the English practice, see Veall, *Popular Movement,* pp. 17, 18.

57. *Lawes and Liberties,* p. 4; Whitmore, *Colonial Laws,* p. 39. Counsel was allowed, within limits; these restrictions were gradually relaxed (Edgar J. McManus, *Law and Liberty in Early New England: Criminal Justice and Due Process, 1620–1692* [Amherst: University of Massachusetts Press, 1993], pp. 94–96).

58. *Lawes and Liberties,* pp. 8, 14–15, 54, 16, 46; Whitmore, *Colonial Laws,* p. 43.

59. *Lawes and Liberties,* p. 50. For the English context, see Veall, *Popular Movement,* pp. 25–26.

60. Whitmore, *Colonial Laws,* p. 43; *Lawes and Liberties,* p. 54; Bozeman, *To Live Ancient Lives,* pp. 183–84; Veall, *Popular Movement,* pp. 3–4; see also Cynthia B. Herrup, *The Common Peace: Participation and the Criminal Law in Seventeenth-Century England* (Cambridge: Cambridge University Press, 1987), chap. 6.

61. Whitmore, *Colonial Laws,* p. 41; John Noble, "A Glance at Suicide as Dealt

With in the Colony and in the Province of the Massachusetts Bay," *Proc. MHS,* 2nd ser., 16 (1902): 521–32.

62. Whitmore, *Colonial Laws,* p. 35. The agitation in England during the 1620s over the granting of monopolies, essential background to the colonists' attitude, is described in William Hyde Price, *The English Patents of Monopoly* (Cambridge, Mass.: Harvard University Press, 1913).

63. Whitmore, *Colonial Laws,* p. 35.

64. Veall, *Popular Movement,* pp. 157–58; *The Book of the General Laws of . . . New-Plimoth* (Cambridge, Mass., 1672), p. 42. That partible inheritance was not rigidly followed is demonstrated in John J. Waters, "The Traditional World of the New England Peasants: A View from Seventeenth-Century Barnstable," *NEHGR* 130 (1976): 3–21, esp. p. 20. Social rank re-entered via rules that prohibited whippings for minor offenses for gentlemen; and as McManus points out, "punishments of humiliation . . . were reserved exclusively for persons of low status," noting other discrepancies (McManus, *Law and Liberty,* pp. 175–76). The social implications of impartibility are sketched in Jack Goody et al., eds., *Family and Inheritance: Rural Society in Western Europe, 1200–1800* (Cambridge: Cambridge University Press, 1976); see esp. Goody's introduction.

65. Capital laws for the several colonies are listed in McManus, *Law and Liberty,* app. A.

66. Haskins, *Law and Authority,* pp. 149, 153–54.

67. Whitmore, *Colonial Laws,* p. 33.

68. Ibid. Similar language appears in *General Laws of New-Plimoth,* pp. 1–2, some of it possibly antedating the Body of Liberties.

69. Whitmore, *Colonial Laws,* pp. 41, 33. So historians of the law have sometimes recognized. George Lee Haskins, who knew the English side thoroughly, has pointed out that "in several respects the Body of Liberties went well beyond protecting the traditional rights of Englishmen" (Haskins, *Law and Authority,* pp. 129–30). William K. Holdsworth, the most thorough student of law and society in seventeenth-century Connecticut, has contrasted the "ponderous" and "intricate" qualities of the English system with "the course of justice" in that colony, where justice was "swifter, the chance of inequities, less pronounced. The courts themselves were more accessible and the people were quick to make use of them," and the law "inexpensive" (Holdsworth, "Law and Society in Colonial Connecticut, 1636–1672" [Ph.D. diss., Claremont University, 1972], p. 157). The clearest recognition of the process described in this section is G. B. Warden, "Law Reform in England and New England, 1640 to 1660," *WMQ,* 3rd ser., 35 (1978): 68–90; see also G. B. Warden, "The Rhode Island Civil Code of 1647," in David Hall et al., eds., *Saints and Revolutionaries: Essays on Early American History* (New York: W. W. Norton, 1984), pp. 138–51.

70. John Brewer and John Styles, quoted in Anthony J. Fletcher and John Stevenson, "Introduction," in *Order and Disorder in Early Modern England,* ed. Fletcher and Stevenson (Cambridge: Cambridge University Press, 1985), p. 15. See also William M. Lamont, *Godly Rule: Politics and Religion, 1603–1660* (London: Macmillan, 1969), chap. 6, on the fragility of "saints."

71. Thomas Shepard, *Subjection to Christ, in All His Ordinances and Appointments, the Best Means to Preserve Our Liberty* (London, 1652), in Shepard, *Works,* 3:293, 294, 289.

72. Hall, *AC,* pp. 209–11, 307–8, 308–9, 301–3. Another example of this rhetoric is Shepard's *Subjection to Christ,* with its dark warnings that the alternative to accepting the authority of Christ is the reign of the Antichrist and, instead of peace, bloody warfare and persecution.

73. English critics of the Congregational Way hurled the word "popular" at its empowering of the laity; see, e.g., Thomas Lechford, *Plain Dealing: Or, News from New England* (London, 1642).

74. John D. Eusden, "Introduction," in William Ames, *The Marrow of Theology* (Boston: Pilgrim Press, 1968), pp. 22–24; Hall, *Faithful Shepherd,* pp. 55–60; David F. Wright, "Calvin's Accommodating God," in *Calvinus Sincerioris Religionis Vindex: Calvin as Protector of the Purer Religion,* ed. Wilhelm H. Neuser and Brian G. Armstrong, Sixteenth-Century Essays and Studies 36 (Kirksville, Mo.: Sixteenth Century Journal Publishers, 1997), pp. 3–19.

CHAPTER FIVE. "ALREADY IN HEAVEN"?

1. John Pratt, "Exposition" or "Answer," in *Records of the Court of Assistants of the Colony of the Massachusetts Bay, 1630–1692,* ed. John Noble and John F. Cronin, 3 vols. (Boston, 1901–28), 2:109–11, a retraction exacted of Pratt in 1632 after it was learned of his writing "thinges which were untrue & of ill repute" to English friends; Winthrop, *Journal,* pp. 160–61; Edward Johnson, *The Wonder-Working Providence of Sions Saviour in New England,* ed. J. Franklin Jameson (New York: Scribner, 1910), p. 106; Winthrop, *Journal,* p. 115. See also *Winthrop Papers,* 3:203, for a contemporary judgment that Cambridge was "straitened."

2. The regional origins of the families that settled after 1635 in Cambridge and their connections with Shepard are described in Roger F. Thompson, *Cambridge Cameos: Stories of Life in Seventeenth-Century New England* (Boston: New England Historic Genealogical Society, 2005), pp. 3–5.

3. *Recs. Mass.,* 1:119, 122, 130. Shepard's reasons for considering a move are indicated in undated notes he wrote to himself, printed in Michael McGiffert, *God's Plot: The Paradoxes of Puritan Piety, Being the Autobiography & Journal of Thomas Shepard* (Amherst: University of Massachusetts Press, 1972), p. 89

n. 6. That a decision to move was close to being made is indicated by a letter of 1640 from Hooker to Shepard, printed in John A. Albro, "Life of Thomas Shepard," in Shepard, *Works,* 1:cxlii–clv. Two persons appointed to survey Shawsheen in 1642 reported to the General Court that, "for the quality, in our apprehensions, no way fit, the upland being very barren, and very little medow there about, nor any good timber almost fit for any use" (*Recs. Mass.,* 2:10).

4. Of the English studies that ask similar questions, the most apt is David Underdown, *Fire from Heaven: Life in an English Town in the Seventeenth Century* (New Haven: Yale University Press, 1992). The central arguments of that book—that the program of reform in Dorchester drew from all social levels, had its enlightened elements (e.g., extra help for the deserving poor), brought about a surge in charitable contributions, and, in its impact on social behavior, was both successful and intermittently enforced, with courts attempting mediation—provide interesting points of comparison with my own, although Dorchester was a far larger town, with far more social stratification. On the whole, the workings of godly rule or the "reformation of manners" is not described in studies of seventeenth-century New England towns.

5. Winthrop, *Journal,* pp. 168–70. The text of the covenant does not survive.

6. George Selement and Bruce C. Woolley, eds., *Thomas Shepard's Confessions,* in *Pub. CSM* 58 (1981): 159.

7. McGiffert, *God's Plot,* p. 50; Thomas Shepard and John Allin, *A Defence of the Answer made unto the Nine Questions* (London, 1648), pp. 3–4.

8. Printed from a manuscript, no longer surviving, in [Cotton Mather], *The Temple Opened* (Boston, 1709), pp. 30–31.

9. Selement and Woolley, eds., *Shepard's Confessions,* pp. 107–9, 83, 63, 64, 191; Mary Rhinelander McCarl, "Thomas Shepard's Record of Relations of Religious Experience, 1648–1649," *WMQ,* 3rd ser., 48 (1991): 451.

10. Thomas Shepard, *The Parable of the Ten Virgins* (London, 1660), in Shepard, *Works,* 2:65, 20, 622; Shepard and Allin, *Defence of the Answer,* p. 80.

11. McGiffert, *God's Plot,* p. 126; Shepard, *Works,* 3:329.

12. Lucius R. Paige, *History of Cambridge, Massachusetts, 1630–1877* (Boston, 1877), pp. 254–58; "Abstracts of the Earliest Wills upon Record in the County of Suffolk," *NEHGR* 2 (1848): 103, 182; Robert H. Rodgers, *Middlesex County . . . Records of Probate and Administration, October 1649–December 1660* (Boston: New England Historic Genealogical Society, 1999), pp. 11, 3.

13. Edmund S. Morgan, ed., *The Diary of Michael Wigglesworth, 1653–1657: The Conscience of a Puritan* (New York: Harper Torchbooks, 1965), pp. 59, 60, 67, 101; McGiffert, *God's Plot,* pp. 225, 236; David D. Hall, *Witch-Hunting in Seventeenth-Century New England: A Documentary History, 1638–1693* (Boston: Northeastern University Press, 1999), chap. 8; Thompson, *Cam-*

bridge Cameos, pp. 87–97. On note-taking as the basis for some of Shepard's printed sermons, see David D. Hall, *Ways of Writing: The Practice and Politics of Text-Making in Seventeenth-Century New England* (Philadelphia: University of Pennsylvania Press, 2008), pp. 99–101.

14. Rodgers, *Middlesex County,* pp. 37, 15; *Recs. Mass.,* 4, pt. 1:65; *NEHGR* 49 (1896): 146; Thompson, *Cambridge Cameos,* pp. 67–73.

15. Selement and Woolley, eds., *Shepard Confessions,* pp. 66, 140, 185.

16. Stephen Paschal Sharples, ed., *Records of the Church of Christ at Cambridge in New England, 1632–1830* (Boston, 1906), p. 10; Cotton Mather, *Magnalia Christi Americana,* 2 vols. (1702; reprinted, Hartford, 1853–54), 2:111; McGiffert, *God's Plot,* p. 36; Thomas Shepard, *The Church-Membership of Children Cleared Up in a Letter in Answer to the Doubts of a Friend* (Cambridge, Mass., 1663), in Shepard, *Works,* 3:522–24, 536.

17. Shepard, *Works,* 3:536; "Considerations Comended in a Brotherly Way to Those Brethren That Doe Scruple . . . the Seale of Baptisme to Theyr children," Shepard Family Papers, folder 2, American Antiquarian Society; Thomas Shepard, *Wine for Gospel Wantons* (Cambridge, Mass., 1668), p. 10.

18. Richard Mather, *A Farewel-Exhortation to the Church and People of Dorchester in New-England* (Cambridge, Mass., 1657), pp. 12–13. Popular religiosity around baptism is sketched more fully in Anne S. Brown and David D. Hall, "Family Strategies and Religious Practice: Baptism and the Lord's Supper in Early New England," in *Lived Religion in America: Toward a History of Practice,* ed. David D. Hall (Princeton, N.J.: Princeton University Press, 1997), pp. 41–68.

19. *NEHGR* 49 (1895): 146.

20. Thomas Shepard, *The Sincere Convert* (London, 1640), in Shepard, *Works,* 1:57. A few pages later, he disparaged the parish model of church membership as one of nine "easy ways to heaven" that actually led to hell (p. 65). Shepard's one-out-of-a-hundred was a rhetorical means of adding weight to a conditional "might be": if graceless sinners who happened to be church members were actually hypocrites and did not prepare for grace, it might happen that Christ would pass them by.

21. Almost from the beginning of his ministry in New England, Shepard fretted about spiritual decay and indifference; see, e.g., Shepard, *Works,* 2:377, 169; 3:310. My argument in these paragraphs coincides with the thoughtful treatment of Shepard's ministry in Susan Drinker Moran, *Gathered in the Spirit: Beginnings of the First Church in Cambridge* (Cleveland: United Church Press, 1995), esp. pp. 92–99; see also Selement and Woolley, "Introduction," in *Shepard Confessions,* pp. 22–24, and George Selement, "The Meeting of Elite and Popular Minds at Cambridge, New England, 1638–1645," *WMQ,* 3rd ser., 41 (1984): 32–48.

22. Hall, *AC*, pp. 50–51. This sentence summarizes a wider-ranging debate embodied in John Cotton, *Sixteene Questions of Serious and Necessary Consequence* (London, 1644), and two sequels, the ministers' "Reply" and Cotton's "Rejoinder," all in Hall, *AC*. Shepard's leading role in turning back the antinomians is described in Michael P. Winship, *Making Heretics: Militant Protestantism and Free Grace in Massachusetts, 1636–1641* (Princeton, N.J.: Princeton University Press, 2002).

23. Shepard, *Works*, 2:77, 83–84, 184. In a direct retort to Wheelwright, Shepard insisted that hypocrites were concealing themselves behind professions of the Holy Spirit, not, as Wheelwright had alleged, behind the uses of the law (ibid., 2:191).

24. Shepard and Allin, *Defence of the Answer*, p. 13; Shepard, *Works*, 2:188–89; McCarl, "Thomas Shepard's Record of Relations," p. 434; Selement and Woolley, eds., *Shepard Confessions*, p. 118.

25. Roger F. Thompson, *Sex in Middlesex: Popular Mores in a Massachusetts County, 1649–1699* (Amherst: University of Massachusetts Press, 1986), p. 121. Mitchell's catalogue is printed in Sharples, *Records of the Church of Christ at Cambridge*. In the immediate aftermath of the congregation's founding, wives were joining before their husbands, a pattern pointed out in Bruce Chapman Woolley, "Reverend Thomas Shepard's Cambridge Church Members 1636–1649: A Socio-Economic Analysis" (Ph.D. diss., University of Rochester, 1973), pp. 52, 42; a separate analysis I made of the Mitchell register shows that, in the late 1650s and 1660s, wives were much likely to join before their husbands.

26. Walker, *Creeds and Platforms,* chap. 11.

27. Indebted to Gerald F. Moran, "Religious Renewal, Puritan Tribalism, and the Family in Seventeenth-Century Milford, Connecticut," *WMQ,* 3rd ser., 36 (1979): 236–54, this interpretation of baptism in the context of family life strategies is argued more fully in Brown and Hall, "Family Strategies and Religious Practice," and in my introduction to *The Works of Jonathan Edwards,* vol. 12, *Ecclesiastical Writings* (New Haven: Yale University Press, 1994). In these three places, Puritan "tribalism" is regarded as a mechanism for expanding church membership; see in particular Brown and Hall, "Family Strategies," p. 65 n. 26. In contrast to English practice, the cemetery in Cambridge was not consecrated ground, which made it available to everyone—church members, the excommunicated, et al.

28. Winthrop, *Journal,* pp. 301–3; Samuel Eliot Morison, *The Founding of Harvard College* (Cambridge, Mass.: Harvard University Press, 1935), chap. 17; McGiffert, *God's Plot,* pp. 52–53. Eaton is a ghostly presence in the *Parable* sermons and Shepard's journal.

29. *NEHGR* 39 (1885): 373. Shepard endorsed one of the premises of godly rule in

Massachusetts, that the welfare of the churches depended on limiting the franchise in civil governance to church members ("Thomas Shepard's Election Sermon," *NEHGR* 24 [1870]: 366).

30. Thompson, *Cambridge Cameos,* pp. 47–54, 67–73, 99–103; Shepard, *Works,* 3:289, 292.

31. Margaret Spufford, "Puritanism and Social Control?," in *Order and Disorder in Early Modern England,* ed. Anthony Fletcher and John Stevenson (Cambridge: Cambridge University Press, 1985), pp. 41–57; Shepard, *Works,* 3:349–50, 325, 330, 354.

32. Thompson, *Cambridge Cameos,* pp. 17–18.

33. Woolley, "Shepard's Cambridge Church Members," has provided some of the information that follows, supplemented by Robert E. Wall, *The Membership of the Massachusetts General Court, 1630–1686* (New York: Garland, 1991). In *The Puritan Moment: The Coming of Revolution in an English County* (Cambridge, Mass.: Harvard University Press, 1983), William Hunt places the patronage of the Harlakendens, described below, in a broader context.

34. See, e.g., *Aspinwall Notarial Records* (Boston: Municipal Printing Office, 1903), pp. 32, 116, 163. John Winthrop owed Edmund Angier 140 pounds in 1643, and Shepard was owed minor sums by fourteen people at the time of his death (*Winthrop Papers,* 4:413; "Autobiography of Thomas Shepard," in *Pub. CSM* 27 [1932]: 399).

35. Johnson, *Wonder-Working Providence,* pp. 246–48. On the economic life of the town, see Thompson, *Cambridge Cameos,* pp. 22–24.

36. Rodgers, *Middlesex County,* pp. 7, 353–61; Thompson, *Cambridge Cameos,* pp. 111–15.

37. *Cambridge Records,* pp. 18, 17, 24, 32–33, 50.

38. Ibid., p. 75.

39. Robert E. Wall, *Massachusetts Bay: The Crucial Decade, 1640–1650* (New Haven: Yale University Press, 1972), p. 25.

40. Shepard, *Works,* 3:349, 345.

41. *Cambridge Records,* p. 92; *Recs. Mass.,* vol. 4, pt. 1:93; Wall, *Massachusetts Bay,* p. 39; Wall's data also indicate that the highest percentage for a Middlesex County town was 65. B. Katherine Brown, "Puritan Democracy: A Case Study," *Mississippi Valley Historical Review* 50 (1963): 377–96, placed the percentage of men eligible to become freemen at 75, and, taking into account that some who were eligible chose not to be registered as freemen, the percentage who did so as somewhere between 50 and 75. Her methodology (essentially, deciding who should be counted as an adult male resident of the town) was contested in Robert E. Wall, "The Franchise in Seventeenth-Century Massachusetts: Dedham and Cambridge," *WMQ* 34 (1977): 53–58. According to Wall's count of voters (men twenty-one and older), half of the

men in the town were not paying taxes, a finding at odds with town-meeting and selectmen's records. (In nearby Charlestown, only a tiny fraction of householders were delinquent, a fact I owe to Roger F. Thompson.) Two uncertainties stand in the way of precision, knowing whom to count as a resident of Cambridge at any given moment and whom to count as a church member; Jonathan Mitchell could not have known of some of the people who lived in the town briefly, possibly as church members, and some of the men Wall counts as residents were also there briefly. For these reasons, and bearing in mind the percentages elsewhere, I would split the difference between Wall and Brown.

42. *Cambridge Records,* pp. 34–35.
43. Ibid., pp. 34–35, 53, 52.
44. Ibid., pp. 54–56, 117–18, 161.
45. Ibid., pp. 67, 85, 131, 79; *Coll. MHS,* 2nd ser., 10 (1843): 187.
46. *Cambridge Records,* pp. 100, 75.
47. Ibid., pp. 74–75.
48. Ibid., pp. 96–98.
49. *Recs. Mass.,* 3:405.
50. *Cambridge Records,* pp. 99–100.
51. Whether, as a general rule in towns throughout New England, the men who became church members made out better in the distribution of town lands is unclear, in part because church membership may have been secondary to some other social or political factor, as John Frederick Martin argues in *Profits in the Wilderness: Entrepreneurship and the Founding of New England Towns* (Chapel Hill: University of North Carolina Press, 1991).
52. Henry A. Hazen, *History of Billerica, Massachusetts, with a Genealogical Register* (Boston, 1883).
53. Shepard, *Works,* 3:486.
54. Ibid., 3:332.
55. Paige, *History of Cambridge,* pp. 228–29 (undated).
56. Albro, "Life of Shepard," in Shepard, *Works,* 1:cxliv. Serious informed challenges to the argument that religion fell apart as the local economy improved—or, to put things more starkly, that religion gave way to self-interest—may be found in Philip H. Round, *By Nature and By Custom Cursed: Transatlantic Civil Discourse and New England Cultural Production, 1620–1660* (Hanover, N.H.: University Press of New England, 1999); Martin, *Profits in the Wilderness;* Mark A. Peterson, *The Price of Redemption: The Spiritual Economy of Puritan New England* (Stanford, Calif.: Stanford University Press, 1997); and Stephen Foster, *Their Solitary Way: The Puritan Social Ethic in the First Century of Settlement in New England* (New Haven: Yale University Press, 1971).

CONCLUSION

1. Sylvester Judd, *History of Hadley* (Hadley, Mass., 1905), pp. 73–75.

2. Samuel Maverick, "A Briefe Discription of New England and the Severall Townes Therein, Together with the Present Government Thereof," *Proc. MHS*, 2nd ser., 1 (1884–85): 231–49; Edward Randolph, "An Answer to Severall Heads of Enquiry Concerning the Present State of New England," in [Thomas Hutchinson], *A Collection of Original Papers* (Boston, 1767), pp. 477–503.

3. William G. McLoughlin puts the figure for Baptists, Quakers, and Anglicans in the orthodox colonies (not including Rhode Island) at around 1 percent by the first quarter of the eighteenth century (*New England Dissent, 1630–1833: The Baptists and the Separation of Church and State*, 2 vols. [Cambridge, Mass.: Harvard University Press, 1971], 1:121).

4. Some of these assertions are conveniently assembled in B. Katherine Brown, "The Controversy over the Franchise in Puritan Massachusetts, 1954 to 1974," *WMQ*, 3rd ser., 33 (1976): 212–41. See also Horace E. Ware, "Was the Government of the Massachusetts Bay Colony a Theocracy?," in *Pub. CSM* 10 (1907): 151–80.

5. Stephen Foster, "New England and the Challenge of Heresy, 1630–1660: The Puritan Crisis in Transatlantic Perspective," *WMQ*, 3rd ser., 38 (1981): 626–29; John Milton, *The Readie & Easie Way to Establish a Free Commonwealth* (London, 1660).

6. Too many to cite in this brief conclusion, episodes of severe conflict between town proprietors and others are well documented in town histories. For one example, see Samuel Sewall, *The History of Woburn, Middlesex County, Massachusetts* (Boston, 1868), pp. 36–37; for another, focusing on growing inequalities of wealth, see Andrew Raymond, "A New England Colonial Family: Four Generations of the Porters of Hadley, Massachusetts," *NEHGR* 129 (1975): 198–220.

7. Glenn W. LaFantasie, ed., *The Correspondence of Roger Williams*, 2 vols. (Hanover, N.H.: University Press of New England, 1988), 2:389; Michael Wigglesworth, "God's Controversy with New-England" (1662), in *The Poems of Michael Wigglesworth*, ed. Ronald A. Bosco (Lanham, Md.: University Press of America, 1989), pp. 87–102.

8. G. B. Warden, "The Rhode Island Civil Code of 1647," in *Saints and Revolutionaries: Essays on Early American History*, ed. David Hall et al. (New York: W. W. Norton, 1984), p. 150.

Index

A NOTE ABOUT THE AUTHOR

David D. Hall received his A.B. from Harvard and his Ph.D. from Yale. From 1970 to 1989 he was at Boston University as Associate Professor and then Professor; he also served as Director of the American and New England Studies Program (1970–76). In 1989 he became Professor of American Religious History at Harvard Divinity School, and in 2008 John A. Bartlett Research Professor of New England Church History there. From 1984 to 1993 he chaired the Program in the History of the Book in American Culture at the American Antiquarian Society and was General Editor of the five-volume *A History of the Book in America*. He is the author of *The Antinomian Controversy, 1636–1638: A Documentary History* (1968, 1990), *The Faithful Shepherd: A History of the New England Ministry in the Seventeenth Century* (1972), *Worlds of Wonder, Days of Judgment: Popular Religious Belief in Early New England* (1989), *Witch-Hunting in Seventeenth-Century New England: A Documentary History, 1638–1692* (1991), *Puritans in the New World: A Critical Anthology* (2004), and *Ways of Writing: The Practice and Politics of Text-Making in Seventeenth-Century New England* (2008). His *Worlds of Wonder, Days of Judgment* was awarded the Organization of American Historians' Merle Curti Prize and the Philip Schaff Prize of the American Society for Church History. He lives in Arlington, Massachusetts.

A NOTE ON THE TYPE

This book was set in Adobe Garamond. Designed for the Adobe Corporation by Robert Slimbach, the fonts are based on types first cut by Claude Garamond (c. 1480–1561). Garamond was a pupil of Geoffroy Tory and is believed to have followed the Venetian models, although he introduced a number of important differences, and it is to him that we owe the letter we now know as "old style." He gave to his letters a certain elegance and feeling of movement that won their creator an immediate reputation and the patronage of Francis I of France.

Composed by North Market Street Graphics, Lancaster, Pennsylvania
Printed and bound by Berryville Graphics, Berryville, Virginia
Book design by Robert C. Olsson